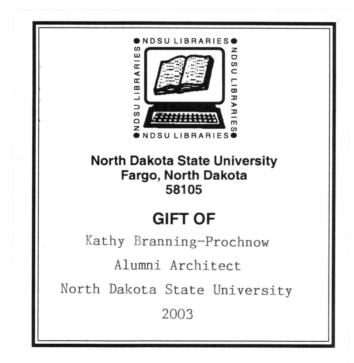

DATE DUE
SUBJECT TO RECALL
AFTER 2 WEEKS

CIRCULATION
You Must Wand Two (2) Barcodes
Disc, Disk, or CD-ROM in book

WARNING
Circ: DO NOT PUT THROUGH
THE DESENSITIZING MACHINE

A WORLD'S FAIR
FOR THE
GLOBAL VILLAGE

CONTRIBUTORS

Graphic Designer: Becky Pranger

Audio and Multimedia Production: Corinne Becknell and Martin Lucas

Book Production: Larry Pranger

Systems Programming: Brad Burdick and Philippe Tabaux

Developmental Editing: Stephanie Faul

Fair Train: Rob Pierce

Fair Mascot Development: Nick Gressle

Primary Photographers: Deb K. Roy, Somkid Chaijitvanit, *Doors Magazine*

Artists: Alan Brown/Photonics Graphics, Mercedes Ferrari

Video Editing: Natasha Tsarkova

Mac and Java Overdrive: Phillip R. Tiongson

Java Development: Noah C. Lehmann-Haupt, William R. Wallis

Contributions of computers and services for the production of this book were provided by IBM, Sun Microsystems, BBN Planet, First Virtual Holdings, NIKHEF, and WIDE.

A WORLD'S FAIR
FOR THE
GLOBAL VILLAGE

Carl Malamud

The MIT Press
Cambridge, Massachusetts
London, England

The following publishers have generously given permission
to use quotations from copyrighted works: From *Ship of
Fools* by Robert Hunter © 1974 by Ice Nine Publishing
Company, Inc. From *Strange Angels* by Laurie Anderson
© 1989 by Difficult Music. The quote from Jorge Luis
Borges on the dedication page is from *The Circular Ruins,*
published in *A Personal Anthology* by Jorge Luis Borges
© 1967 by Grove Press, Inc. *The Love Song of J. Alfred
Prufrock* by T.S. Eliot © by Harcourt Brace and
Company and Faber and Faber, Ltd. Copyright is also
acknowledged for the following works: *The Songlines* by
Bruce Chatwin © Bruce Chatwin 1987, Picador edition.
The Wizard of Oz by Salman Rushdie © Salman Rushdie
1992, British Film Institute edition. *A Supposedly Fun
Thing I'll Never Do Again* by David Foster Wallace ©
David Foster Wallace, Little Brown edition. Screen
captures from the World Wide Web remain the copyright
protected property of their original owners, whose
address is noted on the pages in which they appear.
The black and white pictures of world's fairs are ©
The Smithsonian Institution.

Library of Congress Cataloging-in-Publication Data

Malamud, Carl.
   A world's fair for the global village / Carl Malamud.
      p.   cm.
   Includes index.
   ISBN 0-262-13338-5 (alk. paper)
   1. Internet 1996 world exposition.   2. World Wide Web (Information
retrieval system)   I. Title.
ZA4226.M35   1997
907'.4—dc21   97–11146
                                                                CIP

To weave a rope of sand
Or mint coins of the faceless wind.

Jorge Luis Borges

*This book is dedicated to the people
around the world who have worked to
build a public park for the global village.*

Illustration/Alan Brown/Photonics Graphics

Contents

A crusade to transform the Internet computer network into a combination of a global Main Street and digital Library of Alexandria.

—*New York Times*
December 25, 1995

Foreword

His Holiness the Dalai Lama

The Internet 1996 World Exposition was intended to acquaint the international community with the wonders of the information age. With five million visitors and a huge infrastructure, this fair was an assembly of many things. Principally it showed that cyberspace has become part of the real world. However, building a global village through these new communications networks is not a reason for neglecting our local communities. The technology that lets us span the world, to communicate instantly across oceans, is a tool that we can use to preserve diversity, to enrich our understanding of each other, and enhance our sense of community.

At the Internet 1996 World Exposition the Tibetan people and our culture were represented by our musicians and craftsmen, who told the world something about our heritage. The Tibetan Institute for Performing Arts played its music as part of a year-long concert in Central Park. Tibetan metalworkers and woodworkers told the world about their crafts, steeped in traditions that are centuries old. Tibet is otherwise inaccessible to most people in the world today and yet information about it can be found almost instantly on the Internet.

The combination of computer, telephone, and television has recently created a communications revolution. In this context, the Internet's contribution to the diffusion and dissemination of knowledge and information is truly remarkable. Moreover, the Internet has the potential to be truly democratic because no one owns it, no single organization controls it. It crosses international boundaries and answers to no sovereign. Thus, it gives disenfranchised and marginalised groups a powerful voice to express their grievances and aspirations.

Perhaps as a consequence, some authoritarian governments view the Internet with great alarm. They see it as a tool by which oppressed people can make themselves known, gather support and work to throw off their oppression. Certainly, the Internet provides a nonviolent means for people who have no other voice to give expression to their aspirations for freedom.

One of the goals of the Internet 1996 World Exposition was to build Central Park, a public park for the global village. As they develop, global networks will be an invaluable tool for commerce and trade. However, leisure is as important as business and the Internet is a means for ordinary people to communicate and express themselves. Our communities are diverse and rich in creativity. Like an ordinary public park, Central Park was intended to provide a site in cyberspace for people to share and enjoy these riches together.

For as long as space endures,
And for as long as living beings remain,
Until then may I, too, abide
To dispel the misery of the world.

—Shantideva
Eighth-century Buddhist saint

May I be a wishing jewel,
a magic vase,
Powerful mantras,
and great medicine;
May I become a wish-
fulfilling tree
And a cow of plenty
for the world.

—Shantideva
Bodhisattva Vow

In this book, Carl Malamud gives an account of the Internet 1996 World Exposition. He shows how it provided opportunities for people to begin to think about the Internet and how this technology should fit into our lives. It is important that we do not lose sight of the fact that one of the prime goals of technological progress is to improve the quality of life. Such developments are to help and serve human beings, rather than make human beings serve them. Besides this, we need to consider how to protect the very openness of the Internet from abuse. For example, the potential for exposing children to pornography is alarming. Preserving freedom does not mean we can overlook responsibility. We need to understand that while the Internet cannot feed the poor, defend the oppressed, or protect those subject to natural disasters, by keeping us informed it can allow those of us who have the opportunity to do so to give whatever help we can.

TENZIN GYATSO
THE 14TH DALAI LAMA OF TIBET

STRANGE ANGELS —SINGING JUST FOR ME
THEIR SPARE CHANGE FALLS ON TOP OF ME
RAIN FALLING FALLING ALL OVER ME
ALL OVER ME
STRANGE ANGELS —SINGING JUST FOR ME
OLD STORIES —THEY'RE HAUNTING ME
BIG CHANGES ARE COMING
HERE THEY COME
HERE THEY COME.

LAURIE ANDERSON
STRANGE ANGELS

Preface

This book is the result of a four-year odyssey during which I thought I was building a radio station and found instead that it had turned into a world's fair. With the Internet, many metaphors are possible. With an invisible infrastructure, we can easily call ourselves a global schoolhouse, a telephone company, or a radio station. Sometimes, though, chance intervenes and we are able to go beyond metaphor and create something tangible.

In January 1993, I started work on a new project. The idea was simple enough: I would record interviews with people who were building the Internet, package these interviews as a series of audio files, and let people download and then listen to them on their computers. I called my program "Geek of the Week" and threw in the label "Internet Talk Radio" for good measure.

The *New York Times* wasn't impressed with the Geek of the Week label, but they sure went for the Internet Talk Radio metaphor, writing a front-page story that went into national syndication with headlines like "Move Over, Larry King." Larry King didn't notice, but the rest of the press pack certainly did. The number of listeners to Geek of the Week was quite low, certainly less than the number of reporters covering the story.

The thing about it was, we weren't a radio station. What we were really doing was communicating with our audience using a new technology. Our programs were audio intensive, but this wasn't radio. This wasn't radio any more than television was, as David Sarnoff said in his initiation of service for RCA, "radio sight" added to "radio sound." The Internet is a new medium and we were feeling our way trying to understand what that meant.

To go beyond the radio metaphor, we supplemented Geek of the Week with a web site devoted to Santa Claus, with free on-line databases we liberated from the U.S. government, and with a service to allow free international faxes. This motley collection of services was packaged together under the corporate name of the Internet Multicasting Service, the nonprofit corporation I started to house these projects. Though we weren't talk radio, we were deluged with offers from PR flacks wishing to place their clients and significant others on our "program." The metaphor had stuck.

Metaphor was clearly important, but with any nonprofit, so is funding. In late 1994, I sat down with Dr. Vint Cerf, one of my board members. We were trying hard to figure out how to get more corporate sponsors for the Internet Multicasting Service. The radio metaphor had brought in some important companies, as had

The legacy of the Internet 1996 World Exposition could be enduring, spacious and well-designed public parks at the center of cyberspace.

—*San Jose Mercury News*
March 15, 1996

Quiero expresar mi más firme apoyo a la celebración de la Exposición Mundial Internet 1996. Estoy convencido de que esta iniciativa permitirá; conocer las claves de uno de los factores fundamentales del futuro más inmediato.

—**Pasqual Maragall**
Mayor of Barcelona

the on-line government databases, and other projects. Yet, even with our modest offices in the National Press Building and our production studios above a Chinese restaurant on Capitol Hill, funds were limited and the prospects weren't looking good. What would convince a focused, financially responsible corporate executive to part with some money and send it our way?

"How about a world's fair?" I suggested to Vint. His eyes lit up. "What a great idea!" More important, he went to his boss and *his* eyes lit up. I went to a friend who is a staff member in the White House and his eyes lit up. This seemed like a winner. I went back and informed my staff of three that we were now no longer a radio station, we were a world's fair. The big question, of course, was what in the world did it mean to host a world's fair on the Internet?

Over the course of 1995, I made seven trips around the world to enlist people in this wild scheme. All over the world people saw that this was more than a way of building a web site, or installing a large computer, or getting a cybercafé off the ground. World's fairs attract international attention. As the local representatives for this global event, they were able to go to government ministers and heads of state, wheedle their corporate leaders to keep up with their foreign competitors, and approach their national artists to show off their cultural heritage.

By January 1996 a world's fair had come into being. To my astonishment, it was truly a world's fair. A dozen heads of state endorsed our efforts, corporations contributed close to $100 million in resources, over 85 regions of the world opened pavilions, and over five million people came to visit us. This fair may have been intangible, perhaps even invisible, but it turned out to be very real.

It is a great pleasure and honour for us that our country may participate in this worldwide event.

—Árpá Göncz, President
Gyula Horn, Prime Minister
The Republic of Hungary

CARL MALAMUD (carl@malamud.com)
CAMBRIDGE, MASSACHUSETTS

Global Organizers and Sponsors

Secretary-General
Dr. Rob Blokzijl
NIKHEF, The Netherlands

Fair Architect
Carl Malamud
IMS, United States

International Executive Committtee

Dr. Jun Murai
Keio University, Japan

Dr. Vinton Cerf
MCI, United States

Dr. James Lee
ITRI, Taiwan

Dr. Kilnam Chon
KAIST, South Korea

Joichi Ito
Digital Garage, Japan

Audio and Graphic Design

Martin Lucas and Corinne Becknell
Audio and Web Production

Becky and Larry Pranger
Graphic Design

International Secretariat
Alexander Blanc, Herman van Dompseler, Roos Spier, Philippe Tabaux

Central Park Commissioners

Brad Burdick
Global Project Manager
UUcom, Washington

Philippe Tabaux and
Herman van Dompseler
NIKHEF, Amsterdam

Dr. Yoichi Shinoda
JAIST, Tokyo

Andrew Rutherford
Internode, Adelaide

Stephan Olbrich
RRZN/RVS, Hannover

Lee McLoughlin
Imperial College, London

Internet Railroad

Marten Terpstra and Robin Littlefield
Global Project Managers
Bay Networks, United States

Dr. Osamu Nakamura
Director of Asian Operations
Keio University, Japan

Country and Regional Commissioners-General

Simon Hackett
Australia and England

Deb K. Roy
India, Tibet, and Ecuador

Dr. Kilnam Chon
Korea

Dr. Tan Tin Wee
Singapore

Martin Lucas
San Blas de Cuna

Dr. Rob Blokzijl
The Netherlands

Dr. Hans Frese
Germany

Janez Stefanec
Slovenia

Dr. Wade Hong
Canada

Josep Saldaña
Spain

Dr. Kanchana Kanchanasut
Thailand

Luther Brown
At-Large

Members of the Network Operating Team (NOT)

Toshiya Asaba
IIJ, Japan

Geoff Baehr
Sun Microsystems, US

Nancy Barry
MCI, US

Alexander von Berg
RRZN/RVS, Germany

Bernd Boeker
RRZN/RVS, Germany

Somkid Chaijitvanit
Bangkok Post, Thailand

Yi-Wu Chen
Chunghwa Telecom, Taiwan

Woohyong Choi
KAIST, Korea

Chung-Chi Chuang
Chunghwa Telecom, Taiwan

Clark Fu-kuei Chung
Chunghwa Telecom, Taiwan

Peter Detlefs
MFS, US

Rick Dunbar
Uucom, US

John Gage
Sun Microsystems, US

Curtis Generous
Uucom, US

Dave Grossman
IBM, US

Atsushi Hagiwara
Bay Networks, Japan

Bob Halliday
Bangkok Post, Thailand

Jane Harper
IBM, US

Chung-Yung Kang
Chunghwa Telecom, Taiwan

Akira Kato
University of Tokyo, Japan

Hiromi Kawakami
Keio University, Japan

Kazunori Konishi
KDD, Japan

Hsueh-wu Kuo
RDEC, Taiwan

Chris Liljenstolpe
SSDS, US

Peter Lothberg
Oy Inc, Sweden

Stuart McRobert
Imperial College, UK

Mike Millikin
Softbank, US

Seiichi Morikawa
Cisco, Japan

Kazuhiko Nakamura
NTT, Japan

Yukiteru Nanase
We's Brain, Japan

Tim O'Reilly
O'Reilly & Associates, US

Taeha Park
I.Net, Korea

Anthea Robinson
MCI, US

Tomoaki Sakurai
WIDE, Japan

Cyrus Shaoul
Digital Garage, Tokyo

Noriyuki Shigechika
Keio University, Japan

John Stewart
MCI, US

Paul Vixie
Vixie Laboratories, US

Jinhyoun Youn
Korea Telecom, Korea

Jeff Young
MCI, US

Katherine Webster
Sun Microsystems, US

Official Organizers†

United States

Auspex
Bay Networks
IBM
MCI
MFS Communications
Quantum Corporation
SSDS
Sun Microsystems
UUNET Communication Services

Netherlands

Ministry of Economic Affairs
The City of Amsterdam

Canada

Corel Corporation

Korea

Computer Communication Promotion
    Association of Korea
Dacom
Korean Broadcasting System
Korea Electric Power Corporation
Korea Telecom
LG Electronics
National Computerization Agency
Samsung
The Chosun Daily News
The Kyunghyang Shinmun
The Maeil Shinmun
Trigem Computer
Digital Equipment Korea
IBM Korea, Inc.
Jaeneung Educational Institute, Inc.
KUMHO Group
Posco
SAMMI Corporation
The Han-Kyoreh Daily News
The Joong-Ang Ilbo
The Taejon Ilbo

Taiwan

NII Steering Committee, ROC
DGT Taiwan

Japan

AT&T Jens Corporation
Bekkoame Internet Inc.
City of Kobe
CSK Corporation
Dai Nippon Printing Co., Ltd.
Fukui Computer Inc.
Fujitsu Limited
Hitachi, Ltd.
IBM Japan Ltd.
Internet Initiative Japan Inc.
JAPAN Satellite Systems Inc.
Kokusai Denshin Denwa Co., Ltd.
Kyoto Executive Committee
Kyushu Pavilion Executive Committee
Matsushita Electric Industrial Co. Ltd.
Microsoft Corporation, Ltd.
Mitsubishi Corporation
NEC Corporation
Nihon Sun Microsystems K.K.
NIPPON Telegraph And Telephone
    Corporation
NTT Data Corporation
PSI Japan
Rimnet Corporation
Softbank Corporation
Sony Corporation
Tokyo Internet Corporation
Tokyo Telecommunication
    Network Co., Inc.
Toppan Printing Company, Ltd.
Toshiba Corporation

Germany

Siemens Nixdorf Informationssysteme
Deutsche Telekom AG

Additional Sponsors††

Asian Institute of Technology
Allied Telesis, K.K.
Becknell and Lucas Media
BBN Planet
Cambridge Quality Management
Cisco Systems
CRYPTOCard
Digital Garage
Empire Technologies, Inc.
Enviromedia, Inc.
First Virtual Holdings
I*NET Technologies, Inc.
Intel Corporation
Internode Systems
Japan Advanced Institute of Science and
    Technology
Gateway 2000
Keio University
Kurashiki University of Science and
    Arts
Itochu Techno-Science Corp.
Mori Building Co.
Motorola, Inc.
National University of Singapore
Nara Institute of Science and
    Technology
The Netherlands Design Institute
Net One Systems Co., Ltd.
Nick Gressle Productions
Nihon Silicon Graphics K.K.
NIKHEF
Nissho Electronics
NLnet
Oki Electric Industry Co.
O'Reilly & Associates
Progressive Networks
RIPTech
Schroff K.K.
Space Shower, Inc.
SURFnet
Tokyo Institute of Technology
UUcom
WIDE
Worldwide Solutions, Inc.
Xing Technology
Yamaha Corporation

† Official Organizers have contributed at least US$200,000 (and in many cases, much more) to make Central Park, the Internet Railroad, and the Internet 1996 World Exposition a reality.

†† Additional sponsors have contributed computers, money, software, or other resources to the World Exposition.

The Invisible Fair

1

OFFICIAL SOUVENIR
WORLD'S FAIR- ST. LOUIS 1904

Palace of Mines and Metallurgy.

1904 ST. LOUIS WORLD'S FAIR

A World's Fair for the Information Age

1

A World's Fair for
Modem Times.

—*Washington Post*
March 15, 1995

It was a dark and stormy afternoon. The atmosphere in the meeting room was as cold as the Washington winter outside. Tom Kalil, an aide in the Clinton White House, had wrangled an invitation for Dr. Vinton Cerf and me to brief an industry group on our newly hatched plans for an Internet world's fair.

We were addressing a body that went by the august name of the National Information Infrastructure Testbed, composed of lobbyists and executives for companies such as Hewlett-Packard and AT&T. In early 1995, the political rhetoric in the information policy circles of Washington was sticking close to the antigovernment backlash of the times. Our national information infrastructure, so the catechism went, would most definitely not be built by the government. This was a job in the domain of our brave private sector. The White House might lend moral support, but groups like the NII Testbed had positioned themselves as the movers and shakers of the information revolution.

As a courtesy to the White House we had been granted a slot on the busy agenda. The meeting was not a huge success. In fact, you might say it was a total disaster. Vint Cerf, one of the founders of the Internet and a senior vice president at MCI, gave an inspirational pep talk about our emerging global community and the need to reach out to people and introduce them to technologies that would change their lives. I gave a little speech about the grand fairs of the last century and the opportunity before us to create a world's fair for the information age.

We finished our song and dance and looked around at a long table of bemused, perplexed, and blank faces. The lobbyist for Hewlett-Packard spoke up first.

"An Internet world's fair?" he asked rhetorically. "Why Internet?"

The Internet wasn't the NII, he elaborated for us. It was simply an early prototype that pointed the way to something that would emerge in the future. Who would build that national infrastructure? The group around the table, of course. Why celebrate the Internet, a primitive predecessor of the wonders yet to come, a historical artifact of a few government subsidies?

One of my tasks as the head of a small nonprofit Internet service had been maintaining the north.pole.org web site, the home of Santa Claus and his surly elves. Over the few days preceding our audience with the NII Testbed, we had received over 680,000 mail messages to Santa from 70 countries. From my perspective as the elfmaster for Santa Claus, the Internet sure looked real and resembled an early prototype only in the sense that the interstate highways of the 1950s were an early prototype of our national highway system.

The meeting went downhill from there. The lobbyist from AT&T gave us her "welcome to the big city" speech, explaining that she admired our verve but this idea was simply not going to happen. World's fairs belonged to the last century and, here in Washington, there were more important things to worry about. We should look to the future, not the past.

The rest of the group took their turn around the table, patiently explaining to us why we were as confused as goats on AstroTurf. A token government attendee at the NII Testbed, the representative from the National Library of Medicine, gave a little talk about how the time for large government projects had passed.

Getting the world's fair started through Washington obviously wasn't going to work, particularly if it meant spending all of our time in meetings, such as the classic one we had just attended. Beltway Bandits refer to these exercises in futility by the acronym BOGSATT, for Bunch of Guys Sitting around the Table.

They beat us up for 45 minutes. It was time to leave while our dignity was still intact. Vint Cerf, the distinguished father of the Internet and co-inventor of the Internet Protocol, led the way, getting up from the table and walking straight into a closet. We did an about face, smiled at the assembled BOGSATT, and found the real door.

"Tough crowd," murmured Tom Kalil with a sympathetic smile, as we straggled into the hall.

Time for Plan B. I bought an around-the-world airplane ticket and sent email to colleagues in several countries asking if I might buy them dinner, as I just happened to be coming by.

Around the World in 20 Days

My first stop was Tokyo, where I met with Dr. Jun Murai, the man who created the Japanese Internet when he connected two computers together with a modem many years ago, an act that at the time violated all sorts of telecommunications regulations in his country.

Over a snack of beer and barbecued eel livers, I explained the basic premise. World's fairs create huge sites, which are often turned into public parks and other permanent improvements to the local infrastructure when the fair is over. Jun Murai and I were in the business of building big networks, like thousands of our colleagues around the world. My idea was that a world's fair might give

Tom Kalil

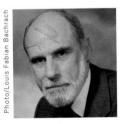

Vint Cerf

us a common focus, a lever we might use to raise the visibility of the Internet. In both Japan and the United States, many corporations and government groups desperately wanted to do something about the national information infrastructure, but each group was going off on its own. Perhaps a world's fair would get their attention and provide a common focus.

Even more important was the global card. If Jun Murai was representing a global exposition, he would have more weight in Japan than as a simple engineer. The same was true in the United States: if I could point to strong activity in Japan, perhaps the American corporations would pay attention.

The timing was perfect for Jun. Internet mania was just about ready to explode in Japan and Japanese corporations understood world's fairs. Tokyo was supposed to be hosting a real world's fair in 1996, but the project was in deep trouble and looked like it was about to be canceled. Here was a metaphor that Jun Murai could use.

Throughout the next two weeks, I stopped in Bangkok, Singapore, London, Amsterdam, and other cities and signed up colleagues. In each city, there was at least one engineer or researcher who was worried about how the Internet would scale, how it would reach out into society. Each saw the power of this lever, of this metaphor.

What in the World Is an Internet Fair?

Mike Millikin, a long-time member of my board of directors, offered us a special session at Networld+Interop, the industry's largest trade show. This special session would be used to announce our fair. The announcement was scheduled for late March 1995, giving us a few months to get the bandwagon rolling and, more important, to figure out what it meant to have a world's fair "on the Internet." While it was easy to proclaim that we were going to create such a beast, the devil would surely be in the details.

The architecture that developed over those months consisted of three key concepts. First was a *pavilion*, an on-line presence such as a World Wide Web site. Since this was an Internet fair, we came up with our first rule: in this fair anybody could open a pavilion. No fancy rules or juries. If you wanted to be a part of this fair, you were part of it.

We didn't want this fair to be simply a web site, a virtual world's fair, so a second concept of *events* was developed. An event would be anything happening live. The challenge to the event teams was to figure out how to present the event on the Internet in a meaningful way, and also to use their presence at the event as a way of showing people the fair.

World's fairs have traditionally been where technology is introduced to new communities. A world's fair visible only to people already on the Internet

Design the "global village" at World Net expo.

—**New Scientist**
March 15, 1995

Internet Expo provides boost to Asia's computer networks.

—**Nature**
September 7, 1995

Perhaps the most ambitious undertaking on the Internet to date: a 1996 world exposition modeled on world's fairs of the past.

—*Newsweek*
July 24, 1995

would be a charade. The third key concept was for *places* in the real world where people could visit the fair.

The two questions we kept getting were "where" and "when." When was easy: an arbitrary decision was made that the fair would last all of 1996. A few people wanted to defer the event until 1997, but Vint Cerf and I felt we'd have an easier time getting support from American politicians during an election year and the Japanese team was eager to start as soon as possible.

Where was also easy: this world's fair would take place all over the world. It was suggested that we register ourselves with the Bureau of International Expositions in Paris, the official certifying body for real world's fairs. Unfortunately, the first question on the application form is the location of your fair. We somehow didn't feel that the august BIE was quite ready for "everywhere," so the Internet 1996 World Exposition became a rogue exposition.

During early 1995, my mailbox started exploding. Messages were arriving from all over the world at the rate of hundreds per day. Jun Murai in Japan was going nuts, enlisting companies like NTT and Sony, and getting prime places in the real world such as the Tokyo Aquarium. In the United States, companies such as MCI and Sun Microsystems quickly signed up, and were joined by organizations such as the Kennedy Center for the Performing Arts. Tom Kalil, our man in Washington, secured an official letter of support from Vice President Al Gore.

It was time to roll this project out the door.

The Launch

Trade shows like Networld+Interop are a great place to reach the computer and communications corporations. Presenting to these companies was a way to get corporate support. However, we wanted this fair to reach beyond the already converted, and the press who come to trade shows are dry industry rags such as *Communications Week* (known to some as *Communications Weak*).

Instead of leaving ourselves in the hands of the trade press, I leaked the story to mainstream publications like the *San Jose Mercury News*, the *New York Times*, the *Wall Street Journal*, and the *Washington Post*. All four papers wrote nice long stories, with the *Mercury News* story appearing on the front page.

The story in the *Washington Post* had an interesting result. Soon after it appeared, I was summoned to meet with the director of the Progress and Freedom Foundation (PFF), a think tank founded by Newt Gingrich, the newly elected Speaker of the House of Representatives. PFF fancied itself at the cutting edge of twentieth-century thought, issuing documents with titles like *A Magna Carta for the Information Age* and acting as the home institution for intellectual heavyweights like Arianna Huffington.

The Republicans in Washington were riding high, and the folks at PFF were as euphoric as the rest of their colleagues. I pitched the fair to them, giving the usual spiel about the dawn of the information age, a talk I could give in my sleep by then. They quickly stopped me and got to the real point of the meeting. They had just happened to notice that the story in the *Washington Post* had mentioned Vice President Gore's support, but there was no mention of any Republicans in the story. Was this a world's fair or a partisan event?

Not a problem. We would be delighted to get any support we could get. Perhaps the Speaker could appear via satellite at our announcement, using the occasion to underscore his commitment to high technology and family values. It was agreed that this would be our plan. We exchanged email addresses, which was simple in the case of PFF since the entire organization was sharing a single email account on America Online.

I had spent enough time in Washington that I had learned that "yes" and "no problem" don't have the same meaning here as in the rest of the world. I decided to hedge my bets. I called the White House, apologized profusely, and explained the situation to them. The Speaker's staff had said that Mr. Gingrich would appear live at our announcement. Of course, we could wave our letter

Postcards were invented for the 1893 Chicago Columbian Exposition. These original postcards became an important graphic design element for the Internet 1996 World Exposition.

from the vice president from the podium, but was there something a bit more impressive the White House could do?

We flew out to Las Vegas with 104 boxes of computer equipment and various other components (some of which we had even used or had at least packed the manuals for) to get the announcement ready. Faxes started zipping back and forth between Las Vegas and Washington. It turned out that the Speaker wasn't available for a live announcement. The Speaker also wasn't available to send out a videotape. The Speaker wasn't available to send a letter of support. I asked for a postcard, but the folks from PFF didn't feel that I was paying due homage to the seriousness of their positions. Then, to my delight, a letter signed by the president of the United States came rolling off the fax machine at the convention center.

Meanwhile, last-minute calls were coming in from corporations that wanted more details. One call was from Barbara Fagan-Smith, the director of public relations for Quantum, one of the leading disk drive manufacturers. She had read the article in the *San Jose Mercury News* and wanted to know what she could do. I asked for a terabyte of disk drives, equivalent to 1,000 gigabytes of storage capacity. That was a fairly breathtaking request to make, but two days later Barbara called back to say we had a deal.

The formal announcement was great fun. Marty Lucas, audio director for the Internet Multicasting Service, composed a beautiful fanfare, modeled somewhat on Aaron Copland's *Fanfare for the Common Man.* We gathered every image we had stored on disks and copied them over to a few portable 4-gigabyte drives, supplemented with several hundred photos from our clipart collection.

Pipo, Official Mascot of the World Exposition.
Illustration/Nick Gressle

Using practically every computer we owned, we projected hundreds of images from around the world onto four big screens in the hall. Photos from the Smithsonian archives and postcards from old world's fairs were projected on the screen, and live audio and video from the announcement were sent out to the Internet.

A dozen senior corporate executives got up and expressed their support. We waved our letter from the president from the podium. Jun Murai and representatives from other countries got up and told of their emerging plans.

We were in business.

A Public Park for the Global Village

There was one piece still missing to make this a real world's fair. This had to be more than just a one-year show. Real world's fairs create new infrastructure. They leave something behind.

Our first "Eiffel Tower" was easy to conceptualize, though actually running it proved to be very tough. We called this "Central Park," a set of very large computers spread throughout the world. The computers would mirror each other, taking data created on one machine and copying the data to all the other machines. If the Japanese pavilions created a web site, the data would be copied to the other machines throughout the world. A user would visit the primary on-line portion of the fair by visiting Central Park. Each machine would be "close" to the user, alleviating the need for a user to travel over scarce and slow international lines to visit information from another region.

Our terabyte of disk from Quantum was a great start for making Central Park real. Supplementing the disk were several large donations of systems from Sun, IBM, and Auspex. There were huge computers: a typical system had over 1 gigabyte of main memory, several hundred gigabytes of disk, and eight very powerful central processing units. Just as important as the hardware, laboratories in London, Amsterdam, Tokyo, and other locations agreed to host the machines, providing the people necessary to run such a complex system.

The other piece of infrastructure created for the fair, the Internet Railroad, almost didn't happen. I've traveled extensively to visit colleagues making the Internet around the world, and the one single factor that holds up development is the lack of fast connections between countries. There is no global backbone for the Internet and telecommunications capacity is very expensive on an international basis.

Jun Murai, for example, was spending over $1 million a year for the main line connecting the United States to Japan. This line, known in the industry as a T1 line, was running at a paltry 1.5 million bits per second and was totally saturated. User demand from Japanese universities could easily pump many megabytes of traffic to the United States, much more traffic than an T1 line could hold. The result was that the line was full 24 hours per day, running so far over capacity that packets were dropped, response time was awful, and Japanese

On-Line Internet Expo Will Promote Cyberspace to the Whole Wired World.

—Wall Street Journal
March 14, 1995

Wettstreit der Melker: Zwei amerikanische Manager organisieren eine digitale Weltausstellung im Internet.

—Der Spiegel
October 9, 1995

Jun Murai

James Lee

students were avoiding communications to the United States because it had become so painful. Sadly, the T1 line to Japan was one of the fastest international lines on the Internet. Many other countries had a total connectivity of only 64,000 bits per second, equivalent to two or three modems.

Our dream for the Internet Railroad was to build a line circling the globe at 45 million bits per second. This dramatic increase in connectivity, I believed, would be enough to spur market development in each of the countries and was thus going to be a big win for the telecommunications industry. The telecommunications industry, I convinced myself, would make contributions to us based on a solid business case. By giving us one fast line, they would convince corporations to buy many of these expensive facilities.

We checked the maps of underground cables, and there was enough unused capacity to circle the globe at 45 million bits per second. If I had $250 million in my checkbook, it would have been a simple matter to purchase the unused capacity for a year. Unfortunately, my checkbook had closer to $250 than $250 million, so we resorted to begging.

The way international capacity is allocated is a bit byzantine. A cable is laid between two points, say Los Angeles and Tokyo. Since laying a cable across an ocean costs $500 million, the cable is owned by a consortium of a dozen or more telecommunications providers. When you lease a line between two countries, owing to a variety of arcane international regulations, you need two companies. Each provides service running in one direction, known as a half-circuit. By putting the two half-circuits together, you get a full line. The bottom line for us was that it wouldn't do any good to convince one company. To get the ball rolling, we needed two companies to agree to make a donation.

Our best bet appeared to be starting with a line across the Pacific Ocean. Both the United States and Japan had very strong fair activities planned, and we had good friends in telecommunications companies in both countries. Jun Murai set to work on KDD, the main international provider in his country. In the United States, I went to AT&T and MCI, brandishing news clips from the *New York Times* and the letters from Clinton and Gore. After a month of trying with AT&T, including numerous letters, phone calls, faxes, and even a briefing to the chairman, it became evident that AT&T would only play if we paid them the full retail price.

MCI was a different story. Serge Wernikoff of MCI dug through the cable charts and identified some unused capacity and Vint Cerf came back to say he was interested, but only if KDD would confirm a donation of their half-circuit. A quick call to Jun Murai confirmed what I suspected would happen: KDD had also been very positive and would happily make the donation, if MCI would confirm their half-circuit. Neither company could make a unilateral move and we had reached a temporary deadlock.

I flew to Tokyo where Jun Murai and I engaged in a week of 24-hours-a-day telecommunications poker. It started with email from the White House to the Ministry of Post and Telecommunications (MPT), which got us a meeting with ministry officials. They were impressed by our letter from the vice president, which emphasized the synergy between our initiative and a recent agreement by the G-7 countries to promote a Global Information Infrastructure. While MPT was supportive, it couldn't order KDD to do anything.

We spent a week of long dinners, faxes, phone calls, and even the occasional email, slowly nudging the U.S. and Japanese governments and the two telecommunications companies. Everybody wanted to do this, but there were all sorts of little issues that kept cropping up. For example, KDD was under strict tariff regulation. It was only allowed to sell lines at carefully set prices. A price of zero was not on the tariff schedule, making it illegal for KDD to make the donation. That particular issue was resolved by specifying that our 45-million-bit-per-second line, being the first of its kind, was in fact not a donation or a sale, but a research experiment for one year.

Finally, Jun and I scheduled a press conference to announce Japanese participation in the fair. By sheer luck, the Tokyo World's Fair had been canceled the week before. Just before going on stage, we had our formal commitments from the companies involved and clearance from MPT, and we were ready to roll. The story of the death of a real world's fair and the subsequent birth of a world's fair for the information age was too much to resist, and over 200 reporters showed up for our press conference.

Our donation from KDD and MCI of a line worth over $20 million for the year, the fastest international line in Internet history, was the centerpiece of that press conference. KDD and MCI were joined by Bay Networks, one of the leading companies that builds routers, the specialized computers that provide the links between long-distance lines and local area networks. In addition to $2 million in routers, Bay Networks also lent us two of their best engineers.

Building the Fair

The rest of 1995 was a whirlwind of activity. I ended up traveling around the world seven times that year. In one particularly intense five-day period, I went from Washington, DC, to Rio de Janeiro, Brazil, to Almaty, Kazakhstan, ending up the week in Atlanta, Georgia.

Support started popping up out of the blue. In Tokyo one day, I received email from a Dr. James Lee in Taiwan, inquiring if Taiwan could participate. I sent a note back, emphasizing that we were really, really busy, but if he was serious I'd try and divert my schedule and stop in Taipei. Several days later, I found myself in Taipei meeting the minister in charge of NII programs for his

With great interest and satisfaction, I have learnt about the Internet 1996 World Exposition. I am confident that this will be one of the global events in our World.

—Asakar Akayev
President of Kyrghyzstan

Vitrine da aldeia global: A Internet sedia a Exposiçaõ Universal de Era De Informação.

—ISTOÉ (Brazil)
September 9, 1995

country, followed by a formal banquet hosted by the head of Chunghwa Telecom, the national telephone company. In just a few days, Taiwan had mobilized a huge effort, drafting Stan Shih, the chairman of the computer giant Acer, as the vice-chair of their organizing committee and enlisting people from dozens of other organizations. This certainly was serious.

The organizing efforts were important, but there was one crucial effort that needed to be finished before the fair opened on January 1, 1996. Specifically, we needed a web site. While many of the pieces could be built throughout the fair in 1996 (one of our mantras was that "this fair would evolve throughout the year"), we needed something credible to open the fair.

In late November, with the issue weighing heavily on my mind, a bit of serendipity happened. I got a note from Becky Pranger, a web designer in Cincinnati whom I had never met. She had seen our Santa Claus site and really liked some of the audio we had produced of cranky elves who said things like "how's an elf supposed to get any sleep with all that jingle, jingle, jingle?"

Becky and Larry Pranger, her husband and partner, wanted to know if we might be willing to trade our audio for a little free design work. A little design work was just what we needed; two days later, Becky and Larry Pranger came to DC and we explained this rather strange web design project. We had our graphic design team, and just in the nick of time!

December was a blur of early mornings and late nights. Becky and I exchanged a hundred mail messages per day as we built the main web site. Martin Lucas, our audio producer, slaved in his studio in Indiana to produce audio files and Expo Radio, a series of interview shows with people who were participating in the fair. Philippe Tabaux, the voice of the elves, worked on building pavilions for India, Tibet, and many other countries. All over the world, teams were frantically working to meet my daily pleas that something, indeed anything, be ready from their countries.

On December 31, we moved hundreds of audio, graphic, and text files in place and I flipped the switch turning on the fair. Washington was in the middle of a huge blizzard, but Philippe and I trudged through three feet of snow to find the only open bar on Capitol Hill where we could have a glass of cheap champagne and toast the world's fair and the new year. I sent Becky a quick email in Cincinnati telling her to go home and sleep and waded back through the snow to my house, a few blocks away from the office.

January 1, 1996, I trudged through the snow back to the office. Had the computer crashed? Were people mailbombing us? Everything was quiet and nothing major was broken. I went and looked at the guestbook for the fair and realized that this world's fair was real. People from all over the world were writing in, from exotic locations such as Japan, Taiwan, Colombia, and Arkansas.

The fair was off and running.

A group of pioneering researchers who have been involved in shaping the Internet since its inception are preparing a world's fair to bring this technology into the lives of millions of people in over a hundred countries.

—*Bangkok Post*
March 15, 1995

In the stations where the papers fly,
Past the peasants of our fears.
Just nerves of sand infused with light,
It's nowhere and it's here.

It's the distances between us
It's the atmosphere and land
It's the water and the fiber
And the borders that we span.

Martin Lucas and Corinne Becknell
Distances

OFFICIAL SOUVENIR POSTAL

THE AGRICULTURAL BLD.

CERES

WORLD'S
COLUMBIAN EXPOSITION

President.

Secretary.

SERIES Nº 1.   DESIGN Nº 4.
COPYRIGHT, 1893, BY CHARLES W. GOLDSMITH, AGENT FOR THE UNITED STATES, THE ISABELLA, 45 VAN BUREN ST. CHICAGO.   AMERICAN LITHOGRAPHIC CO. N.Y. LITHO.

1893 WORLD'S COLUMBIAN EXPOSITION

The Tempo of Our Times

2

The middle of the nineteenth century marked the birth of the industrial revolution, the beginning of our modern era. The power of steam was building factories and railways, soon to be followed by electricity, the internal combustion engine, radio, and the telephone. The world was about to change.

In January 1850, Prince Albert convened a commission for a universal exhibition that would display every machine known to man. Over 233 designs were submitted for the building to house the "Great Exhibition of the Works of All Nations." Joseph Paxton produced a sketch for a Crystal Palace on a piece of blotting paper, then submitted the final plans in less than nine days. The building itself, a remarkable edifice with 293,655 panes of glass, 330 huge iron columns, and 24 miles of gutters, was erected in just six months.

The building featured the largest roof ever made at the time and stood out among London's architecture. To complement the mass of glass, the building was decorated in red, green, and blue, and the iron columns were variegated with yellow stripes.[1] Despite fears in the press that the building was unstable and would dissolve on spectators in a torrent of shards of glass, the building proved to be a popular icon.

The committees putting together the Great Exhibition gave a great deal of attention to their system of classification. The British proposed a system that included five major divisions, such as "Raw Materials," "Machinery," and the ever-popular "Miscellaneous." Countless subdivisions and subclassifications were used to put all mankind into appropriate categories. The French, then as now, had slight philosophical differences with their British colleagues. At one point, the French commissioner, to show why the British system wouldn't work, held up his walking stick and demanded to know its classification. The British commissioner assigned it to "Class XX: Articles of Clothing for Immediate Personal and Domestic Use: Miscellaneous Objects." The French commissioner pointed out that he believed that it would better fit in as a "Class V: Machines for Direct Use: Machines for the Propagation of Direct Motion."[2]

Inside the building was just about everything you could imagine, and many things you wouldn't have thought of. America brought stuffed squirrels and a McCormick reaper. Lucifer matches were the latest modern convenience,

Yesterday, I went for the second time to the Crystal Palace. It is a wonderful place, vast, strange, new, and impossible to describe. Its grandeur does not consist in one thing, but in the unique assemblage of all things.

—Charlotte Brontë
Letter of 1851

The Crystal Palace, erected in just six months, was a remarkable building with 293,655 panes of glass, 330 huge iron columns, and 24 miles of gutters.

an envelope-making machine could produce 60 units a minute, and, of course, there were steam engines everywhere you turned.

Many of the objects shown for the first time were things that we take for granted today. William Brockeden, for example, had an exhibit that showed how powdered graphite could be reformed into a block without binder. This was the birth of the classic yellow pencil. At the time, high-quality pencils were made of cedar or other expensive woods. By painting the pencils, manufacturers could use a cheaper wood by covering up the imperfections. But why did Brockeden choose yellow? Since the inside of the pencil was black and the device had been developed in Vienna, he decided that the outside must be yellow in honor of the yellow-and-black Austro-Hungarian flag.

Brockeden sold these relatively cheaply made pencils for three times the price of his competition, trumpeting the supposedly high-quality "Siberian Graphite" and sleek shiny yellow color as the marks of quality.[3]

Over 100,000 exhibits on 17 acres under one remarkable roof drew the world to London for the first of what were to be 75 years of great exhibitions and world's fairs. The palace was moved to another location after the fair, where it was a meeting place for many years until it burned down.

The Great Paris Expositions

After the resounding success of the Crystal Palace, the focus shifted across the channel to France as Paris hosted a series of great exhibitions. In 1855, the Palais d'Industrie was built and the exhibition it housed brought in 5.1 million visitors from all over the continent. In 1867, 15 million people came to the next exposition.[4]

When it came time for the 1889 Centennial Exposition, the organizers wanted a symbol people would remember. The idea of a 1,000-foot tower was something that had been bandied about for years by architects. At the time, the Washington Monument was the largest tower in the world at 555 feet.

Edouard Lockroy was the minister of commerce and industry who drew the initial plans for the Centennial Exposition in Paris. Lockroy published a note in the *Journal Officiel* and announced that bidding was open for a tower that would be the centerpiece of the exposition. The responses were fairly diverse. One proposal was in the form of a giant guillotine, another was a giant garden sprinkler that could water the city in case of drought.

This was an era of great change, and one with no parallels in history. It was the engineers, not the generals or politicians, who were leading this revolution, and an engineer named Gustave Eiffel had been at the forefront, helping to build bridges, railways, and the Statue of Liberty.[5]

Eiffel won the competition and was awarded a subsidy of $300,000, putting an additional $1.3 million of his own money on the line. Eiffel would be allowed to operate the tower (as well as the restaurants, cafés, and other ways of separating people from their money once they got on the tower) for 20 years, after which ownership would revert to the city of Paris.

Although Eiffel won the tower competition, there was another serious contender for the honor. Electricity and lighting were the key technologies during this period. Edison's carbon filament lamp had first been made public at the Paris Electricity Exposition of 1881. Until then, public electric lighting was all arc lighting.[6] Arc lighting was quite popular in the United States. Detroit had 122 towers lighting 21 square miles. Cities ranging from San Jose, California, to Flint, Michigan, all had built huge arc lighting towers.

A young French electrical engineer named Sébillot toured the United States and was hooked. When the 1889 exposition committee launched a competition for a "monumental landmark," Sébillot teamed up with the architect Jules Bourdais.[7] In 1885, the team submitted a proposal for a 360-meter Sun Tower, designed to light "tout Paris." The tower narrowly lost the competition to the one submitted by the bridge designer Gustave Eiffel. Why did the Sun Tower lose out? The committee was worried that "the light would dazzle rather than illuminate," blinding viewers with its glory.

Writers, painters, sculptors, architects, passionate lovers of the heretofore intact beauty of Paris, we come to protest with all our strength, with all our indignation, in the name of betrayed French taste, in the name of threatened French art and history, against the erection in the heart of our capital of the useless and monstrous Eiffel Tower, which the public has scornfully and rightly dubbed the Tower of Babel.

—*La Protestation des Artistes* including Charles Gounod, Guy de Maupassant, and Alexandre Dumas fils[8]

By the time all the competing and awarding were done, however, there was only two years left to build the tower. Eiffel got the job done on schedule, with the loss of only one life. By early 1889, visitors were climbing hundreds of steps to get on the first and second platforms of the towers. The elevators almost didn't make it because French procurement regulations required that the bid by the Otis Elevator Company be rejected the first time. When no French company would bid on the crucial elevator from the first to the second platform, Otis was allowed to rebid; he completed the job by mid-June, not long after the opening of the Exposition.

On June 10, Eiffel held his grand opening, squiring royalty to the top, including tours of his private apartments. In the coming weeks, guests to the tower included the shah of Persia, the prince of Wales, the king of Siam, the bey of Djibouti, the president of France, Buffalo Bill, and Thomas Edison. Young women purchased special dresses made for the occasion, called the "Eiffel ascensionniste." Over 1.9 million people came to the tower, and over 32 million attended the Centennial Exposition.[9]

The tower was used extensively by Eiffel over the next years as a serious science instrument. Working with the French Central Weather Bureau, Eiffel installed thermometers, barometers, and anemometers. Later, Eiffel began experimenting with aerodynamics, building the world's first reliable wind tunnel in the tower. Today, the Eiffel Tower still receives twice as many visitors as the Louvre.[10]

The Philadelphia Centennial Exhibition

While there had been a few half-hearted attempts before, the United States entry into the world's fair sweepstakes came in 1876, the 100th anniversary of the birth of the republic. The nation's first capital, Philadelphia, was the natural site for this Centennial Exhibition, which centered on a vast machinery hall with 13 acres of new devices, widgets, and gadgets.

One of the most popular exhibits in the Machinery Hall was a prototype slice of the galvanized cable that Roebling Brothers would use for the Brooklyn Bridge. The bridge would end up using 6.8 million pounds of these cables, covered with zinc and with a strength of 160,000 pounds per square inch (double that of the iron wire used for the bridge over Niagara Falls).

The Machinery Hall also featured other novelties, such as the first typewriter and a telephone. Emperor Dom Pedro of Brazil put Bell's strange device to his ear, then quickly dropped it, exclaiming "My God, it talks!"

Telephones and typewriters were interesting gadgets, but what drew people was power. Towering over the hall was the gigantic Corliss steam engine, taller than a house, powering 13 acres of machinery in the great hall.

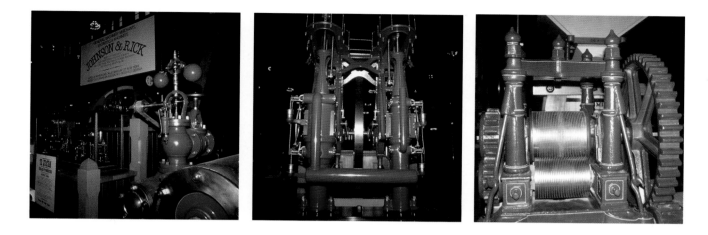

The 1500-horsepower double Corliss steam engine connected to five miles of shafting used to move this power throughout the vast machinery hall.[11]

On opening day, the hall was full of people but dead silent as President Ulysses S. Grant and Emperor Dom Pedro climbed up on the engine platform and hit the levers that allowed steam into the cylinders. The engine hissed and the floor trembled. Then, huge walking beams slowly started moving up and down, feeding a giant flywheel, which spun around, gaining momentum and storing energy. Belts started moving and shafts and pulleys started turning as power went out into the hall.

The amount of activity in the hall was daunting. The *New York Herald*, *Sun,* and *Times* all printed their daily editions in the hall. Machines started sewing, pins got stuck into paper, wallpaper was printed, logs were sawed. What really amazed people, though, was the Corliss engine that powered it all. The machine had only one attendant, who sat calmly on the platform and read newspapers.[12]

To preserve the results of the Centennial Exhibition, the Smithsonian Institution built its second building on the Washington Mall. The Arts and Industries Building still contains many replicas of the devices in the Machinery Hall, including a model of the great Corliss engine.

The Chicago Columbian Exposition of 1893

In 1890, in the middle of America's rush to industrialize, Congress authorized a World's Columbian Exposition in Chicago to celebrate the 400th anniversary of the "discovery" of America.

Chicago had come into its own in the decade before the exposition. In 1871, the city had been razed by a fire, but in just 22 years had raised skyscrapers over the prairie and was ready to play host to the world. Nervous about how

Replicas of machines at the Philadelphia Centennial Exposition are on display at the Smithsonian Institution in Washington, DC. In the middle is a replica of the Corliss steam engine.

I am reminded of Chicago's 1893 World's Fair and subsequent fairs that heralded technology as the Promised Land. Technology's siren still calls to us today. Is the Internet's promise of electronic democracy, instant communication, and virtual information our long-lost Eden? Probably not. A better land? I think so.

—**Randy C. Bunney**
Laramie, WY, USA
bunney@uwyo.edu

The Chicago Columbian Exposition featured spacious grounds and beautiful parks, complements to the Beaux Arts architecture of the Great White Way.

their brash new architecture would seem to the rest of the world, the city fathers established a commission of the best architects and designers, who produced a classical Beaux Arts "white city" from 686 acres of marshes on the city's south side.

In charge of construction was Daniel Burnham, who, based on the grand success of his work in Chicago, was later put in charge of rescuing the dusty plans L'Enfant made in 1792 and reconstructing Washington, DC, as a "city of parks and vistas." It is ironic that Chicago, which helped invent modern architecture, ended up with a fair full of imitations of the Renaissance and Classical Greece.[13]

Chicago set a new standard for world's fairs, bringing in 21.5 million paid subscribers while letting in another 6 million people on free passes. The gate receipts of $14 million surpassed the previous record holder, the Paris Exhibition of 1889, which had collected a then-astounding $8.3 million.

Electricity ran all over the Chicago fair and became one of the most notable features of this exposition. The fair telephone system, for example, was connected to the Chicago Exchange, with special links to police, fire alarm, and telegraph services. The Edison Tower of Light was an 82-foot high tower at the center of the Electricity Building. The tower had been ringed with mirrors, and incandescent bulbs that sparkled and flashed in changing patterns of color. The shaft was topped by a gilded capital, upon which rested an eight-foot replica of an incandescent light bulb constructed from thirty thousand prisms.[14]

Outside, all the waterways and buildings were illuminated, and every evening 38 colored arc lights played off waterfalls.

Chicago was the kickoff celebration for the birth of the electrical industry. In their three-volume *History of Industrial Power in the United States,* Hunter and Bryant wax almost rhapsodic over "a broad range of potential applications of this astonishingly versatile new form of energy, in transportation and communication as well as in lighting."

At the opening ceremonies, President Grover Cleveland turned the key on the great engine in the Machinery Hall and the exposition came to life. A veil fell from a golden Statute of the Republic, fountains shot water into the air, and cannons thundered. The fair was the place where many people came into their first contact with this new technology, and the use of

striking electrical exhibits … gave thousands of visitors their first direct experience with electrical power and light and also impressed the industrial and engineering world with the surprisingly high level and varied attainments of a group of industries that had hardly existed ten years earlier.[15]

While at the 1876 Philadelphia Centennial celebration the Corliss steam engine was the biggest yet built, by 1893 engines its size had become commonplace. In Chicago, there was an aggregate of 22,000 horsepower of electrical generating capacity, used to power motors all over the fair, not to mention hundreds of thousands of arc and incandescent lights, moving sidewalks, and the Intramural Railway, featuring a 2,000 horsepower dynamo.

Most of the electrical plants of the time, particularly those of Edison, used direct current (DC). George Westinghouse, a young engineer, was working hard on a radical form of electricity, alternating current (AC). He got his big break when he won the contract to do lighting for the 1893 fair. Westinghouse put in a full electrical system, with a generating plant, transformers, motors, the works. The success of his efforts in Chicago was so impressive that, in the summer of 1893, alternating current was chosen for the great Niagara Falls project and Westinghouse got the contract to install the initial 5,000 horsepower generators.[16]

One of the keys to the successful use of AC in Chicago was the rotary converter, exhibited by both Westinghouse and General Electric. This device allowed the coupling of old DC systems to the new AC grid. Chicago Edison, for

It is a privilege to be part of the origins of this emerging technology. The clarity of the vision is yet to come. History has a way of unfolding and giving perspective to the "hasting and evanescent present." In the spirit of the Columbian exposition, I give my best regards.

—**Dan Garigan**
Dallas, OR, USA
d.garigan@ieee.org

Photo/Smithsonian Institution

Photo/Smithsonian Institution

A Ferris wheel is visible in the background of this 1904 picture from the rooftops of St. Louis.

example, was able to start shutting down its local DC stations, using AC for long-haul transmission and converting to DC at the local districts.[17] Backward compatibility has remained one of the key requirements for any technology to be successful.

At the Chicago World's Fair

Surrounding the grand structures of the formal center of the fair was a teeming amusement park, with George Ferris's huge new wheel at its center. The axle for the 1,200-ton Ferris wheel was the largest steel forging in the world. Other technologies also had their debut at this world's fair: the postcard and the hamburger were both born in Chicago in 1893.

People started with the Great White City at the center of the fair, but invariably migrated to the Midway Plaisance, a street one mile long and six hundred feet wide. A series of model villages offered food and dance, and the entertainment included the notorious Little Egypt, the scandalous "hoochie-coochie girl of the Nile" in *The Streets of Cairo*. Everything from German beer gardens to Samoan wrestlers were present in this prototypical amusement park. Scott Joplin played his newfangled music and people could sit and write home on a postcard while enjoying the most modern of libations, a carbonated soft drink.[18]

I've always been a great fan of World's Fairs, and am very pleased to have found yours! I'm looking forward to exploring your Fair and all its Pavilions, Places and Events! I think this is a great idea, and I hope that you'll do it again in future years!

—Loren A. Herrigstad
Littlerock, WA, USA
lbhrgstd@isomedia.com

Corn was everywhere in Chicago. Almost all the State Pavilions featured corn objects. In the definitive *Story of Corn,* Betty Fussel tells us how "Iowa's palace was 'Pompeiian style,' with a grapevine frieze of purple popcorn." Other photos showed "corn draperies, pyramids, corbels, Roman arches, Gothic arches, buttresses, arabesques" and any other architectural motif that could be applied to the great grain.[19] Reid's Yellow Dent was "the corn that changed the face of the American continent" and was crowned the grand prize winner in Chicago. This was the first of the hybrid corns that swept over the farms of the American midwest.[20]

Another technology that came into its own in Chicago was standardized time, an invention of the modern era. The railroads needed to coordinate time among their stations and with each other, lest two trains sharing a stretch of track share it too closely. In 1883, the U.S. Naval Observatory agreed to telegraph standard railway time throughout the country, a great boon for Western Union, which also happened to own the Self-Winding Clock Company. To celebrate its accomplishments at the World's Columbian Exposition, Western Union built a network of 200 clocks, all regulated from their central pavilion, topped with a 150-foot clock tower.[21]

Electric-powered streetcars hauled people to the exposition, trains of four cars jammed with people inside, on the roof, and hanging off the sides.[22] Visitors came from all over the world, but the fair also brought farmers, school children, and residents from small towns from throughout the midwest to Chicago to learn about culture and technology and to entertain themselves.[23]

One group that came in droves to Chicago were the world's engineers. At the time, engineering wasn't considered a real profession, and there was considerable tension between the engineers who wanted to build things and the corporate employers who wanted to build businesses. In fact, throughout the next 100 years, technology deployment would be marked by tension between the societies that represent technology, such as the Institute of Radio Engineers at the turn of the last century or the Internet Engineering Task Force at the turn of this next one, and the groups that represented engineering as a business.[24]

The Louisiana Purchase Exposition

Wireless became the hot application of the turn of the last century. For the St. Louis World's Fair in 1904, the great Guglielmo Marconi was personally invited to exhibit by the governor of Missouri. Marconi heard that his arch-rival Lee DeForest and other competitors would be there.

As the market leader, Marconi decided he shouldn't be lending legitimacy to his competitors, particularly at what he figured would be a short-term exhibit. Instead, Marconi concentrated on "real things," such as sending a message

I went to the University of Chicago surrounded by the history of the 1893 World's Fair. I loved seeing the building from the fair [at the Internet World Expo, reminding me of how people went there to learn the latest technological innovations of the day. I am so happy to see what you have done creating this ability in the worlds latest technological achievement.

—**Caroline Katzin**
Ft. Lauderdale, FL, USA
caroline@shadow.net

Photo/Smithsonian Institution

Brilliantly lit domes and towers were one of the hallmarks of the U.S. world's fairs in the early 20th century, such as this 1901 night view of the Pan-American Exposition in Buffalo, New York.

Absolutely fantastic idea. I was born in St. Louis and love all the old 1904 St. Louis World's Fair illustrations. This is a great way to learn more about other cultures, share information and promote cooperation.

—Steve Simons
Austin, TX, USA
Steve_Simons@US.Dell.Com

across the Atlantic Ocean on December 12, 1902, a stunt that got him on the front page of the *New York Times*.[25]

While Marconi turned down the offer to participate, Lee DeForest was never one to miss an opportunity for exposure. He spent $10,000 to take a sightseeing tower from Niagara Falls and re-erect it in St. Louis (with the not-so-discreet addition of his name emblazoned in lights across the top). The tower was more than a giant billboard and was used for experiments such as supporting the first automobile equipped with a wireless receiver. Just to make sure that people saw all these experiments (and the DeForest name), the operators were told that whenever crowds started to thin around the tower, they were to emit as loud a spark as possible, audible a quarter-mile away.

The 300-foot tower DeForest built was the largest structure in St. Louis and the zenith of his career. Although DeForest had a beautiful three-bedroom house near the fair, complete with cook and servants, he had a cot brought to the top of the tower. At night, he would enjoy the cool night air, then fall asleep. During the day, the tower was used to send messages to the "Wireless Auto. No. 1," but also to Chicago, Illinois, and Kansas City, Missouri.[26]

On Electricity Day, DeForest received the Grand Prize Medal for General Excellence in Wireless Telegraphy. At the time, people didn't know what would happen with their technologies. While the telephone was first considered to be a broadcast medium, wireless AM was envisioned as a point-to-point communication mechanism. AT&T was making big money acting as the transportation network to bring feeds from one radio station to another. Edwin Armstrong's invention of frequency modulation (FM) turned the tables, and soon the airwaves were being used to send broadcasts out to huge audiences and the telephone became the way individuals talked to each other.

The 1939 New York World's Fair

> In the darkest days of the Depression, they dreamed of orderly hygienic cities and houses. … They looked ahead to safe, fast travel on luxurious streamlined aircraft, trains, buses, ships, and automobiles. Unlike modern architects, whose utopias rarely develop beyond the drawing stage, the first American industrial designers were able to build their model city, the 1939 New York World's Fair.[27]

The 1939 New York World's Fair suffered from unfortunate timing and the investors lost two-thirds of their investment when World War II broke out shortly after the fair opened. Before the war, however, the fair attracted large crowds to Flushing Meadow Park in Queens. Many of the people who came liked not only the fair, but Queens as well. The communities of Forest Hills and Elmhurst sprang up after the war.[28]

The 1893 World's Columbian Exposition in Chicago had inspired the creation of the Coney Island amusement park. The 1939 New York World's Fair set a new price performance point, with amusement parks and rides and "stage-set representations of vernacular architecture" that inspired Walt Disney to create Disneyland.

Sharon Zukin draws some telling parallels between Chicago in 1893 and New York in 1939. Both fairs had ideal communities, the 200 idealized buildings of Chicago's White City and the Town of Tomorrow in New York. Both fairs featured visions of a world led by brave corporations (though by 1939, it was a new generation, led by General Motors, GE, Eastman Kodak, and AT&T).[29]

The future was the topic of this world's fair, even more so than most. Norman Bel Geddes designed a Futurama ride for General Motors, putting the riders in chairs that moved across a model of an idealized United States. From one coast to another you flew across cities of the future, with cars on spacious roads and pedestrians on elevated walkways.

Geddes forgot one detail: his model city had no churches. This omission was noticed (repeatedly) when the fair opened in 1939, and by the 1940 season of the fair churches had magically appeared in the Futurama.[30]

When you were done with the Futurama, you might then go to the Perisphere, a huge dome. Inside was Democracity, a perfect model of a perfect

The Internet World Exposition is not only in a neat location … it also gives much needed information on a pivotal event in United States history, the 1939 New York World's Fair!

—Frank Barton
Parsippany, NJ, USA
75275.1351@compuserve.com

world with a thriving central core and pleasant suburbs for nuclear families. The Democracity was high art for model making, requiring over 100 people to keep the exhibit running.

You left the Perisphere by walking down the Helicline, a long ramp that snaked around the dome. Next to the Perisphere was the huge spike of the Trylon. The Trylon and Perisphere, painted white and lit brightly at night, were the visual icons of this world's fair, appearing everywhere you went in New York.[31]

A Medium Is Born

While the radio world was expanding quickly in the 1930s with the stunning success of Armstrong's implementation of FM, David Sarnoff had staked RCA's future on the newfangled medium of television. Television had been percolating into the public consciousness through experiments in the 1930s in Britain, Germany, and the United States. RCA was ready to roll this new service out as a major new product. Sarnoff scheduled his first program to coincide with the opening of the 1939 New York World's Fair.

RCA built its pavilion on the Avenue of Progress. Only a few hundred people around the city had television sets, but that didn't stop Sarnoff from putting a camera on the Avenue of Patriots. On April 20, 1939, Sarnoff stood in front of the camera, talking to just a few people, and proclaimed "now we add radio sight to sound."[32]

Like many inventions, television was only partly the creation of the RCA Corporation. Though Sarnoff did the PR blitz, he built on the work of many inventors, including an unsung engineer named Philo T. Farnsworth. One of the surprise submissions in the Internet 1996 World Exposition was *The Farnsworth Chronicles,* a fascinating account of the inventor's life based on the personal archives of his widow and put together by Paul Schatzkin, a devoted follower of Farnsworth.

Just as Baron Haussmann crowned his achievements with the Universal Exposition of 1867 in Paris, Robert Moses wanted to crown his own achievements with the 1964 New York World's Fair. The fair left huge debts behind, but it also left Shea Stadium and "the hollow fretwork of the Unisphere, with its abandoned dedication to man's aspiration towards Peace through mutual understanding."[33]

The 1964 World's Fair in New York also featured the future, but was somehow different, less striking. There was no brave new future to show. The fair had AT&T's Video Phone and a few new cars, but lacked the feeling that a whole generation of technology was about to spring out into society, or perhaps the fair participants were unaware of the changes that were about to occur in communications and computers.

The following saying is off the "Donut Casino" postcard that was given out at the 1939 New York World's Fair: As you ramble on thru Life, Brother, Whatever be your Goal, Keep your Eye upon the Doughnut And not upon the Hole!

—**Rich Hayden**
New Haven, CT, USA
haydenrm@aol.com

The Tempo of Their Times

The era of the Great Exhibitions started in 1851 at the Crystal Palace and ended in 1939 at the New York World's Fair. During those 88 years, the world saw an industrial age come into being. They were where people went to understand what this new world would be and how it would affect their lives.

The world's fairs of the industrial era played a crucial role in cushioning the shock of technological change. The fairs were a place where engineers could meet to advance the state of their art: rising to the challenge of the mammoth expositions by inventing new buildings and towers, power plants, and Ferris wheels. The fairs left a lasting impression on the landscape in the form of their Eiffel Towers, but they also left lasting impressions in the minds of their visitors.

The world's fairs marked the tempo of their times. They set the pace of our modern era; they were the icons that symbolized the dawn of the industrial age.

Notes

1. Asa Briggs, *Victorian Things*, Penguin Books (London, 1990), pp. 52–53. Along with the other two volumes of this series, *Victorian Cities* and *Victorian People*, this trilogy gives a compelling look at Victorian life.
2. Ibid., 55.
3. Henry Petroski, *The Pencil*, Knopf (New York, 1993), pp. 127–134. Everything you wanted to know about pencils. Petroski is the author of a series of books about engineering and design, including *To Engineer Is Human* and *The Evolution of Useful Things*.
4. Joseph Harriss, *The Tallest Tower: Eiffel and The Belle Epoque*, Regnery Gateway (Washington, 1975), pp. 7–11. Fascinating biography of Eiffel with particular focus on the tower and the Exposition.
5. Ibid., p. 37.
6. Wolfgang Schivelbusch, *Disenchanted Night*, University of California Press (Berkeley, 1988), p. 58. Highly recommended history of lighting. Also recommended is *The Railway Journey*, the first volume in Schivelbusch's trilogy on the dawn of modern life.
7. Ibid., pp. 126–128.
8. Hariss, *The Tallest Tower*, p. 26.
9. Ibid., pp. 95, 122, 230.
10. Roland Barthes, *The Eiffel Tower and Other Mythologies*, Noonday Press (New York, 1979), p. 9.
11. Louis C. Hunter and Lynwood Bryant, *A History of Industrial Power in the United States, 1780–1930. Vol 3: The Transmission of Power*, MIT Press (Cambridge, MA, 1991), pp. 207–208.
12. David McCullough, *The Great Bridge: The Epic Story of the Building of the Brooklyn Bridge*, Touchstone Books (New York, 1972), pp. 351–352.
13. Daniel J. Boorstin, *The Creators*, Random House (New York, 1992), pp. 549–550. A panoramic sweep of man's creations and creators through history.
14. Carolyn Marvin, *When Old Technologies Were New: Thinking About Electrical Communication in the Late Nineteenth Century*, Oxford University Press (Oxford, 1988), pp. 171–172.

The Crystal Palace, 1850 … The breadth of Prince Albert's vision of an industrial future for England in the first World's Fair is nothing compared to what we can achieve with the Internet. Seize the power to shape our own future. Jack In.

—**Ericka Fowler**
New York, NY, USA
175551@newschool.edu

This site has given me great insights for a paper I'm writing on the Columbian Exposition in Chicago, 1893 due tomorrow ... who knew that procrastination could be so productive! Thank you.

—**Leslie Hermanson**
Princeton, NJ, USA

15. Hunter and Bryant, *A History of Industrial Power*, pp. 207–208.
16. Ibid., p. 248.
17. Thomas P. Hughes, *Electrification of America, Technology and Culture*, vol. 20, no. 1, January, 1979, reprinted in Terry S. Reynolds, ed., *The Engineer in America*, University of Chicago Press (Chicago, 1991), p. 210.
18. Neil Baldwin, *Edison: Inventing the Century*, Hyperion (New York, 1995), p. 235.
19. Betty Fussel, *The Story of Corn*, Knopf (New York, 1992), pp. 318–319. The ultimate story of corn. What more can we say? A fascinating look at the grain that changed the world.
20. Ibid., p. 71.
21. Michael O'Malley, *Keeping Watch: A History of American Time*, Penguin Books (New York: 1990), pp. 153–154.
22. Brian J. Cudahy, *Cash, Tokens, and Transfers: A History of Urban Mass Transit in North America*, Fordham University Press (New York, 1990), p. 4.
23. William Cronon, *Nature's Metropolis: Chicago and the Great West*, Norton (New York, 1991), p. 344. The story of Chicago's growth from empty prairie to the rail capital of the United States.
24. Edwin T. Layton, Jr., *The Revolt of the Engineers*, Johns Hopkins (Baltimore, 1986), p. 45. Looks at the politics of the engineering societies. Must reading for anybody involved in Internet standardization who wants to understand why committees proliferate when there is still real work to do.
25. Susan J. Douglas, *Inventing American Broadcasting: 1899–1922*, Johns Hopkins (Baltimore, 1987), p. 72.
26. Tom Lewis, *Empire of the Air*, HarperCollins (New York, 1991), p. 44. The story of radio's early days. This book was made into an excellent PBS documentary by Ken Burns.
27. Donald J. Bush, *The Streamlined Decade*, Braziller (New York, 1975), p. 3. The birth of planes, trains, and automobiles in the 1950s.
28. Geoffry Moorhouse, *Imperial City: The Rise and Rise of New York* Spectre (London, 1989), pp. 242–243.
29. Sharon Zukin, *Landscapes of Power: From Detroit to Disney World*, University of California Press (Berkeley, 1991), p. 225.
30. David Gelernter, *1939: The Lost World of the Fair*, Free Press (New York, 1995), pp. 23–25. A wonderful book about the New York fair written by a prominent computer scientist.
31. Ibid., pp. 66–82.
32. Lewis, *Empire of the Air*, p. 275.
33. Moorhouse, *Imperial City*, p. 297.

HOLIDAYS, PARADES, SUMMER TRIPS, SPORTING
EVENTS. FAIRS. HERE THE CHILD'S MANIC
EXCITEMENT IS REALLY EXULTATION AT HIS
OWN POWER: THE WORLD WILL NOW NOT ONLY
EXIST FOR-HIM BUT WILL PRESENT ITSELF AS
SPECIAL-FOR-HIM. EVERY HANGING BANNER,
BALLOON, GILDED BOOTH, CLOWN-WIG, TURN
OF THE WRENCH ON A TENT'S ERECTION—
EVERY BRIGHT BIT SIGNIFIES, REFERS.

DAVID FOSTER WALLACE
A SUPPOSEDLY FUN THING I'LL NEVER DO AGAIN

General View of Irish International Exhibition, Dublin, 1907

1907 IRISH INTERNATIONAL EXHIBITION

Places in the Real World 3

Our most compelling concept for the world's fair was also the hardest to realize. A strictly on-line virtual world's fair had no attraction for us. World's fairs are how you reach out to new people, how you solve new problems. Places in the real world were our way of putting computers into public locations and using these places to show people our world's fair.

Integrating the computer into society is not just a problem faced by world's fair planners. It is the next big challenge for the Internet. Today, there are a few Internet cybercafés, coffee shops with computers taking up table space and hooked into the Internet by a few modems. These early prototypes are attractive to the already converted as a place to socialize, drink a cup of coffee, or read their electronic magazines.

If these places are really going to succeed, however, the computers must disappear, becoming part of the facilities instead of a showcase on stage. In the early days of electricity, there were no electrical outlets. Wires ran all over the place and homeowners became adept at stringing new appliances directly into the mains. Over time, we learned how to make the infrastructure disappear, to become a natural part of buildings.

The challenge of putting places on line is more than just technical. There has to be a reason to bring the technology into a building. "Because it's cool" may work for a few places, but a more compelling reason is needed. This technology also requires people: people to install the computers and telecommunications lines, people to run the computers, and, most important, people who have a reason to use them.

Our places in the real world program for the world's fair had mixed results. We had dreams of thousands of places around the world. That didn't happen, but in a few locations some very surprising results did occur. In Taiwan, hundreds of computers were installed in showrooms to help spread the Internet, but computers were also installed in national treasures such as the National Palace Museum and the Sun Yat Sen Memorial.

In other countries, the fair was used to bring about partnerships between places for people and the Internet engineers who maintain the infrastructure. In Amsterdam, for example, the fair helped to cement the relationship between the national backbone engineers and the operators of an innovative facility in downtown Amsterdam dedicated to the study of old and new media.

This fair embraces the idea of "World Exposition" perhaps more so than past efforts. In a society immersed in cutting-edge technology, and with the web virtually eliminating geographical barriers, it's only fitting that the next grand exposition be played out in the domain of cyberspace.

—Todd Blackburn
Knoxville, TN, USA
killdozer1@aol.com

Where will this fair take place? What city? When?

—Lis Maria Rabaco
Serra Fina, Brazil
lis@cenpes.petrobras.gov.br

31

The Digital City of
Harajuku, located
in a busy Tokyo
shopping district.

The Digital City of Harajuku

Harajuku is one of the prime shopping districts in Tokyo, a crowded warren
of shops specializing in fashion, cosmetics, and other products that attract the
young shoppers of Japan. Our most successful place in the real world was
installed here, a most unlikely location. In Japan, only a small percentage of
Internet users are women. The Digital City of Harajuku project proved that
this is more a historical and cultural accident than a lack of interest.

The Digital City of Harajuku was the brainchild of Joichi Ito, a multimedia
producer and well-known celebrity in Japan. His partner in this project was
Reiko Chiba, a teen idol best known as the pink ranger on the *Mighty Morphin
Power Rangers*. They convinced the merchants of Harajuku to give them some
space to install computers aimed specifically at showing women what the
Internet is and how to use it.

At first the merchants were quite skeptical, but Joichi is nothing if not
persuasive. He pointed out the vast marketing potential of the Internet, and

Reiko Chiba
and Joichi Ito.

Photos/Hiroshi Tokuda

also mentioned that the computers and the Internet hookup would be free. He went to IBM and persuaded them to help support the operation. "A fashion shopping mall? Is that our market?" was the first reaction.

In early 1996, Joichi Ito and Reiko Chiba opened the Digital City of Harajuku. Banners featuring the exposition were installed on the sidewalks of Harajuku. A big fashion show kicked off the site, complete with an IBM logo in pink, certainly a first for Big Blue.

Over 20,000 women ended up using the Digital City facility. Seventy-five percent of them said they had never used the Internet before and all said they would want to do so in the future. My favorite part of the Digital City was a little sign on the wall reading "No Oyaji." Oyaji are old folks wearing suits, who are the typical denizens of a place with computers. Reiko Chiba was adamant that her facility was to be used for the intended audience and Oyaji were politely whisked away to keep the computers free for real people.

I'm just browsing around in a department store in Japan. It's great to look into a world where there are no boundaries and where people can communicate. I hope to buy a computer and participate in this world. Thank You.

—Toshio Tanaka
Tokyo, Japan

33

Taiwan

The country that really took the concept of places to heart was Taiwan. Taiwan is one of the world's leading producers of personal computers. The local industry banded together and came up with a donation of over 1,500 computers to install throughout the country. With the help of the government and a cast of hundreds of volunteers, these computers were installed in many high-profile locations.

The National Palace Museum is one of the treasures of Asia, housing artifacts from the Imperial Palace in Beijing and numerous other historical objects from throughout China. In March, I stopped in Taipei and was handed the usual agenda full of meetings in various locations. Near the bottom of the agenda was "Visit to the National Palace Museum."

I assumed this would be a tour of the museum, probably because there was a hole in my schedule and people didn't want to just send me back to my hotel room to read email (though a few unoccupied hours to read email in a hotel is certainly one of the highlights of the day if you're traveling all the time). When we arrived at the National Palace Museum, we were ushered into the grand entrance hall. To my shock, the entrance hall was festooned with Expo96 posters.

A half-dozen computers had been installed in the reading library of the museum as a way for scholars to access materials on the Internet. Special classes were sometimes conducted in the facility. More important, the museum had begun the process of digitizing photographs of many of their objects in cooperation with the Industrial Technology Research Institute, a high-tech think tank that spearheaded many of the world's fair activities for their country.

Later in the year, when I was back in Taipei, the agenda had another perplexing item: "Open train station." This time I was less skeptical and half expected to be opening a new train station someplace in Taiwan. Instead, we went to the main station in Taipei, a facility that serves over 1 million people per day.

We were met by Peter Li, the exuberant leader of the Taiwan Internet Alliance. He had installed two dozen computers in the main lobby of the train station and had huge exposition banners fluttering throughout the hall. High-speed Internet access had been installed by Chunghwa Telecommunications, and members of the Taiwan Internet Alliance were standing by to help people use the computers. Peter Li's efforts with Taiwan industry were supplemented by assistance from Sher-Jenn Lee, a senior government official who tirelessly canvassed major institutions such as Chunghwa Telecommunications and the National Palace Museum to convince them to participate.

*Hello, my friend.
My name is Wei-peng Chang, I come from Taipei, Taiwan, Republic of China. This is the best fair I've ever been to. I hope that every day is like today, and every site is like this fair. Enjoy it!*

—Wei-peng Chang
Taipei, Taiwan
pong@cc.nccu.edu.tw

Grand opening of the computers at the Taipei Central Train Station. Opposite, Peter Li shows the crowd his stone soup.

*This is just the future world.
Greetings to everybody in
the whole virtual-real
world! Aquest és el mon del
futur. Salutacions a tothon
en tot el mon virtual-real!*

—**Ramon Cervelló i Eroles**
Vallirana, Barcelona, Spain
ramon2@lix.intercom.es

Mr. Li gave an interesting speech that told how he and others had been able to get such an effort mobilized. Indeed, the story applies to the fair as a whole. Mr. Li, in opening the site, told the story of stone soup. You put a stone into a pot and call it stone soup. You call your friends and ask them to come over to sample this delicacy, and while they are on the way, would they mind bringing a few carrots, or an onion, or a chicken or two?

Stone soup is how Taiwan was able to put computers into 31 public locations and into an additional 454 retail outlets, all available for the public to use to visit the fair. The effort started with Dr. James Lee, a researcher at the Industrial Technology Research Institute. He got the government interested, not in a single agency, but across multiple agencies and at the ministerial level. They were joined by the local computer association, by the telephone company, and by a host of volunteers. It was the kind of collaboration you can't plan, but when it happens, the stone soup tastes very good indeed.

Places in Europe

Throughout 1996, people sent in their requests to be listed as a "place in the real world." Obviously, our explanations had not been very clear, because the vast majority of those places were actually on-line sites. So much for our crystal-clear architecture of places, events, and pavilions!

In Europe, two sites joined up that proved to be quite interesting. Europe seems to be in the lead in the art and the Internet movement, with serious juried competitions such as Ars Electronica and a host of web sites, public demonstrations, and other explorations of how this new medium can be used properly. An example is the Institute for New Cultural Technologies in Vienna. This group is an example of the serious (sometimes very serious) exploration of art taking place in cities such as Copenhagen, Amsterdam, and Berlin. In Vienna, the institute has a mission statement on its home page:

> Digital telecommunication towards hypermedia and the global
> connectivity of the infosphere provokes an interdisciplinary
> intermediation of art and science on the basis of a society that is
> determined through new technologies. The data-matrix as a model
> of a culture that is based on electronic information-technology
> demands a new understanding of art and space of maneuver for
> the forthcoming models of art production.

The Internet café at the institute is termed the "Depot for Art and Discourse." A class is held every Monday evening with a target audience of artists and other cultural workers. The café itself is open six hours per day. Rather than

De Waag in Amsterdam, home of the Society for Old and New Media.

just offering surfing lessons, the café has a series of projects that are part of the Zero Zone, an on-line space that complements the public space.

Siberian Deal, for example, is sort of an on-line travelogue and experiment in cultural transformation. The artists purchased ten items in Vienna, then went to Siberia and "transformed" the items into their Siberian counterparts. A Walkman from Vienna, at the conclusion of its journey, had turned into canned beef. A pair of high heels had turned into a Siberian salt bowl. The entire experience is documented on line with movies, pictures of the objects, and travel narratives.

On the other side of Europe, in the middle of a public square in Amsterdam, is a building called De Waag. Built in 1488 as a weigh house for goods, the building became a headquarters for the labor guilds of Amsterdam, including the masons and the medical guilds. By the late 1500s, the facility was used for public (and illegal) dissections as a way of training medical practitioners of the time. By 1619, an anatomical theater had been erected inside the building, the place where Rembrandt painted his famous *Anatomy Lesson of Dr. Nicolaes Tulp*.

In late 1995, the facility was turned over to Caroline Nevejan and Marleen Stikker, two of the most innovative practitioners of new media in Europe. They are most famous for constructing the Digital City of Amsterdam, the first real on-line presence for a city. The Digital City included public access points for Amsterdam citizens, extensive links inside of city hall to put government information on line, and a variety of innovative public spaces on the Internet. It had extensive participation from both citizens and politicians.

Photos/De Waag

De Waag was turned into the Society for Old and New Media. The anatomical theater has been restored and turned into a public meeting room. A media laboratory on the second floor features some very innovative projects, such as "Amsterdam in the 21st Century," which links a variety of public planning databases together to let people see how the city will change over time.

On the ground floor is a restaurant and café, the "place in the real world" registered with the fair. The restaurant features dining in a space over 500 years old. Off to the side is a long reading table, very similar to the tables throughout coffeeshops in Holland. Built carefully into the furniture are terminals with Internet access. Also on the table are daily newspapers and journals, and off to the side readers are invited to make their own contributions to the *Reading Table Chronicle*.

What is interesting about De Waag is the combination of the old and the new. The Internet will not replace existing media and it will not replace existing infrastructures. Rather, it has to fit into the fabric of our everyday lives. Marleen Stikker, one of the founders of this facility, speaks passionately about the need for making the Internet a part of our cities. Instead of making cyberspace a new frontier, a new world, she sees this technology as a way of changing our current cities and making them more responsive to the people who live in them.

One of our mantras for the world's fair was to "bring the real world into cyberspace and cyberspace into the real world." We succeeded very well in bringing the real world into cyberspace, bringing heads of state, national arts centers, and individuals on line. However, the real challenge for the Internet over the next 20 years will be bringing cyberspace into the real world, integrating the technology into our daily lives until the Internet, like our other infrastructures, adapts and disappears. We'll know that the Internet is successful when it becomes invisible.

Australia

On the other side of the world, in Australia, Simon Hackett has been waging a one-man war to bring cyberspace into the real world. Hackett first made his name on the Internet by putting a toaster on line. The genesis of this toaster net was at Interop, the trade show that helped bring engineers together once a year to put a mammoth network into a convention center.

At one of the early Interop shows, founder Dan Lynch surveyed the trade show floor and was marveling at the work that over 100 volunteers had done putting in the show network. "You guys are incredible," he exclaimed. "Look at all these different kinds of computers all talking to each other! Hell, I bet you guys could get toasters to talk on the Internet." He was kidding, but Internet engineers tend to take things literally.

hello all from the hudson valley in new york. i just spent an interesting couple of hours exploring the exposition. now the real world beckons me back to it, so i must go. i'll revisit often. good job.

—**Corky Ray**
Washingtonville, NY, USA
cork@ny.frontiercomm.net

Simon Hackett, along with Stuart Vance and John Romkey, two long-time Internet developers, took the challenge seriously. The next year, they showed up at Interop with a computer-controlled toaster that allowed any computer on the show network to command the toaster to activate. While impressive, it did require the user to insert the bread manually into the slot. The following year, they showed up with a Lego-based crane that would pick the bread up from a stack and insert it into the toaster.

Putting a toaster on line may seem frivolous, but it was an eye-opening demonstration of the power of a new set of network management protocols that had been developed. Simon Hackett continued his tinkering with new devices for the Internet. He developed an Internet-controlled CD player that allowed remote workstations to control music. He even developed one of the first audio delivery systems for the Internet, putting the speakers on the network at a trade show in California and the sound sources in Australia, running his own software that connected the computers to regulate the audio streams and control the radios, CD players, and other sound sources.

When Hackett was not playing with new devices, he was working on building the Internet in his home town of Adelaide. He founded Internode Professional Access, the largest regional Internet service provider in South Australia. Internode provides everything from dial-in and ISDN access to home consumers to high-speed dedicated lines to government and corporate clients.

One of the things that has made Internode distinctive has been Simon's quest to put the thriving cafés of Adelaide on line. His office is located on a street with several of these cafés. Rather than call the telephone company to install wiring for each café, Simon ran his own wires down the block, providing a neighborhood network.

Cybercafés were the hot item in 1994 and 1995 in Adelaide, but as in much of the world, many of these operations have folded. The problem with many of these cybercafés is that the emphasis is on the cyber, not on the coffee. People go to coffee shops for a variety of reasons. Checking mail on the Internet is one good reason, but it is not enough by itself to sustain a business.

For the world's fair, however, Simon found two sets of businesses that seem to have the longevity to stay around. One is the East End Precinct, a building housing a row of great cafés on the ground floor, and a dozen multimedia development houses on the floor above. Simon ran wires throughout the building, then over to his offices and back out to the Australian backbone.

Just down the street, a new multimedia development center had just opened, called the Ngapartji Co-Operative MultiMedia Centre. Ngapartji is Aboriginal for multimedia. The center was set up to provide a place for developers to learn about the latest technology, but the founders wanted to make it more than just a computer showroom.

Greetings to all from the country with the largest number of Internauts per capita in the world.

—**Nathan Cochrane**
Perth, WA, Australia
nathan@wanews.com.au

Simon Hackett

Pipo

Top: The Ngapartji Multimedia Café.
Bottom: Simon Hackett and his fabulous flying machines.

Bongiorno's Café, one of the inhabitants of the East End Precinct, provided the first crucial ingredient, helping set up the food and drink that would attract people to stay for more than just a demonstration. Simon used a wireless infrared link to connect Ngapartji to the rest of his neighborhood network at a speed of 10 million bits per second.

Ngapartji took it from there. The founders certainly have a flair for marketing. The sign on the street spells out the name of the café in binary. To attract people, they placed 10 Macintosh computers on the street for people to use for free. Inside, more powerful computers (and more powerful air conditioning) are available for $5 an hour.

When Simon Hackett isn't putting cafés and toasters on line, he indulges in his other passion, gliding. On a slow day at the office, he'll tell the staff that he is off to do research and then drives down to his motor glider. Even when 3,500 feet in the air, he isn't totally out of touch, however. He brings a little palmtop computer and a wireless RadioMail system just in case he has to descend back to earth and fix an appliance, such as a computer or a toaster.

An infrared wireless link on the side of the building.

The Invisible Fair

"How interesting, a virtual world's fair," was the most common reaction from people when they learned about the Internet 1996 World Exposition. Virtual somehow implies something that isn't real, that exists only in our imaginations and not in the real world. This was not a virtual fair, and I tried to discourage use of that word whenever possible.

The nature of our world's fair did, however, make this different from the great fairs of the last century. The fact that this fair was located all over the world and not in one place gave it a rather strange quality. The fair was an iceberg, with a little bit visible in any one place, but with a great deal below the surface, hidden across the world and only visible through the Internet.

The lack of a single venue made it very different from events in the last century such as the Chicago World's Fair, or our present-day spectacles such as the Super Bowl. A single venue makes the scale of the event immediately apparent. Even those of us working in the fairgrounds had a tough time visualizing the scope of an event that had locations in places throughout the world, five million visitors, and thousands of people working on the fairgrounds.

An invisible thing is something real. The Internet 1996 World Exposition was certainly not virtual, but it may have been the first invisible fair.

THE 1915 PANAMA PACIFIC EXPOSITION

Events at the Fair

4

We needed a grand opening. The fair went on line on January 1, and our hit rates were very impressive, but the fair had just started and many of the pavilions were not ready to open. Pressured by our sponsors for some gala event, and feeling the need for a definite deadline to prod some of the groups around the world that hadn't yet reached full steam, we wanted to declare ourselves to be open in some suitably momentous way—digital fireworks, if you will.

In addition to building pavilions in January, over 100 people worked frantically to put the infrastructure for Central Park and the Internet Railroad into operation. Engineers from KDD and MCI worked to put the first-ever high-speed line across the Pacific. The Bay Networks engineers were shipping and installing routers all over the world and a dozen teams were working on the Central Park servers. We officially projected that everything would be working by the end of January, projections based as much on hope as on fact.

Coincidentally, there was a big event already scheduled to happen in early February. Judith Donath, a Ph.D. candidate at the MIT Media Lab, had been trying to figure out a way to celebrate the lab's tenth anniversary on October 10, 1995. She came up with the idea of documenting a day in cyberspace, having people all over the world contribute material to build a massive web site.

The Media Lab contacted Rick Smolan, a photographer known for his photo series *A Day in the Life,* where he would dispatch teams of photographers around a particular country and edit the photos into a glossy picture book. Rick had recently discovered the Internet and agreed to work with the team at the MIT Media Lab. Rick's previous projects had been focused on producing books and it was not unusual for him to postpone one of his days in the life until he thought it was ready. In late summer of 1995, the Media Lab was deep into preparations for its big birthday bash when Rick proposed a delay of several months.

Nicholas Negroponte, the formidable director and founder of the Media Lab, was not amused. He wanted his birthday party actually to occur on his birthday. So, Judith Donath and the others went ahead, but Rick split off and formed his own event. On October 10, 1995, the Media Lab's Day in the Life of Cyberspace went on line, directed by Michael Hawley, a professor at the

The World is becoming smaller they say. Now it seems there all on my desktop, thanks to all those who are helping to make this Expo 96 happen. Good luck to you all and hope that this monumental exercise will truly benefit all mankind.

—Kang Seung-Ha
Seoul, Korea
hans@chosun.com

This feels like a few small clicks by my fingers, but may signify great leaps for mankind!

—Nick Reid
Amsterdam, Netherlands
nick@ripe.net

lab, and produced by the Art & Technology Group, a small multimedia group headed by Donath's husband.

Rick continued work on his own project, now dubbed 24 Hours in Cyberspace, and had scheduled his day for February 8. One of our big sponsors at the Internet Multicasting Service was Sun Microsystems, and they frequently called us in for a reality check or to work together on live Internet events, particularly ones where they had invested a lot of money. Smolan's event had cost them a cool $1 million cash as a sponsorship fee and would cost them much more after they threw scores of machines and people into the preparation efforts. By the time the other sponsorship fees were added in, this was turning into a $10 million tab for the one-day event, far more than the Internet Multicasting had spent in its entire period of existence.

At Sun's request, we went and talked to Rick Smolan and his team. Smolan is a very personable ex-hippie who works with a team of high-powered PR consultants and business managers. We agreed to have the world's fair grand opening day coincide with his 24 Hours in Cyberspace. My feeling was that this would give meaning to his event. He needed to document a day, and what better day than the inauguration of the Internet Railroad and the grand opening of the first world's fair for the information age?

It turned out that the 24 Hours team had a slew of business people, but the technical side of the house was a bit weak. The entire system for the event was being run out of a contractor's house until only shortly before the big day. A flurry of activity was going on in California, but most of it was focused on a PR campaign of major-league proportions. To get the technical systems in place, Sun finally threw all the resources they could muster at the problem, shipping in close to 100 workstations, servers, and other equipment and bringing in their top consulting SWAT team to the event site in San Francisco's China Basin Building and get the systems up and running.

MFS, one of the railroad suppliers, had installed a 10-million-bit-per-second cross-country link from the 24 Hours site into the world's fair systems in Washington, but the line was never used. The activity was so frenzied and last-minute that it didn't seem wise to further complicate an already confused situation with a second route from the event site out to the net. When a site becomes multihomed, routing becomes significantly more difficult, since multiple links carry with them the possibility of routing loops and other disasters.

The 24 Hours event went off, but the result was a disappointing four million hits, with about a million coming from the Central Park servers that served as the "international" sites. *International* is a term often used on American web sites and has always seemed to imply that the United States is the natural home of cyberspace, with the rest of the world aliens come for a visit. Only four million hits put the event down in the middle of the pack if sheer volume were the judge. Big Internet events in late 1995 and early 1996, such as major tennis opens or soccer games, would typically get 10 million hits per day or more.

The world's fair lent minor support to the event, but we were invisible, listed way down on a long list of additional sponsors. We had thought we were part of the content, but ended up being a vendor. On the Internet, it is very easy to link one web page to another, and therefore it is just as easy to link one big event with a huge list of sponsors, partners, and other affiliates.

We cheerfully pursued this strategy ourselves in the world's fair, whenever it was convenient. Some of the early pavilions were simply links to other sites, and to flesh out our "places in the real world" category, we added pretty much anything that could remotely qualify as a place. Certainly, a cybercafé that simply put our logo on the web page doesn't have the same significance as the 1,500 places that Taiwan put together.

The same was true with events. Some events were true world's fair mass activities. Others were true partnerships. But a simple site full of linkage for linkage's sake wasn't going to cut it if this was going to become a real world's fair. The World Wide Web was already one huge directory, and repackaging that directory wasn't going to work.

Luckily, the real work of the fair was progressing nicely. On line, we were raking in awards and, more important, our guestbook was filling up with thousands of comments from visitors all over the world. We had all year to get it together for events, so we informed our sponsors that we had made the grand opening a soft rollout, a technical term in the PR lingo that means you didn't do anything and hoped people would somehow hear about it anyway. One of the first lessons you learn as a consultant is to couch bad news in technical terms— I didn't break your computer, I merely activated a technical malfunction that had previously been dormant.

A soft rollout was another way of saying we didn't have a grand opening, but luckily we had a second chance.

Kasparov v. Deep Blue

February 1996 was the fiftieth anniversary of the electronic computer and a series of events was scheduled in Philadelphia to mark this momentous occasion. Seminars, symposia, conferences, and a gala dinner ball were all part of the celebration sponsored by the Association for Computing Machinery (ACM).

The world's fair team was called in to help add a little on-line pizzazz to the ACM celebration. We split into two groups. IBM had a team already working on a chess match between a computer and Kasparov, and asked us to include their computer networks into the Central Park infrastructure.

"Go Kasparov"

—Joe Magyar
Fairmont, WV, USA
magyarj@mantech-wva.com

45

HA HA on My desk,
IBM PC working for me.
He said, I want to visit
World Expo, so I let him
as he like. There are
many PCs, so he would
feel very glad, I hope so.
I feel this place is nice.

—Akio Morimoto
Nagoya, Aichi, Japan
akio@na.rim.or.jp

Let The Games begin!
Marshall McLuhan
was right!

—T.A. Simpson
Montreal, Canada
tasimpson@vir.com

Meanwhile, the Internet Multicasting Service trucked in 62 boxes of equipment, set up real-time audio and video out to the Internet, and put a production studio in the back of the Hyatt ballroom to produce multimedia web sites from the conference. Our local hosts, distinguished computer science professors, scheduled a global schoolhouse event with astronauts, children, celebrities, and a big balloon that would inflate in the middle of the event, acting as a replica of a space capsule. The children would invite Dr. Guion Bluford, the astronaut, into the space capsule and show him their understanding of space science.

Over 100 schools were supposed to participate interactively via the Internet and by calling an 800 number. Speakerphones were dispatched all over the world, our producers hammered a script out of the whirlwind of plans, and the systems people frantically hooked up computers, video mixers, cameras, lights, and microphones. The results were less than stellar. Only two schools participated on the speakerphones. The balloon inflated ahead of schedule and had been shifted in position so it exactly obscured both cameras that broadcast to the Internet. The video producer in the back saw the image on his monitor go from a pretty picture to a white cloud that filled the screen. He went sprinting out to the front of the hall to see what had happened. By then, though, the balloon was full of kids giving a tour to a somewhat bemused Guion Bluford, and for the rest of the show our audience of six Internet viewers saw a test pattern and listened to a rather chaotic program.

Hotel ballroom gigs are an interesting part of an Internet broadcaster's life on the road, though we had come to view some of these as cheap stunts because the whole point of the broadcast was for the people on site to prove how trendy they were. Internet multicasting is often one of those things you add when you can't get a really good speaker or the balloons didn't come in.

Throughout our five days of camping out in the back of the hotel ballroom, a steady stream of ACM officials had come in to plead for us to stay yet one more day to put another session on line. We had done a half-dozen productions during the week, people had flown in from all over the country, and I decided that it wasn't worth the logistical nightmare of rescheduling our freight service and our people. We wouldn't be available to work on Saturday.

What the ACM wanted was access to the T1 leased line that we had secured from MCI to put our network operating center on the Internet. Friday night, with all the freight packed up and under the careful watch of our security guard, we were sitting in the bar having a drink, when Luther Brown, our vice president of programs, came walking up with a big smile on his face.

"You're not going to believe this," he said. I followed him back to the ballroom. ACM had dismissed our security guard and three people were huddled around a wall jack, trying to reactivate the T1 line. A dedicated line like this runs between two fixed points, in this case the hotel ballroom and a router port that had been assigned to us on the MCI special exhibit network. Borrowing the line would be about as meaningful as borrowing an airplane without also getting a place to land.

The burly director of operations for the ACM came up and blocked my way when I walked over to inspect this bizarre activity. I explained that for a variety of technical reasons, he really couldn't use the line, and in any case it wasn't his to use: it had been donated to the Internet Multicasting Service. It was 1 A.M., but he got Dr. John Buck, the conference chairman, on the phone.

"John, you can't just take that line," I complained (in more colorful language), "it was donated to me by MCI."

"Well," he responded, "you just donated it to me."

The next morning, I went back to supervise the loading of our freight onto the trucks. Three very tired ACM officials were still huddled around the wall, but weren't having much luck. I had called my friends at MCI that ran the national backbone and explained that somebody was trying to steal their T1 line. That was certainly a first for them, but these folks are extremely security conscious and had promptly deactivated the port on the router. Even if ACM had made the line work, it would have been a road to nowhere.

Across town, however, there occurred an event that nobody was paying attention to. One of the sideshows for the 50th anniversary celebration was a chess match between Garry Kasparov, the world champion, and a computer called Deep Blue. IBM, developer of the Deep Blue computer, was one of the sponsors of this event, and had put together a web page to be part of the chess match. This one was a real world's fair event, boasting our logo on the web page and a set of computers inside Central Park.

Dave Grossman, part of an elite IBM SWAT team whose responsibilities included doing large events, had a rare night off and was watching the first match at home on Saturday afternoon with his eight-year-old kid. He knew the site was in deep trouble when he couldn't get his on-screen chessboard to refresh with the current position of the pieces.

When a site gets swamped, performance doesn't just degrade gradually—it plummets. If a computer has too many requests, it spends all its time managing the overflow requests and none servicing the ones already in line, making the problem progressively worse. On a PC, if you open too many programs, you will see the same effect until performance reaches the point where only a swift kick to the power button can make the system move.

The group that initially built the site for IBM had been told to prepare a system that could handle a quarter of a million hits per day. After all, how popular could chess be? To everyone's surprise, more than 1 million hits per hour came in from all over the world, overwhelming the event team that had prepared the site.

I was trying to get in to see the chess match, I could not get in to see. so here i am checking out your expo 96 page. I know i am not that smart, so where and when the expo going to be held. thank you very much for your page.

—**Harry E. Sears, Jr.**
Sayreville, NJ, USA
gamesmst@ix.netcom.com

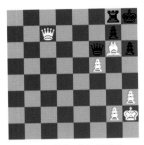

Game 4: Feb. 14, 1996

Game 6: Feb. 16, 1996

http://www.chess.ibm.park.org/

This is my first (but not last) look at your fantastic presentation. The chess match brought me here!

—William McKay
Satsuam, FL, USA
mckayw@mail.firn.edu

Early Sunday morning, Grossman received a phone call. He tracked down Sean Martin and Andy Stanford-Clark, two members of his team who were in a hotel room in New York recovering from a flight from London. They all dialed in to see what was wrong on the system. They tried some quick fixes, like moving all the images off the main web server over to two large computers at IBM headquarters in New York. This helped a little, but it wasn't enough, and the site was still swamped all day Sunday.

Monday there was no match, and Grossman's team went to IBM headquarters in New York. They changed the address of the web server to point to a bank of six SP2 processors. A single SP2 is equivalent to a very powerful workstation, but you can put several central processing units together. These multiprocessor configurations were the same type we used in Central Park, using an equivalent system from Sun Microsystems that put eight Sparc processors on a single system. Put six or eight processors together, add a gigabyte or two of random access memory and a few hundred gigabytes of disk, and you have the equivalent of a powerful supercomputer.

Simply adding processing power, however, was not enough to handle the load that the team was estimating would come in the next day. The system that had been put together for the event was a dynamic site. When a browser would connect to the server, a special program would run that would do such things as determine the type of browser the user had so that appropriate graphics and advanced formatting features could be applied, but only if the browser supported those features. These special programs are known as *scripts*.

A web server is a single program that sits in memory on a computer. When it receives a request, it spawns a job for that request. A script, however, requires yet another job to be spawned. Dynamic web sites can do a lot, but they significantly increase the number of jobs that each request needs. Grossman's team rewrote the server software so that it put the most common jobs in the core program. Hacking up the web server to know about functions specific to one particular application is messy, but it can really speed up the system.

Grossman's team also found another way to speed up the site by changing the way the chessboard was drawn. The page showing the current position of the pieces was the most popular on the site. When the user requested that page, a chessboard would be drawn with the current position. The original implementation had each square of the board as a graphics file. A request for that page was translated into 30–40 connections back to the server, each one for a different component of the chessboard, the text accompanying the page, the IBM logo, and the other elements from which the page was constructed. Grossman's team changed the code, so that when Deep Blue wrote out a log file with the current position it was a single image, reducing the number of connections back to the server by an order of magnitude.

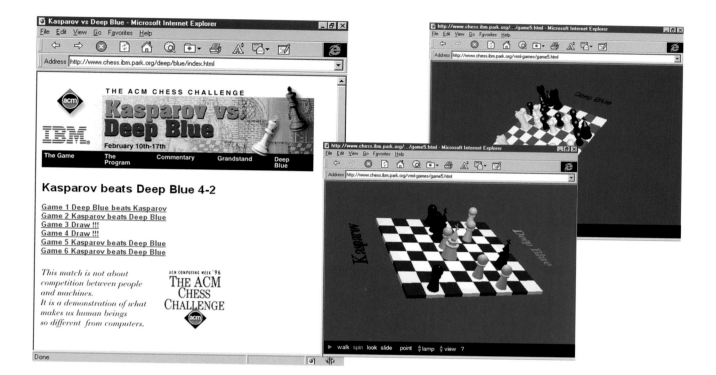

One more change was necessary, however, before the system would work. If you have multiple systems that are on line, there has to be a way of distributing the requests among the processors. The typical way to do this is known as DNS load balancing. The Domain Name System (DNS) is how a computer finds another system on the Internet. When a user types in the name of a computer, such as park.org, that name gets translated into an Internet address.

The usual way to do load balancing is to hack the DNS. A set of Internet addresses is put into the DNS and the system answers each request with a different address, cycling through the set of potential addresses in a round-robin manner. There are two problems with this. The first is caching: if a system in, say, Australia, asks for an address, it remembers the answer. The next time another computer asks for the address of that same domain, the system doesn't go back over the ocean to check, it simply hands in the cached answer.

Grossman likes to say that load balancing with the DNS is like trying to steer an oil tanker. The response time is bad. The entire university system of a major state, for example, may have cached a particular address and tens of thousands of users will continue to try that address for many minutes even though the computer behind it is overloaded and not responding.

The second problem with DNS load balancing is that it doesn't take into account the load on a system. If you have six computers masquerading as one

No comments. The fair says it all !

—George Zeibekis
Nicosia, Cyprus
drbones@spidernet.com.cy

name, each one will have different load characteristics. One might be running low memory because all the requests it received were for big graphics files. Another might be bombarded by too many Internet connections, saturating the Internet code in the operating system. Another might be saturating the paths into disk drives, or might have too many jobs that require extensive use of the central processing unit.

IBM had a project in one of its laboratories that had never been put into operation before, but Grossman dragged in the lab team and asked them to help. The system was called a *TCP sprayer* and it combined several different computers together so they looked to the Internet like a single system. When the sprayer received a web request, it would route that request into a bank of SP2 processors that were behind them. There was no need for DNS load balancing since this looked like a single Internet address to the rest of the Internet. The system had a sophisticated internal load balancing system that was able to route incoming request to an appropriate processor based on a profile of the different resources being used on the system.

The changes to the web server and the use of the TCP sprayer were both untried solutions. Throughout Monday, the team was tearing apart the source code for both systems trying to figure out how they worked, making changes, recompiling, and testing. By Monday night, it appeared that the system was ready to go. Tuesday morning, with another match scheduled, was the real test. The first hour or so was a bit tough as the system was fine-tuned and engineers discovered the remaining bugs. By the end of the day, though, the system was easily swallowing peak rates of 1 million requests per hour, one of the largest Internet events to date.

The Brain Opera

Perhaps the biggest and most successful Internet event for the world's fair was the Brain Opera, the brainchild of Tod Machover. Machover is a professor at the MIT Media Lab and is also a noted composer. Groups such as the Los Angeles Philharmonic have debuted his pieces. His opera *Valis,* based on the novel by Philip K. Dick, was called the "best new American Opera" by the *New Yorker* when it first came out. When Machover read about the world's fair in the *New York Times,* he immediately called me for more information.

Machover was one of the first major artists to sign on for the World Exposition. His new opera, to be based on the groundbreaking book *Society of Mind* by Marvin Minsky, had been in the planning stage for over two years. Machover and his students had developed a line of new musical instruments they called *hyperinstruments.* Tod describes these instruments eloquently:

I am really impressed and can't wait to check out the Brain Opera!

—**Jonathan Epstein**
Carlisle, PA, USA
epstein@dickinson.edu

Photo/Madoka Sakaguchi

Tod Machover

My view of technology has always been that it should respond to human intentions, rather than simulate or replace them, and I started developing Hyperinstruments at the MIT Media Lab in 1985 towards this end. The first generation of hyperinstruments was designed for virtuosic professional musicians, such as Yo-Yo Ma. These hyperinstruments measured many nuances of performance expression, using this information to enhance and expand the instrument's capabilities. Starting in 1991, we began building hyperinstruments for non-professional music lovers. Our Joystick Music System allows a piece of music to be steered, modified, and shaped by manipulating two videogame joysticks. A Sensor Chair, designed for magicians Penn & Teller, uses an invisible electric field to detect body motion and turn it into sound. Such instruments are easy to learn but difficult to master, with enough depth to make them worth practicing and exploring.

The Brain Opera was set to open as one of the featured pieces of New York's Lincoln Center Festival. The Juilliard School's recital hall and huge marble lobby had been allocated to Machover's crew, who filled the space with a jungle of hyperinstruments. The audience could meander through this space for an hour, painting music on a melody easel, exploring harmony by means of a harmonic driving machine, or even have a sort of dialogue with Marvin Minsky, who had been encapsulated in interactive workstations, musing and posing questions on such topics as "what do we hear when we listen?"

After an hour in the marble lobby, people were ushered into the performance space. Three of the more sophisticated hyperinstruments were aligned on the stage, and three virtuoso hyperinstrumentalists would come out once an hour and play the Brain Opera. The sensor chair, the digital baton, and the rhythm tree manipulated a stream of music emanating from a bank of computers and electronic music equipment backstage, all piped through a very sophisticated sound system. On three screens in back of the performers, a rack of laser discs played streams of images and expressive text that moved and morphed on the screen to help express the mood of the words.

For Machover, the Brain Opera was a new kind of opera because it really involved the audience. Experiences from the lobby were sampled and inserted into the stream of music in the performance space. He saw the world exposition as a way of extending the Brain Opera even more, allowing the Internet to be a meaningful part of the experience. The Internet joined the performance space and the lobby as one of the three faces of the Brain Opera.

The July debut of the Brain Opera was set for seven performances per day for 10 days. A team of 40 MIT Media Lab students, assisted by professional

We have always wanted to play our music at the World Fair and thanks to you we now play it here everyday, 24 hours a day! Thanks for all you do for the Net.

—The Bluefields
Banner Elk, NC, USA
Mturbyfill@Skybest.Com

Don't Stop The Music!!!

—Paco Garcia
Valencia, Spain
pgarcia@ibm.net

The Brain Opera

Top: Teresa Marrin plays the digital baton, her master's thesis at the MIT Media Lab.
Middle: Composer Tod Machover in the sensor chair.
Bottom: Maribeth Back, interactive sound designer, plays the rhythm tree.
Opposite: In the lobby, people learn about music in a forest of instruments and experiences.

Photos/Johannes Kroemer

I am a System-Programmer in IBM Main-Frame, and sometime Artist, Poet, or Musician. Anywhere, I can be in Cyber-Space.

—**Toshihiro Oimatsu**
Tokyo, Japan
tien0028@mxa.meshnet.or.jp

architects, logistics experts, and a whole slew of others, set the opera up in the MIT Media Lab, then tore the systems down and reassembled them in New York. The scene for the two months preceding the debut was one of controlled chaos, as sophisticated electronic instruments and stage constructions that had never been used before were hotstaged, debugged, and dressed up. The instruments all had sophisticated software systems controlling them, in many cases the result of a student's doctoral or master's thesis. Quite a few of these systems were still being debugged even in the middle of performances.

Throughout the Brain Opera, the instruments used sensors extensively to detect how hard a person was hitting a surface or how fast the hands were moving over the melody easels, allowing computers to measure the expression and personality inherent in ordinary body movement, touch, and voice. Much of the sensor design was the product of Joe Paradiso, technical director of the Brain Opera. A physicist by training, he has worked at high-energy accelerator sites such as CERN in Switzerland. He also has a rather extensive hobby, having built one of the world's largest home synthesizers. As a research scientist at the MIT Media Lab, Paradiso is able to combine his natural interests in physics and music on projects like the Brain Opera.

The debut was a huge success. The web presence for the opera had been hosted onto eight different computer servers in Central Park, and Nynex and MCI ran a 45-million bit-per-second line into Lincoln Center for the performance. Xing Technology shipped a half-dozen realtime video and audio encoders in to allow a series of realtime streams to go out to the Internet, including one feed that ran at 15 frames per second of video with CD-quality sound. Of course, that stream was over 1 million bits per second, making the average home user unable to swallow it. However, because the Brain Opera was directly connected to the Internet Railroad, we were able to ship that stream of data over to Japan to people gathered at the Makuhari convention center, where the exposition had set up a exhibit in the middle of a trade show.

Participation over the Internet was more than just reading about the opera or seeing the show live. Eric Metois, a doctoral student at the MIT Media Lab, had directed a team that constructed a series of musical instruments that could be played on the net. These instruments were built with an innovative set of tools constructed from the Java programming language, allowing people on the net to construct scores, experiment with rhythm, or play with nature of sounds.

The centerpiece of these Java tools was the Internet instrument known as the Palette. At the beginning of movement three in the performance, Teresa Marrin, the player and developer of the digital baton, would turn to the screens and begin conducting the Internet. Users on the net would click their mouse on the special instrument, a series of levers you could shift that would in turn affect a stream of music flowing by. One lever would change the type of instrument,

Joe Paradiso at home with his synthesizer.

Award-winning Internet instruments allow net users to compose music. At right, Andrew Garcia, director of Internet activities for the Brain Opera in a rare moment of repose.

another the amount of randomness, and another the coherence of the piece. When Teresa pressed a sensor on her baton, it would select a new user from the Internet, allowing her to cycle through the different soloists.

Setup in Lincoln Center took a week of early mornings and late nights. On opening day, almost everything was ready, but there was the usual flurry of last-minute changes. The Internet team spent hours rewiring the cameras mounted in the performance space to try and remove interference from the huge web of electrical lines. The laser discs weren't working properly with the projectors and a team of four people hovered anxiously over manuals trying to see where the problem was. The code for the baton had a mysterious bug and programmers were trying to figure out how to make the device restart in the middle of a performance without crashing the rest of the systems.

When the first performance went on the air, we looked up from our consoles in the middle of the second movement and realized that no users had yet signed onto the Internet instrument and that the solo was coming in a few minutes. Andrew Garcia, the student assigned to the Internet portion, and I quickly fired up web browsers on our network management stations and flicked rapidly through the menu options until we got to the instrument page.

"How does this thing work?" I asked Andrew.

"Not sure," he replied. "I think you click on these things, but I'm not sure what they do."

The solo started and we frantically started clicking on the little levers. Our sound system was tuned to the Internet feed and, while the rest of the opera had come in loud and clear, during our big solo we couldn't hear much of anything happening. Our video monitors showed Teresa Marrin gamely conducting an orchestra that didn't appear to have returned from the luncheon buffet.

At the break, we dragged down the master's thesis on which the Internet instrument was based. I discovered the tempo switch and instructed Andy to max it out, then click randomly on other characteristics. My theory was that

So Funky Funky Expo!

—Ko Shimada
Nara, Japan
na6k-smd.asahi-net.or.jp

Cool links, Crescendo muzik and more ...

—Roman Pihel
Tallinn, Estonia
roman@online.ee

55

this would at least generate noise, if not music. At the next solo, we frantically clicked away, only to discover that putting the tempo switch on the highest setting produced a tempo of zero. More silence.

We read the thesis more carefully at the next break and the Internet instrument started to become useful. The performance systems worked their bugs out, the marble lobby proved to be a huge hit, and thousands of people ended up coming to the Brain Opera debut at Lincoln Center, joined by countless more on-line users.

The Brain Opera hit the road, with all the equipment sent over to the Ars Electronica festival in Linz, then to an arts center in Copenhagen. In November, the Brain Opera hit Tokyo ready to go. In Tokyo, the event was sponsored by NTT Data Corporation and was produced by an ace team of concert producers led by Yukiteru Nanase of the multimedia production firm We's Brain.

By Tokyo, all the bugs were out of the Brain Opera. Elaborate sound and lighting systems were installed in the Garden Concert Hall in the Ebisu district. With over 300 high-speed expo lines into homes in Japan, our on-line listening audience was larger. The Palette had been revamped from a series of levers into an elegant shape on the screen that twirled around. By hitting one of three corners, you could change the style, coherence, or energy of the stream of music.

The Brain Opera used new instruments and new ways for the audience to be part of the experience, but it was still an opera, filled with music, breathtaking effects, and surprising drama. Although it has no single linear narrative, Machover stresses that there is still

> significant dramatic progression, which is the voyage of each audience member through the maze of fragments, thoughts and memories, to collective and coherent experience. Just the process of understanding the scenario of each instrument—how it is played and what it means—and seeing how these turn into full musical structures in the performance, is a very rich and involving story in itself.

Many people have tried to mount large-scale artistic collaborations on the Internet and many musicians and performers are intrigued by the possibilities of the medium. Making these events more than just TV in a box, however, takes a great deal of planning. Machover's team made the Internet part of the performance, allowing the user to participate by submitting sounds, learning about the opera, playing Internet musical games, and supplementing the experience in the performance spaces. The people who were able to attend both the Internet and on-site versions of the Brain Opera were some of the most enthusiastic fans of the work.

It seems that now the Net has received something it was worthy of. Something nice looking, informative and well-organised. I hope it will last! Visu labu Jums!

—**Aldis Putelis**
Riga, Latvia
aldisp@lanet.lv

The Uitmarkt

In August, the focus of the world's fair shifted to the Netherlands. On August 24 and 25, Amsterdam celebrated the Uitmarkt, the start of its cultural season. For two days, all the theaters in town open their doors for performances, and the streets are jammed with stands where those who have anything to do with the performing arts can present themselves.

The Internet part of the Uitmarkt was coordinated by the same team that also acted as the International Secretariat. Led by Rob Blokzijl, director of networking at the Dutch National Institute for High Energy and Nuclear Physics (NIKHEF) and secretary-general of the fair, the team built a pavilion where people could walk through the Uitmarkt by means of 3-D maps and see what was on the different stages and performance spaces.

The team also secured space for itself at Arti et Amicitiae, an artistic society located in the heart of the Uitmarkt. The team installed 20 public workstations where people could visit the fair. A multimedia guestbook was installed at the entrance of the hall. A team of 18 independent professional photographers who had organized themselves into an agency called Hollandse Hoogte were outfitted with Canon digital cameras and sent out into the streets to give us their view of the festival. The cameras were then rushed back to Arti et Amicitiae where they were immediately processed and published on the site. Over 90,000 hits were received on the site, many of them by local Dutch citizens scoping out the streets before heading into them.

Over 5,000 people visited the Expo pavilion at the Uitmarkt. One elderly man brought his grandson with him, who promptly rushed over to a computer and started madly clicking away. The man stood patiently off to the side with an indulgent smile while he watched his young prodigy adeptly manipulate the computer. Alexander Blanc of the International Secretariat approached and offered him the use of a computer. He protested that he was "he was too old to understand all these new technologies," but our staff politely browbeat him until he reluctantly sat down at a computer. He enjoyed himself so much that later he had to be nudged away as the lines queued up to visit the fair. At the end of the day, people had to be disengaged from their keyboards, and two of them were waiting at the door the next morning half an hour before opening.

The Internet is a global communication mechanism, wonderful for allowing somebody in Kazakhstan to visit a theater festival in Amsterdam. Yet, for many events, the most avid users are people who are local. The Uitmarkt was a fascinating experience for people on the other side of the globe, but the most fervent users were local Dutch attending the festival in person. By integrating itself into the event with 3-D maps and an on-site presence, the world's fair team found that it was not a replacement for the event, but a part of it.

Photographers from Hollandse Hoogte, armed with
Canon digital cameras, descend on the Uitmarkt.

Photos/Hollandse Hoogie

The Closing Ceremony

By December 1996, some of the people who were working hardest were beginning to burn out. After 12 months of planning and almost a year of operation, many of the projects had almost exhausted the funds they had raised. Other groups were just getting going and were clamoring for an extension of the fair into 1997, if not forever.

We decided not to extend the fair beyond a year. Fairs traditionally lasted one year, and we didn't see why we should break this tradition. After the first world's fair in London, the French were inspired to show their cousins across the channel what a real exposition looked like. We felt that by providing a definite end to our world's fair, we would draw a clean line and perhaps others would follow our example and show us how to really throw a party.

We didn't want to quit without some ceremony, some gathering of the people around the world who had worked hardest on the fair. The task of organizing the final ceremonies fell on the Japanese committee, perhaps the most successful of the groups that worked on the world's fair and the only one with a piece of their budget still unspent.

On December 5, teams from the United States, Europe, and Asia all gathered in Kobe, Japan. Many of the people had only met by email or late-night faxes. Representatives from Japanese companies and other sponsors were invited to join us. We started at the Ikuta Shrine, where our time capsule was blessed in a Shinto Ceremony. Our time capsule was a digital videodisc of the main portion of Central Park, a disk archive that had grown to over 10 gigabytes. We had no idea how big the rest of the fair was outside of Central Park, and indeed had lost track of much of what was in the park, so a symbolic disc was placed into a special box and set on the shrine in the temple. A few months later, we would replace the symbolic disc with a real one.

The priests came out, accompanied by slow drumming and flutes. The head priest chanted a long blessing in Japanese, one that surprised the Japanese members present with the depth of knowledge the priest had about our exposition. He chanted about the world's fair, how it opened new vistas for our children, how we must preserve this event for our children in the 21st century.

Each of the five guests of honor was handed a branch of a tree. One by one, we filed up to the shrine and rotated the leaf 360 degrees, placing it next to our time capsule. The branch, called a *tamagushi,* ended up with the base end pointing toward the *kami* or god which is the root. The ritual asks the god to help cleanse and then grow the object being blessed, the twigs symbolizing growth. After placing the twig on the kami, we were instructed to bow twice, clap twice, then bow one more time, turning around to face the attendees and walk back to our seats.

A Shinto priest at the Ikuta shrine cleanses a digital videodisc, the time capsule of the Internet 1996 World Exposition.

The last to file up to the shrine was Deb K. Roy, the director of the pavilions for India and Tibet. Deb walked up to the shrine with his face away from the rest of us, but as he was the last of the guests of honor, all the attendees had stood up and accompanied him in the ritual. Deb placed his leaf on the shrine, then bowed solemnly and slowly. He clapped twice, and I could see him look up quizzically, trying to understand where the sudden echo had come from.

The ceremony concluded, the guests filed over to a large sake barrel, where we each took a symbolic three sips from a little saucer. Our time capsule suitably cleansed, the group went over to the City of Kobe museum where the disc was presented to the assistant mayor of Kobe for eternal safekeeping. The Kobe earthquake was only two years in the past, and the city was still feeling its effects. The Internet had played a vital role right after the quake, having been the only way that information could get out of the city to anxious relatives across Japan and around the world. It was thus particularly symbolic, the assistant mayor observed, that the city, which had benefited so much from the Internet during its time of need, would repay this debt by keeping our disc safe for the ages.

The group then filed back to the Kobe Portpia hotel where the Japanese secretariat organized a lavish party. An official of the Japanese government gave a short speech to welcome us, followed by the consul general of the United States, who gave a long dissertation about global information infrastructures while we all anxiously eyed the tables piled high with sushi. The official welcoming done, 15 people were handed large wooden mallets and on cue broke open three huge barrels of sake, signaling that the festivities had begun.

This event will be remembered forever. Greeting for all "Internaut" of the world. Saludos a todos desde Toledo - España.

—Francisco Garcia
Toledo, Spain
tolfrg@bitmailer.net

CLOSING RECEPTION

Top right: Presentation of the time capsule to the city
of Kobe for safekeeping.
Bottom: Breaking open the casks of sake to celebrate
the closing of the fair.

CLOSING CEREMONY

Bottom: At the presentation of the accomplishments
of the Japan National Committee, Professor Suguru
Yamaguchi unveils the Cyber Kansai project, which
will install high-speed networks in the Kobe and
Osaka regions of Japan.

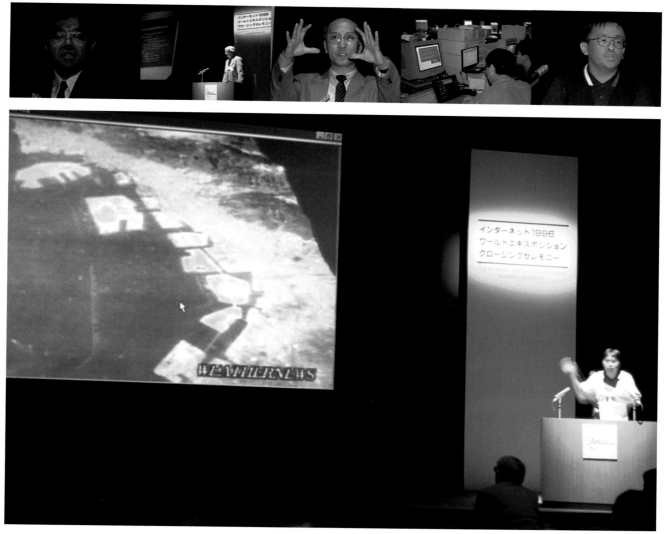

Photos/Doors Magazine

http://www.fix.co.jp/kabuki/movie/manjiro_morph.mov

Ichimura Manjiro

http://www.fix.co.jp/kabuki/manjiro.html

Ichimura Manjiro PRESENTS
KABUKI for EVERYONE

Suitably hung over the next day, we all headed over to a large exhibition hall where the Japanese team had installed dozens of computers and high-speed lines to demonstrate the beginning of a project to wire the Kobe/Osaka area with a high-speed test regional network. Representatives of each of the regions of the world got up and gave presentations on their activities. These speeches were a real eye-opener for many who had only seen their own local activities and had not realized the extent of the participation in countries such as Taiwan and Japan.

The team then boarded the Shinkansen bullet train to Tokyo and headed the next day to the National Theater, where we received a special backstage tour of the world's most elaborate Kabuki theater by Ichimura Manjiro II, a famous actor and the son of Living National Treasure Ichimura Uzaemon XVII. Manjiro is the pioneer behind a series of Kabuki for Everyone performances that have attempted to popularize the ancient art to high school students, to foreigners, and even by means of the Internet.

Manjiro showed us how huge sets could be moved 50 feet up and down on hydraulic shafts to effect the instant and dramatic scene changes for which Kabuki is famous. The team then joined the audience for a performance, which had extensive program notes in English and wireless headsets for those who wished to hear English commentary. Manjiro's web site features movies of the actor morphing from his street appearance into some of his most famous stage roles. The site includes schedules of upcoming performances around the country, and an on-line theatre that includes photos, video, and stories.

The Kabuki performance and the Shinto shrine seemed like an appropriate ending for this gathering of people who had been working together to build a public park for the global village. Technology should not replace our cultural heritage. When properly used, it becomes part of our culture, preserving and extending it. But, when used without foresight, technology can also wipe away our culture. We saw that clearly with the automobile and roads, which in the United States and elsewhere contributed to the gutting of inner cities and the building of faceless bedroom communities and strip malls. With the exposition, we wanted to show that there were alternatives when we build the global village and that we can, to some extent, determine what kinds of cities we want to live in.

In this way, our world's fair was no different from the fairs of the last century, with their idealistic White Cities and other utopian visions. We had our own visions of what the Internet can do and we hoped that the world's fair might show people some of what is possible. With our time capsule safely held at the City of Kobe Museum (and countless other copies of the world's fair still floating around the Internet), we ended our year on the network and set about to the task of turning our fairgrounds into a public park, to wait and see if others would follow our example with their own world's fair.

I have not searched all your options, but the first impression is quite good!! More when I see the rest! Ciao!

—Saso Smole
Ljubljana, Slovenia
saso.smole@kiss.uni-lj.si

A Fair in the Air

Portland Or — Aug 26th · 1905

INDUSTRIAL AND LIBERAL ART PALACE
LEWIS & CLARK EXPOSITION

arrived here yesterday and found Portland quite

1905 INDUSTRIAL AND LIBERAL ARTS PALACE

The Global Schoolhouse Pavilion

5

John Gage has the enigmatic title of science officer at Sun Microsystems. He has had a varied career, from a campus radical at the University of California at Berkeley in the 1960s to press officer for the McGovern presidential campaign and for other politicians such as Ted Kennedy. He got into the computer business when he was working in Cody's, a Berkeley bookstore, helping them to build up a world-class mathematics section.

One day at Cody's, he ran into his friend Bill Joy, a legendary programmer responsible for much of the Unix operating system used in most of the large computers on the Internet. Bill had banded together with some colleagues from Stanford University and they were talking about forming a computer company with the then-radical notion of giving every high-end user his or her own powerful workstation. This was in the era when the VAX minicomputer reigned, called a minicomputer because it only filled half the machine room (as opposed to its mainframe predecessor, which took up the whole machine room). The company was formed, John was hired, and Sun quickly became a major force in the industry after LucasFilm decided to buy a boatload of these machines to make the film *Star Wars*.

The workstations were based on a series of open standards: engineers knew exactly how their operating system worked so they could modify any aspect of the machine. Adding new peripheral boards, or writing a real-time kernel to monitor scientific experiments, or letting the user change the memory manager to do strange scheduling and priority tricks with programs were all things that you could do on these machines.

John Gage had no specific skills in the area of high-end workstations, but quickly became an expert. His computing background until then had consisted of writing an inventory system for Cody's bookstore and using an arcane typesetting language called troff for printing mathematical formulas. He became the so-called science officer for Sun, charged with touring the garages of Silicon Valley, the high-end research laboratories in government and corporations, and pretty much anyplace else he cared to go. In the process, he became a superb matchmaker for the company, bringing in new technology for the Sun engineers to play with and showing potential customers what they could do with Sun's products.

This site is great!

One of my students told me about this, and forever proved the point that you can always learn from your students.

—Roberto Ordóñez
Berrien Springs, MI, USA
ordonez@andrews.edu

Photo/Sun Microsystems

John Gage

Vice President Al Gore and President Bill Clinton take Internet lessons at NetDay96.

Photo/White House Press Office

Thank you!

I have just written a worksheet for my students to go along with your Mola International page. We have a reading in our Spanish IV textbook about the Cuna indians in a lesson on popular arts in the Hispanic world. What a gift to be able to show my students so many wonderful examples of the artwork and motifs described in our text. You even had a category (nautical) that our text missed! The sound files were great, better quality than anything I have used so far. Thanks again from a very grateful teacher in Minneapolis.

—**Robynne Runyon**
Minneapolis, MN, USA
robynne@blake.pvt.k12.mn.us

There's a story about John that is widely told in the computer industry. You are stranded on a remote island in the Pacific Ocean, about to be boiled alive and served as dinner. Your only escape is to ask if the chief perhaps knows John Gage. The answer will come back quickly. "Of course," the chief will reply, "he was here two weeks ago. And where are those damn computers he promised us?"

In the course of John's travels and frequent speeches, he always tries to push the state of the art. When he came to the National Press Club, he encouraged every officer and librarian he ran into to wire the club, put it on the Internet, and become a resource to train every journalist in Washington, indeed the world, how to use the Internet. Another of his visions was the wiring of every school in the nation by having corporations adopt their local schools.

In late 1995, John put together a web page about the idea, sort of a draft straw man proof-of-concept. "Wire our schools!" the page trumpeted. Prominent on the page was a huge list of corporations that he figured would be interested in wiring our nation's schools, and at the bottom of the page was a banner that read "Note: This is only a test. This is not the truth, yet." John showed it to Tom Kalil at the White House.

What happened next is a perfect illustration of the serendipitous nature of doing big projects on the Internet. Tom Kalil showed it to Vice President Gore at his monthly meeting. The vice president loved the idea and marched into the president and showed it to him. The president thought it was a great idea. Somehow the note was overlooked.

John got a call. "The president loves your idea," Tom said. "He'll be out in eight days with the vice president to give a speech on education and wants

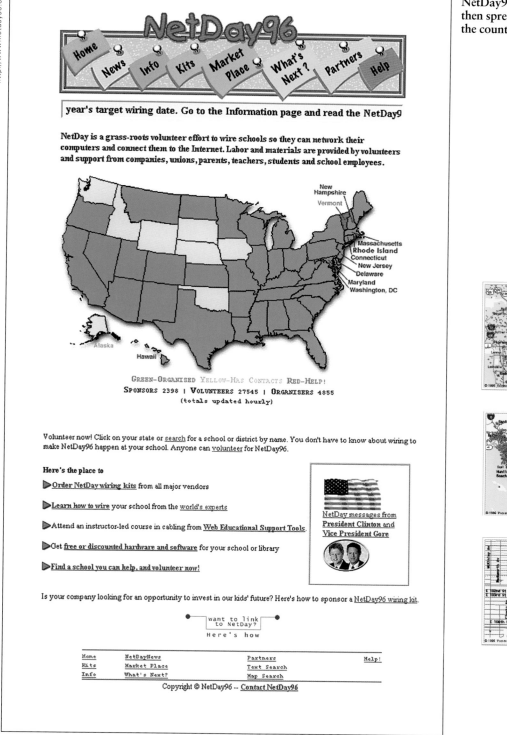

year's target wiring date. Go to the Information page and read the NetDay9

NetDay is a grass-roots volunteer effort to wire schools so they can network their computers and connect them to the Internet. Labor and materials are provided by volunteers and support from companies, unions, parents, teachers, students and school employees.

GREEN—ORGANISED   YELLOW—HAS CONTACTS   RED—HELP!

SPONSORS 2398 | VOLUNTEERS 27545 | ORGANISERS 4855
(totals updated hourly)

Volunteer now! Click on your state or search for a school or district by name. You don't have to know about wiring to make NetDay96 happen at your school. Anyone can volunteer for NetDay96.

Here's the place to

▷ Order NetDay wiring kits from all major vendors

▷ Learn how to wire your school from the world's experts

▷ Attend an instructor-led course in cabling from Web Educational Support Tools.

▷ Get free or discounted hardware and software for your school or library

▷ Find a school you can help, and volunteer now!

NetDay messages from President Clinton and Vice President Gore

Is your company looking for an opportunity to invest in our kids' future? Here's how to sponsor a NetDay96 wiring kit.

want to link to NetDay? Here's how

Home	NetDayNews	Partners	Help!
Kits	Market Place	Text Search	
Info	What's Next?	Map Search	

Copyright © NetDay96 -- Contact NetDay96

NetDay96 started in California, then spread like a wildfire across the country.

California NetDay96

http://town.hall.org/places/SciTech

The SciTech Gluon machine.

I'm very interested in this. We offer English as Second Language classes and are very interested in teaching our students how to use the Internet. Thank you for providing a very useful, attractive, and educational place for them to learn.

—IELS Language School
Austin, TX, USA
iels@88net.net

your project to be the centerpiece. Get the presidents of all those companies you listed to show up at the Exploratorium in San Francisco and we can announce this." John Gage spent a fairly frantic week calling every corporation he could think of and getting them to pledge their support for the project. Having the president of the United States (POTUS) and the vice president (VPOTUS) there worked miracles and almost every corporation decided they would support what became NetDay96.

It started in California on March 9, 1996. Over 19,000 volunteers descended on the schools of California to wire them for Internet access, using cable, components, and installation experts donated by corporations, universities, and small businesses all over the state. The press ate it up, showing the president and the vice president hauling out spools of red, white, and blue cable at Ygnacio Valley High School in Concord. In many cases, the support went beyond merely wiring the school, including computers, Internet access, and local "angels" to assist in keeping things going. On-line dynamic maps allowed volunteers to zero in on a local school, find the organizers for NetDay in their area, and pitch in with their time or contributions.

NetDay spread all over the United States. Governors, members of congress, mayors, and others saw a perfect opportunity, and the project got the full backing of the government. By the end of 1996, NetDay programs had been initiated in every state but Vermont and many other countries were putting together their "Wire Our Schools" programs.

NetDay spread much the same way the Internet has grown. No large staff decided to do this. It was pretty much an accident, but the idea was simple and easy to support for engineers, corporate donors, government officials, and local teachers and school officials. In the early hectic days after the president announced that he wanted to wire every school in America, John and a half-dozen other volunteers ran the whole program. The web site was run by two webmasters and John, in between his speeches and nonstop cell phone calls. Other groups started organizing themselves, and were able to join by linking their efforts with those of others.

More important than detailed guidelines and rules or a formal support organization is a clear, open definition of the concept and the interface—how you can join with the other people doing similar projects. Rather than a single organized system, successful Internet projects, indeed the Internet protocols themselves, work best when control is decentralized. What is defined is the protocol and the network interface: how we communicate with each other if we are sending email, or exchanging web pages, or even trying to mount a world exposition or wire every school in the country.

The Quantum Slot Machine

The year 1996 saw many other projects aimed at children and our schools, projects that the world's fair tried to highlight in the Global Schoolhouse Pavilion. Some projects just happened on their own, like NetDay96. NetDay96 was featured in the world's fair headlines, and was thus part of the fair, but the site was also part of the Yahoo Directory, the Cool Site of the Day collection, and other directories to the World Wide Web. In that sense, part of the world's fair was no different from other directory sites, though we tried to make sure we had some connection with the fair.

In other cases, the on-line pavilions were created specifically for the world's fair, in some cases even receiving help in building their web site or mirroring facilities in Central Park. Other sites got more tangible support from exposition sponsors, such as computers. An example of one of these sites, featured in the Global Schoolhouse Pavilion, was SciTech, a hands-on science museum in the suburbs of Chicago, Illinois. The museum, very similar to facilities such as the Exploratorium in San Francisco, gives kids a chance to play with hands-on experiments to see how to make a tornado or how color works.

The specialty of SciTech is the very big and the very small, with a special emphasis on physics, a natural focus given SciTech's location near the Fermi National Accelerator Laboratory. The link to the world's fair was a natural one: SciTech was started by Olivia Diaz and Ernest Malamud, a distinguished physicist at Fermilab who just happens to be my father.

It is a great pleasure to participate in the Internet World Exposition and I think that it is one of the most important dates in computer history. Visit our system, the first on middle education at South America.

—Prof. Marcelo Kruk
Montevideo, Uruguay
webmaster@reu.edu.uy

SciTech teaches children about quantum building blocks.

Illustration/Nick Gressle

*I'm a science teacher
who looks forward to
expanding my mind.
I know my students will
benefit from anything
I can learn, proving to
them that "knowledge is
power." Thank you all for
providing this site.*

—**Melinda Berg**
Barrow, AK, USA
mberg@arctic.nsbsd.k12.ak.us

SciTech received two computers from IBM and also had their web site mirrored inside Central Park. Mirroring meant that the web site for SciTech was developed by people at the museum. When web pages were completed, they would transfer them over to the large machines that make up Central Park. The world would "see" SciTech as being located on a very large, very fast machine. Mirroring is a common way for a small business, a community group, or an individual to develop a site for the web, and then leave it to a big Internet service provider (or a world's fair) to worry about keeping the computers running, the Internet links flowing, and security enforced, along with other aspects of maintaining a large Internet system.

SciTech's contribution to the Global Schoolhouse was an on-line exhibit that allowed students to learn about how subatomic particles are constructed. On site, people could go up to a real slot machine, hit the lever, and spin quarks around to form neutrinos, protons, and other building blocks of the universe. Two down quarks and an up quark, for example, would appear 13 percent of the time, forming, as any student should know, a neutron. The probabilities of forming different particles corresponded with the probabilities in the so-called real world. On line, a similar slot machine let people on the web conduct the same experiments. Later in the year, a Gluon machine was added, letting people explore not only the flavors of quarks, but the color of the attractions between quarks.

The Global Schoolhouse CyberFair

The Global Schoolhouse is a term that has been in use for on-line, collaborative educational projects since 1993, the year that the National Science Foundation called in some educators, corporations, and the usual motley crew of Internet volunteer engineers. The project was instigated by Dr. Steve Wolff, the visionary director of the Internet group at NSF at that time who had spearheaded projects such as the NSFnet, the first real backbone for the Internet. Steve wanted to "do something big with kids and use the Internet."

What evolved, after a hectic two months of email, was the Global Schoolhouse Project. Students in four sites in England and the United States worked with Yvonne Andres, a curriculum director in Los Angeles. The students all read Al Gore's book on the environment, then went out into their communities to do some activities related to the environment in their area. At the end of the program, an on-line teleconference was scheduled. This was unusual in 1993 in that the teleconference was based on the Internet. It used software that had just been developed at Cornell called CU-SeeMe that allowed an ordinary Macintosh with a cheap video camera to do on-line teleconferencing using a line as slow as a modem connection, though it did work better with faster connections.

Sprint and other corporations contributed resources to put T1 lines into the four schools. The four schools all reported on their individual findings, and in Washington government officials from the vice president's staff, the National Science Foundation, and the British Embassy gathered to hear the reports and ask questions of the students. Yvonne Andres in Los Angeles worked with the Internet Multicasting Service in DC and Internet "angels" at the other sites to support their local schools. The project was rough, as first experiments with technology generally are, but Yvonne Andres took the project and flew with it, forming a nonprofit foundation called the Global SchoolNet Foundation.

By 1996, the concept had evolved into CyberFair96, a project supported first by Cisco and MCI as major sponsors and later joined by Microsoft and other corporations. Over 350 schools from 30 countries signed up with the assignment of putting some part of their local community on line in a meaningful way. Seven categories were available for students to enter. In Local Leaders, for example, the prize-winning entry from Kirby School in Austin, Texas, was completed by 7- to 9-year-olds and featured people such as Barbara Jordan, a civil rights advocate and the first black congresswoman, and Willie Nelson, on whose page where students Casey and Dusty proclaimed:

Willie Nelson is a country dude
He likes Tex-mex food
He has a longhorn for a pet,
which he's never met.
His favorite word is c-c-c-c-c-o-o-o-o-o-l-l-l-l-l cool!
He hates gruel!!!!!!!!!!!!!!!

The sites that were submitted by some of the older students were also impressive, in many cases meeting standards of quality rivaling those of design professionals. A site sent in by high school students in New Jersey, for example, won in the category of environmental awareness. The students split into groups that focused on matters such as local water quality and animals. The students were required to act as ambassadors to their community. The local water quality group created a museum exhibit, while the animals group put on a play that dramatized problems animals faced and created a pamphlet for use by elementary school teachers.

The student ambassador function applied to the on-line site. The web pages they constructed featured photos, on-line quizzes, a sophisticated user interface for navigating the site, and very nice graphic design. How advanced the students were was underscored when I wrote for permission to use screen-dumps of their site in this book. Within minutes of the request for rights being sent in by email I received a warm note back from the systems administrator,

As an art teacher for 6–10 year old children, I found one of the projects the children were most interested in was the biosphere construction project, understanding that the biosphere would need to house and support all their survival and aesthetic needs for two years. I hope you all have great success stories, too.

—Meta Bright Star
Chicago, IL, USA
heybaby@ripco.com

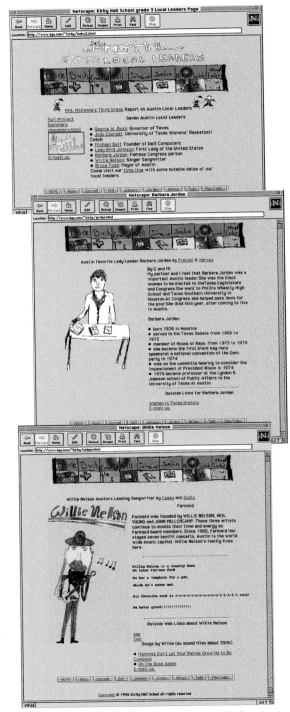

Winning entries from the Cisco/MCI Global
Schoolhouse Cyberfair96 competition, which
was hosted by the Global SchoolNet Foundation.

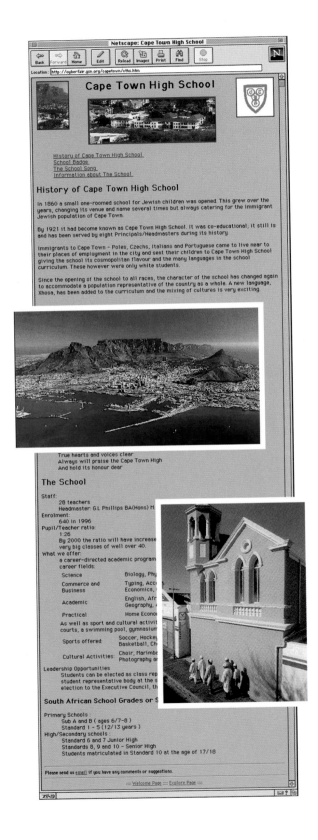

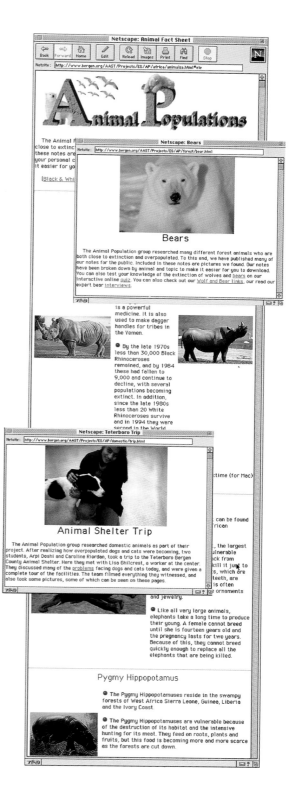

*Simply Marvelous!
Powerful! A place
transcending borders ...
a town hall of the world ...
all are citizens here.
I am awe struck by the
feelings here. This is
absolutely the *best*.
Almost beyond description
... Until the next time,
with my best regards,
Thank you!*

—**Edward Girard**
Jacksonville, FL, USA
jerry@southeast.net

Anne Lucey. The signature line on her electronic mail, after listing essentials such as her SnailMail (postal) address, has the customary whimsical quote or quip. Hers reads:

"But Miss Lucey, I NEED crontabs!"

Crontabs are a Unix systems programming facility that allows a user to have jobs executed at certain times. You might use a crontab to delete garbage files, or archive your system logs, or other functions that one wouldn't automatically associate with high school students.

The winning sites were rewarded at an on-line awards ceremony. Those who did not have lines fast enough to use an Internet videoconference could call an 800 number provided by MCI to listen to the ceremony. Vice President Gore sent in a videotaped message of congratulation to the CyberFair project in particular and the world's fair in general, which was sent out over the Internet as a real-time video during the ceremony and then made available as a movie file for people to download after the fact. Of course, not many people are going to want to download a four-megabyte video clip of a few seconds of the vice president, but it is important to understand that a successful web site spans the technology, looking good to users on different kinds of browsers and those with different kinds of computers. It is also important to remember that web sites are accessed locally as well as from the Internet, and that big video clips are very useful for demos or public award ceremonies.

The Global Schoolhouse theme illustrates the difficulty of trying to corral cyberspace. When people registered their pavilions, many of them were considered educational in nature. Do you put a site like the Environmental Awareness site in a Global Schoolhouse because it was done by students, or do you put it into a Global Interest Pavilion because it concerns us all, or do you create a new Environmental Pavilion to house it?

Luckily, our world's fair had infinite real estate. When people came in with an existing site and wanted to be "part of a world's fair," or when people approached fair organizers with just an idea and a request for helping in making that idea real, they were easy to fit into the fair. This world's fair had a cardinal rule: anybody could open a pavilion. In some ways, this makes the world's fair just an affinity group, a list of people with similar aims. However, when all those people start working together, the world's fair becomes ever more real as the individual activities swell into trends. In this sense, our fair was no different than the old fairs, where people all making similar machines, or promoting their local cultures, gathered under a glass roof or on the banks of the River Seine to celebrate a global holiday.

OUT FLEW THE WEB AND FLOATED WIDE;
THE MIRROR CRACKED FROM SIDE TO SIDE.

ALFRED, LORD TENNYSON
THE LADY OF SHALLOTT

1893 WORLD'S COLUMBIAN EXPOSITION

The Reinventing Government Pavilion

6

W orld's fairs are little cities, and people see different things when they look at cities. At the Chicago Columbian Exposition in 1893, some people came away thinking the fair was about the Ferris wheel and the hamburger. Others thought it was about electricity, lighting, and other public infrastructures. Some went away talking of the White City, a surreal architecture of ornate Beaux Arts palaces, or of Mrs. Palmer's Women's Building, which helped a new generation of young women explore the possibility of careers outside of the home.

The fairs of the last century were well known as gathering places for inventors and manufacturers, places where countries showed off their culture. There was always the public carnival aspect, a grand show of huge light towers, entertainment extravaganzas, and other elements that made the fairs a public party. But another element present from the beginning was exhibits by government bodies. Patent offices, national libraries, arts centers, geographical surveys, and other agencies of different countries would come and show the world their treasured possessions and latest accomplishments.

Government and industry used the fairs as a meeting ground. Agricultural boards used the Chicago world's fair to promote their grain policies. Geographical surveyors worked with miners and developers. Trade officials used fairs to promote foreign investment or trade. And, of course, governments used the fairs, places where millions of people came to learn about the world, to promote their particular corner of that world.

It is no accident that where most of the world's inventors and engineers would gather, groups such as the U.S. Patent and Trademark Office would also be present. A patent office works closely with industries, particularly the rapidly changing ones. The patent office creates value when it declares a particular process or invention to be unique and the sole property of the patent holder. The relationship between the patent office and the industry that creates and sells the inventions is a complex and often uneasy one.

During most of the last century, a world's fair was the perfect place for the patent office to bring a few of the more exotic items from their collection and use the show as a way of generating goodwill toward their customers. The fairs of the last century were a perfect meeting ground, away from the battlefield of the patent process. The Internet 1996 World Exposition became such a meeting ground, but in a different way than one might expect.

The computers in our home will be no more dummy box ... Share the information!

—Chanyoung Jeong
Sherman Oaks, CA, USA
eugene@cinenet.net

81

The U.S. Patent Office
exhibited its wares at the
1876 Centennial Exhibition
in Philadelphia.

Photo/Smithsonian Institution

*Carved in the rotunda of
the Missouri State Capitol
are the words, "Ideas
Control the World."
This Internet World Expo
demonstrates the power of
ideas to connect us ... to
teach us ... to inspire us.*

—Daniel Arnall
Jefferson City, MO, USA
darnall@learfield.com

Government in the Information Age

It was no surprise, then, when governments gravitated toward the Internet
1996 World Exposition. This was a project they could understand. In some
countries, such as Singapore, Korea, and Taiwan, government bodies ended up
having major roles in organizing and running strong world's fair committees.
In Korea, for example, the National Computerization Agency ran a Korean
Secretariat for the fair with a staff of 15 and charged it with drafting sponsors,
building an on-line pavilion, and gathering participation from other government
groups, community centers, or anything else they could find. The Korean
pavilion ended up with over 700 different sets of web pages.

 In addition to running parts of fair operations, there was a flood of requests
to link in Digital City or National Information Infrastructure programs from
governments all over the world. Many of these were simply "please link my page"
requests, which were all sorted into a Digital Cities pavilion. In some cases,
however, there were surprises. In Singapore, the National Computer Board
used the fair as an opportunity to get permission to do Internet "broadcasts"
from events such as the National Day Parade.

 Getting permission simply to be present with your equipment is the first,
and often the hardest, challenge when the Internet wants to participate in large
public events, and it is especially difficult at official public events. Any reporter,
no matter what the medium, has to have special access to an event to cover it

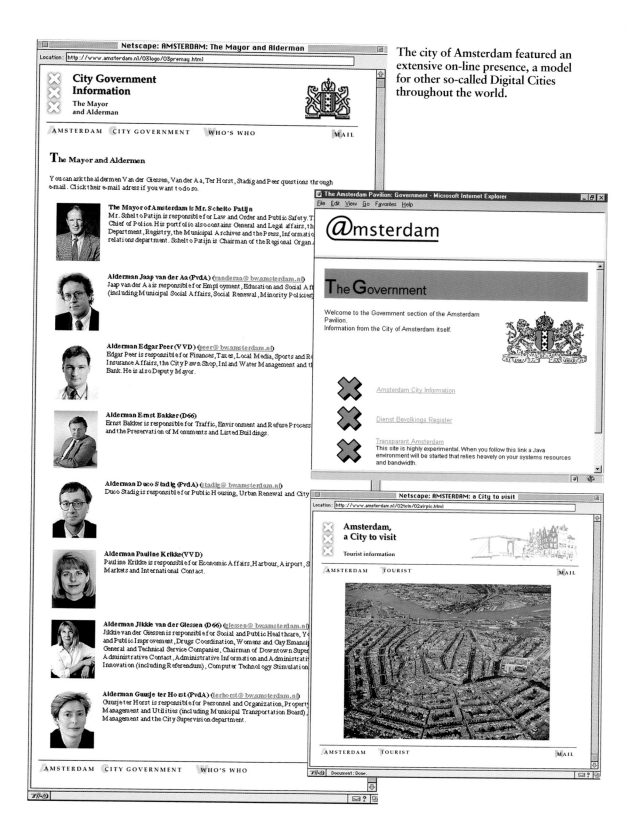

The city of Amsterdam featured an extensive on-line presence, a model for other so-called Digital Cities throughout the world.

Transparent Amsterdam allows
on-line users to navigate through
maps of the city.

Transparant.Net is an initiative of the Society for Old and New
Media, the ARCAM Foundation, The Digital CityFoundation,
NL Design and the city council of Amsterdam.

properly. You have to bring in equipment to take photographs, tape record, shoot movies, talk to officials, and otherwise become part of the event that you are covering.

The Internet is no different. If government is to go on line, be it at a public hearing or a public celebration, getting certified to drag in equipment and then to "broadcast" the information is quite difficult. Taking digital photographs at a computer conference is easy. Getting permission to do so in an august chamber or somber occasion is often viewed in the same category as requests to go rollerblading in the White House or to paint a mural on the front of the Notre Dame cathedral.

Similar problems are faced all over the world by the people charged with maintaining web sites for their organizations: getting permission to get started is often the hardest challenge. World's fair committees were allowed into many places throughout the year, broadcasting not only parades like the Singapore National Day Parade, but also the APEC Summit in the Philippines and other events throughout Asia.

Somehow, these activities didn't strike a chord with many of the world's fair organizers. Surely, there had to be a way to "do government" in a more meaningful way in this fair.

The Congressional Memory Project

Not all exhibits about government were built by government. In the case of one, the Congressional Memory Project, government was not even aware that it was being done. The first requests for credentials by the Internet Multicasting Service to cover the House and Senate were sent in 1993 to the august-sounding Executive Committee of the Radio-Television Galleries of the United States Senate and House of Representatives News Galleries. "We want to do radio broadcasts from the floor of the House and the Senate over the Internet computer network," read our application. The application was promptly routed to the guy who ran the PCs for the senate gallery, at the time a fairly unadventurous computing environment. We chatted briefly about his PC and his goal to get an Internet account at some point in the near future. I confirmed that what we were proposing was indeed possible.

Our application sat for close to a year. Luckily, a new staff member joined the Internet Multicasting Service and he found the magic bullet. Luther Brown had been a senior producer at NBC News and CBS and had won an Emmy award for a PBS documentary. A bar-certified lawyer, Luther had also been director of public relations for the Wilderness Society. For some reason, he gave up that promising career to work on top of a Chinese restaurant three blocks from the Capitol in Washington.

Congressional Memory Project? Does congress have a memory? Does it even have a mind?

—Bob Schatz
Nashville, TN, USA
schatzr@belmont.edu

Superhighway Routed Through Capitol Hill.

—Washington Post
September 19, 1994

Luther Brown

As vice president of programs, Luther had to find new content for the Internet Multicasting Service and to bring professional production techniques to our broadcasts. Luther took a look at our long-standing application for credentials and laughed. He went to his phone and soon the fax machine spouted a list of the names of the members of the committee. His first boss at CBS turned out to be the chair. We were granted a hearing.

Getting the credentials turned out to be fairly easy, taking about five minutes. We explained what we were doing, and gave references to our existing programs, such as the National Press Club luncheon speeches. I didn't mention Geek of the Week, thinking it somehow might take away from our already-thin veneer of respectability. The committee asked one or two questions, and then the chair said he thought the issue was fairly clear cut, that we were obviously journalists, and the committee might as well face the fact that there would probably be others like us who would follow.

Once we had permission, the next trick was to get the signal back out of the Capitol complex and into our computers. The obvious thing to do would be to run a dedicated data line into the basement of the Capitol, then lease fiber optics from the press pool. Unfortunately, bringing the Internet all the way into the Capitol takes space for computers, routers, video mixers, and the other peripherals of running an Internet broadcast operation. Space is very tight in centuries-old facilities like the U.S. Capitol. Press can get rack space in the basement, or special fiber optic runs, or other services, but it often takes a long time and a heavy investment in committee meetings.

We opted for a cheap hack. The local PBS station, WETA, already had an audio feed from the House and another from the Senate that they sent back to their studios in suburban Virginia. Their equipment in the basement of the Capitol building had an extra audio output for each of the two feeds. We called our local phone company and requested a special "conditioned" voice line. A normal telephone line uses 8 khz signals, which is equivalent to a computer sound file of 8000 samples per second. An audio CD, by contrast, uses 44,100 samples per second, each sample is 16 bits, and the sound is stereo, so there are two streams.

The consequence of a normal phone line is that all sounds over 4 khz are cut off. Try playing music on your stereo with the treble switch all the way down and you will hear the effect of cutting off the high end. Then, play music through a telephone and you'll notice the same effect, but with an even greater cutoff. The sound just isn't very good. The conditioned line we requested from the telephone company cuts off less of the high end. Once the lines were installed and hooked up to the House and Senate sound feeds, the signals were run into our mixing board, digitally cleaned up to sound nicer, then sent over to a stack of small Sun workstations. Each Sun was a separate live audio feed out to the Internet, and using a technique called multicasting we were able to reach workstations all over the world.

It seemed a shame, however, simply to dump this information onto the Internet. We set up another computer that "listened" to the Internet sessions. Instead of playing the data through a loudspeaker, however, this computer recorded everything it heard onto a large array of disk drives. Starting in January 1995, when this system went live, we had a complete record of everything that happened on the floor of the House and Senate, an archive that was taking about 400 megabytes of storage for each day of the session.

A database is fairly useless unless you can do something with it and that was the next challenge. The system was handed over to Deb K. Roy, a Ph.D. candidate at the MIT Media Lab who came down to Washington to spend a summer in our studios as a multicasting fellow. As our first (and it turns out only) multicasting fellow, I wanted Deb to focus on one spectacular project instead of getting involved in the nitty-gritty grind of running the radio station.

Deb had done his master's research on audio processing, examining issues such as voice recognition, which focuses on understanding what the speaker is saying, and speaker recognition, which tries to determine who the speaker is. We handed Deb a project with the grand-sounding name of the Congressional Memory Project. His job was to do something with all the audio we had recorded from the floor of Congress.

An audio database is a strange object. If you know exactly what time an event occurred, it is easy to play it back. Making the database more than a massive tape recorder, however, requires some thought. In the case of Congress, we got lucky. There is a formal printed transcript available, called *The Congressional Record.*

The Congressional Record is what we call in the database field a "messy database." Although it purports to be a transcript, it is actually heavily edited. The Speaker can strike things from the record. Members can add additional material. The Government Printing Office, under strong pressure from some members of Congress, put the information on line. You couldn't simply transfer a day of transcripts, but you could do keyword searches for selected parts of the record. We subscribed to the GPO's for-fee service that let us conduct searches directly onto their computer.

We weren't interested in conducting searches, however. We wanted everything. That should have been a simple matter: the transfer of a few files using the FTP protocol. But, because of a fear of a loss of revenue, that service wasn't available and we could only conduct keyword searches using an Internet database search protocol called the Wide Area Information Server (WAIS). We conducted a set of sample searches. The response, while only containing part of a day, also told us which files on the remote system each request had come from.

Deb Roy

CONGRESSIONAL MEMORY PROJECT

The Congressional Memory Project linked
text transcripts with an audio database to
provide keyword searches of speeches.

http://town.hall.org/Congress/Memory/

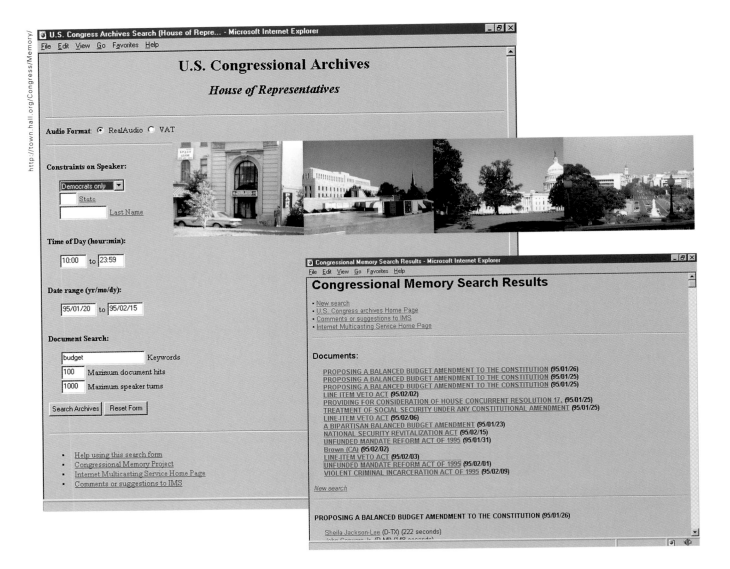

#headline.5 - Microsoft Internet Explorer

File   Edit   View   Go   Favorites   Help

PROVIDING FOR CONSIDERATION OF HOUSE CONCURRENT RESOLUTION 17, (95/01/25)

John Joseph Moakley (D-MA) (351 seconds)
David E. Bonior (D-MI) (80 seconds)
Anthony C. Beilenson (D-CA) (7 seconds)
John Joseph Moakley (D-MA) (9 seconds)
Tony P. Hall (D-OH) (160 seconds)
John Joseph Moakley (D-MA) (34 seconds)
Martin Frost (D-TX) (187 seconds)
John Joseph Moakley (D-MA) (9 seconds)
James A. Traficant Jr. (D-OH) (165 seconds)
John Joseph Moakley (D-MA) (153 seconds)
Ray Thornton (D-AR) (5 seconds)
Charles W. Stenholm (D-TX) (39 seconds)
John Joseph Moakley (D-MA) (7 seconds)
Xavier Becerra (D-CA) (31 seconds)
John Joseph Moakley (D-MA) (5 seconds)
Bill Orton (D-UT) (112 seconds)
John Joseph Moakley (D-MA) (4 seconds)
Richard A. Gephardt (D-MO) (87 seconds)
John Joseph Moakley (D-MA) (20 seconds)
Richard A. Gephardt (D-MO) (26 seconds)
John Joseph Moakley (D-MA) (8 seconds)
Richard A. Gephardt (D-MO) (141 seconds)
John Joseph Moakley (D-MA) (105 seconds)
Thomas M. Foglietta (D-PA) (176 seconds)
John Joseph Moakley (D-MA) (4 seconds)
David E. Bonior (D-MI) (2 seconds)
John Joseph Moakley (D-MA) (20 seconds)
Bill Richardson (D-NM) (166 seconds)
John Joseph Moakley (D-MA) (65 seconds)
Patricia Schroeder (D-CO) (216 seconds)
John Joseph Moakley (D-MA) (12 seconds)

Congressional Records Search Result - Microsoft Internet Explorer

File   Edit   View   Go   Favorites   Help

Congressional Record from 95/01/25

Mr. FROST. Madam Speaker, for some time I have been a supporter of a balanced budget amendment to the U.S. Constitution. In the 16 years I have served in this body, I have seen the public debt triple to well over $4 trillion and have watched as the Congress has struggled to bring the Federal budget and the deficit under control. Until recently, we in the Congress, working with Presidents both Republican and Democratic, have had only limited success in curbing the spriraling growth of Government spending. Thanks to the policies instituted in the last Congress, we are now witnessing a steady downward path of the deficit, but I remain convinced that stronger measures are called for if we are to finally, once and for all, bring the budget of this Nation into balance. And, for that reason, I will support passage of a constitutional amendment when the House votes tomorrow.

However, Madam Speaker, in spite of my record of support for just such a constitutional amendment, I must rise in opposition to this rule. My Republican colleagues made a number of points yesterday during our markup of this rule saying that it provides for the consideration of more options than have been considered in the past few years.

{time} 1320

Start RealAudio Stream

RealAudio Player: segment.010.ra

File   View   Clip   Sites   Help

Title: U.S. House audio for 01/25/95 (segment 010)
Author: Internet Multicasting Service
Copyright: Recorded by the Internet Multicasting Service, No

Playing 14.4 network stream   00:09.0 / 00:51.8

• New search
• Browse this time and day
• Congressional Memory Home Page
• Comments or suggestions to IMS
• Internet Multicasting Service Home Page

Shortcut to http://town.hall.org/Archives/radio/Congress/Memory/tmp/house950125.010.medium.media.org.1310.ram

By looking at the file names, we were able to determine the way that the GPO named its files. There were four ways that you could name a day's worth of data according to their scheme, depending on factors like whether there were graphics present. We wrote a little program that conducted four dummy searches per day until we hit on the file name for that day, then retrieved the full file back into our system.

There was a glitch, though. Normally, with the WAIS system you send in a search request first. That gives you back an answer to ask for a file and the specific portion of the file containing the answer to the search. We skipped the first part and simply asked for the files that we thought might exist. But each access to a non-existent file generated an error. The GPO was kind of new at this and didn't check its log files. On Central Park systems, log files are several gigabytes per day. Each evening, a daemon program recycles our log files: compressing the last day's data, archiving it, and creating a new empty log file.

Because the GPO didn't check its log files, the data kept accumulating. After a few months of this, the log file got bigger and appears to have filled up the temporary file system on their computer, crashing the system. This seems to have prompted the GPO staff to notice the log file and look into it.

What they saw was thousands and thousands of error messages that had accumulated over the months. To make things worse, their WAIS system was misconfigured and on the day their system had filled up a rogue process had stuck in memory and kept trying to re-execute the same non-existent search. This was a standard bug in WAIS and a simple patch to the code had long ago fixed this problem on most systems.

We received several frantic calls from the GPO. We tried to explain what had happened but they were a bit, shall we say, on edge. For people who run Internet services for a living, these kinds of problems are part of the day-to-day operations, but evidently the information systems bureaucrats had decided to configure the system once and hope that it would run perfectly forever. We seem to have put a crimp in that plan and a letter was dispatched to me explaining that we were not welcome anymore and further attempts would be referred to the inspector general.

No matter. By that time we had nine months of transcripts, nine months of audio, and three months to go before the world's fair opened. Deb Roy took the transcripts and worked on coupling them to the audio database. The goal we gave Deb was that we wanted to be able to search for "all congressmen last week who spoke about the budget."

Deb's first task was to analyze the *Congressional Record* database, looking for a hook for our automated analysis programs to hang a hat on. There were time stamps, but they were approximate. We certainly knew on what day things happened, but the exact times were anybody's guess. The labeling of the record was also messy, with speaker names sometimes mislabeled or a single speaker being recorded when the debate in fact had a whole series of people.

Programs were used to parse the record; we tried to discern what an addition looked like, or the header information at the beginning of each day, or any other material to exclude because it wasn't spoken. Because of the ability to "revise and extend" remarks, we knew that even the material that was left might not be an exact match to our audio database.

The parsing of *The Congressional Record* gave a set of clues about who might be speaking. Deb then ran the audio through a series of processors to try to identify and segment the audio into different speakers. He built a database of samples of each of the members of Congress, giving a statistical profile of how a member spoke. Using *The Congressional Record* as a clue, the programs then compared the statistical profile of members to the actual audio, trying to determine the probability that a particular speaker in the audio database was a particular member. Deb then used that information to write out a set of speaker "turns" (when a new person begins to speak), and then linked that information to specific portions of the record.

On January 1, when the project opened in the world's fair, people were presented with a user interface that let them search a date range and confine the search to a particular location, member of Congress, or political party. Key words were used to search *The Congressional Record*, the searches being limited by factors such as date and time. Then, filters such as political party were applied to the data.

What the user saw at the completion of the query was first a series of debates in Congress that focused on their subject. By clicking on the particular debate, the user saw the speeches by members that satisfied the query. Clicking on a member would bring up a transcript of the session, followed by a tape recorder interface that allowed people to hear that particular speech.

Deb Roy finished his coding on the Congressional Memory Project in just three months. The work was not only an interesting way to send out government information and make it more accessible, but demonstrated very innovative uses of audio processing techniques. Deb had several papers accepted to scholarly journals describing the successful use of his techniques.

Deb Roy finished his work at the end of August and was under strict orders to return to the MIT Media Lab to start his doctoral studies. The world's fair bug hit him, however, and Deb paid a call on Dr. Alex Pentland, the chairman of his department and one of the real visionaries at the Media Lab. Deb asked to take a semester off to go travel to India and South America to build world's fair pavilions. Dr. Pentland agreed and Deb set off for four months of intensive travel.

A global change, a global clearer picture, a new language, a global peace that unites, and improves, solutions to total communication and democracy ... thanks for being there for all.

—Joseph Herrera
New York, NY, USA
joseph@flotsam.com

Fuel for the Information Economy

Started with a big effort by Vice President Gore's staff, government had made a big push into the on-line world. The White House home page was put together and shown to every cabinet member and agency chief. Each official was brought in and walked through the pages before they were published. When it got to the list of the agencies in the government, all were there, but if an agency did not have a web page, the name was in a pale gray font, certainly not up to the standards of their information-enabled who sported a bright, bold font with a nice blue underlining for the link. When you bring in a crew of deputy assistant secretaries for the Department of Education, show them their blank link, and then give them an enthusiastic tour of the Department of Labor pages, memos start to fly. Soon, you could click your way through the federal bureaucracy.

Even though every agency had a presence on the Internet in the United States, many of the web sites only featured pictures of the head of the agency, a few press releases, and a few pages describing things such as mission statements. A picture of the secretary is nice, but people are often more interested in the meat and potatoes: retrieving a specific patent filing or examining the annual reports filed with the Securities and Exchange Commission.

The large databases were not showing up on the Internet. Many of the agencies were still using Reagan-era procurement processes. The large databases were nominally available to the public, but only in bulk format on mainframe computer tapes and usually for a lot of money. The Reagan-era philosophy was that the sale of these databases was a profit center for the government. The buyers were typically the retail information industry, companies such as Dialog, LEXIS/NEXIS, and Dow Jones. These buyers, information wholesalers if you will, would add value to the raw bulk data and then make it available using retail information networks.

In 1993, this was exactly how the Securities and Exchange Commission (SEC) ran its operation. Public corporations in the United States are required to file a whole slew of public disclosure statements, annual and quarterly reports that explain their financial position, where they do business, who they do business with, and how they are owned through their public stocks and their debts. Beginning in 1970, a system called EDGAR, which stands for Electronic Data Gathering, Analysis, and Retrieval, had slowly come into being.

EDGAR handled both the filing of SEC documents and the dissemination of that information. The SEC contracted out the system to Mead Data Central, a large information processing firm. Mead would act as the data wholesaler, cleaning up the raw data and adding value. Mead would in turn sell to data retailers, including itself and various other firms. The retailers were in turn selling

http://www.sec.gov/

US Securities and Exchange Commission - Microsoft Internet Explorer

File   Edit   View   Go   Favorites   Help

Text only | Search non-EDGAR documents | Search EDGAR Archives

U.S. SECURITIES
AND EXCHANGE
COMMISSION

About the SEC

Investor
Assistance
& Complaints

EDGAR
Database

SEC Digest
& Statements

Current SEC
Rulemaking

Enforcement
Actions

Small Business
Information

Other Sites
to Visit

"We are the investor's advocate."
William O. Douglas
SEC Chairman, 1937-1939

Current News:

Plan of Distribution Filed Re Wealth International Network

Commission Posts OmniGene Notice on America OnLine

EDGAR RFP Issued, October 30, 1996

About this site | FAQ

Search SEC EDGAR Archives - Microsoft Internet Explorer

File   Edit   View   Go   Favorites   Help

You can search this index. Type the keyword(s) you want to search for:

sun AND microsystems

Search EDGAR Archives

Welcome to the archive of EDGAR documents. This is an index to **1994**, **1995**, and **1996** EDGAR documents stored on this server. The index is a full-text WAIS index of the header information contained in each document. Please enter your query in the search dialog.

ch dialog.

Search SEC EDGAR Archives - Microsoft Internet Explorer

File   Edit   View   Go   Favorites   Help

You can search this index. Type the keyword(s) you want to search for:

Result(s) of EDGAR search

Query: **sun AND microsystems**
Number of matches: **43**

Company name	Form Type	Date Filed	File Size
ROSS TECHNOLOGY INC	SC 13D	(08/20/1996)	37467 Bytes
		(11/13/1996)	104032 Bytes
		(10/31/1996)	44107 Bytes
		(10/02/1996)	85873 Bytes
		(09/26/1996)	837609 Bytes
		(09/10/1996)	84883 Bytes
		(08/09/1996)	50524 Bytes
		(05/20/1996)	0 Bytes
		(05/14/1996)	51151 Bytes
		(03/06/1996)	97689 Bytes
		(02/26/1996)	6689 Bytes
		(02/14/1996)	15449 Bytes
		(02/13/1996)	11490 Bytes
		(02/12/1996)	51817 Bytes
		(02/12/1996)	12471 Bytes
		(12/08/1995)	14922 Bytes
		(11/30/1995)	5159 Bytes

---

http://www.sec.gov/.../0000950005-96-000898.txt - Microsoft Internet Explorer

File   Edit   View   Go   Favorites   Help

```
-----BEGIN PRIVACY-ENHANCED MESSAGE-----
Proc-Type: 2001,MIC-CLEAR
Originator-Name: webmaster@www.sec.gov
Originator-Key-Asymmetric:
 MFgwCgYEVQgBAQICAf8DSgAwRwJAW2sNKK9AVtBzYZmr6aGjlWyK3XmZv3dTINen
 TWSM7vrzLADbmYQaionwg5sDW3P6oaM5D3tdezXMm7zlT+B+twIDAQAB
MIC-Info: RSA-MD5,RSA,
 K94BLerBYr66Vbg2M53TYjAbmBFrgzg/qyt0H+n+5JRq38ekWoUMExxA0hTZ01/S
 5zSZEN9Selkfgt7Oo8pIQA==

<SEC-DOCUMENT>0000950005-96-000898.txt : 19961115
<SEC-HEADER>0000950005-96-000898.hdr.sgml : 19961115
ACCESSION NUMBER:                  0000950005-96-000898
CONFORMED SUBMISSION TYPE:         10-Q
PUBLIC DOCUMENT COUNT:             6
CONFORMED PERIOD OF REPORT:        19960929
FILED AS OF DATE:                  19961113
SROS:            NASD

FILER:

        COMPANY DATA:
                COMPANY CONFORMED NAME:            SUN MICROSYSTEMS INC
                CENTRAL INDEX KEY:                 0000709519
                STANDARD INDUSTRIAL CLASSIFICATION: ELECTRONIC COMPUTERS [3571]
                IRS NUMBER:                        942805249
                STATE OF INCORPORATION:            DE
                FISCAL YEAR END:                   0630

        FILING VALUES:
                FORM TYPE:            10-Q
                SEC ACT:             1934 Act
                SEC FILE NUMBER:      000-15086
                FILM NUMBER:          96661377
```

to the specialized users of the data. Mead was not only the wholesaler, but also sold the data to itself in its retail role.

The first customer for Mead the retailer just happened to be the SEC, which paid $13 million to access its own information; the SEC, however, was quick to point out it was not paying for the raw data, only the "value added" in the form of sophisticated search and retrieval mechanisms. By the time all the value was added to this database, it could easily cost $100 to retrieve a company's annual filing from an information retailer. Needless to say, the people who were willing to pay that much for information tended to be financial professionals and use by other groups, such as students, was fairly limited.

In 1993, a group of public interest firms led by Jamie Love, director of Ralph Nader's Taxpayer Assets Project, started making noise about this system. They caught the attention of Congressman Edward Markey, who was then chairman of the House Subcommittee on Telecommunications and Finance, which had oversight over the SEC. Markey sent the SEC a letter and asked them to explain in his next oversight hearings why the SEC data weren't simply available for free on the Internet.

Many reasons came back. Putting the data on the Internet would pose a security risk. It was technically very expensive. There was no demand among ordinary citizens for this specialized information. And, of course, giving the data away wouldn't be great for the information wholesalers and retailers who had invested so much money in providing this public service.

I attended a meeting in Markey's office where the computer staff of the SEC explained its position. The staff, which has since been replaced by a very progressive set of computer managers, felt at the time that the Internet was not real and that there would be no demand for Internet use. One deputy MIS manager explained that he felt the Internet didn't have the "right kind of people," by which he meant that the Internet was only a few academic researchers. I couldn't help but think of the wide spectrum of users that I saw on our systems and retorted with the cheap shot that I felt that "the American people were the right kind of people." My input was not appreciated.

The Internet Multicasting Service offered to run a service on the Internet as a demonstration project. We asked the SEC for the data, but they said it would be illegal for them to give data to us, exposing them to possible contract violation suits from their information wholesaler. We arranged a small NSF grant, funded by Dr. Steve Wolff's group. The SEC computer staff was dubious about our free-lance nonprofit group and were skeptical that anything was really going to happen, but before they knew it a story appeared in the *New York Times* announcing that the NSF had issued a grant to give the public free access to SEC data on the Internet. The story included strong praise from the Clinton White House for the move.

Some people were not amused. By 1993, there was a $280-million-per-year industry in selling SEC data through retail channels. The Information Industry Association sent its hired guns up to the hill and soon the director of the NSF had received a nine-page letter from Congressman John D. Dingell, the much-feared ruler of the House Energy Committee, asking him to explain why the U.S. government was competing with the private sector, introducing potential viruses into this key government resource, and otherwise conducting itself in ways not to his pleasure.

We made our announcement in late 1993, and immediately contacted the information wholesaler and committed ourselves to paying the fee of $78,000 per year for a daily text feed of EDGAR data. By January 1994 our system was up and running. That was quick enough to moot much of the debate that was still raging among the information retailers. Once the system was up, there was not much the SEC or the industry could do but live with it, though the criticism kept coming. With the public, however, the system was an instant hit. We were flooded with eager and appreciative users.

The White House, in its quest to add more agencies to its home page, decided it would link in our database. The links were in the form of the seals of each of the agencies, so Marty Lucas and Philippe Tabaux were dispatched to dredge up a seal for the SEC to give the White House web designers.

Since no electronic versions of the seal appeared to exist, Marty and Philippe went to the SEC headquarters and explained that they were there for a color seal that they could scan and give to the White House. Somehow, this explanation didn't go over very well. Some unpleasentness occurred, but while Philippe was busy keeping the security guards occupied, Marty grabbed some SEC literature with a black-and-white seal and carefully eyeballed the official seal up on the wall. He couldn't help pointing out to the security guard that there was an error on the seal on the wall, but his comment didn't seem to be appreciated.

Philippe, in the country on a temporary visa, was not pleased. On the way out the door, he grumbled to Marty that working for the Internet Multicasting Service was sure to get him deported. Back at our studios, Marty and Philippe scanned in the black-and-white seal, colorized it from memory, and sent our newly counterfeited seal over to the White House for their web page.

Our EDGAR system ran through all of 1994, and by 1995 we felt it was time to bring the issue to resolution. We weren't running the SEC database because we wanted to be in the database business; we wanted the SEC itself to provide free public access to its information. We had also added another database just to prove that the SEC database wasn't an isolated case where we had benefited from all the value-added processing at the wholesale stage. This database was the full text of all U.S. patents, another set of information that was not available except through retail channels.

What a wonderful time to be alive taking part in all of this. Let us rejoice in what the Internet has to offer, mostly, the Freedom of Expression. Exercising this freedom is necessary for all those who can to free all those who are currently bound to tyranny.

—Pierre Johnson
Monroe, NY, USA
inforev@monroe.ny.frontiercomm.net

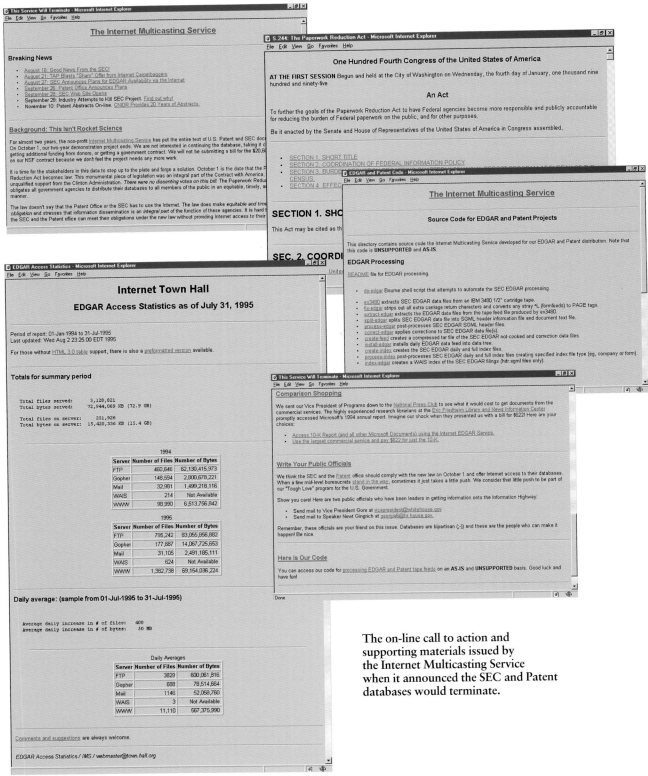

The on-line call to action and supporting materials issued by the Internet Multicasting Service when it announced the SEC and Patent databases would terminate.

In August 1995, we posted a note on the Internet. After sending out several million documents to a user population estimated at 20,000 people per day, we said we would be terminating the service on October 1. When people came in to do their daily search, they saw a headline banner about the death of the service. By clicking on the banner, people were directed to supporting information about our decision to terminate the service.

Our argument was that the SEC and patent office were required to run this kind of service under a recently passed law. One of the first bills to come out of Newt Gingrich's Contract with America was the Paperwork Reduction Act of 1995. Gingrich had held a press conference at the U.S. Capitol within days of his coronation and proudly unveiled the Thomas System, a full Internet service with all text proceedings of the U.S. Congress. He proclaimed that ordinary citizens should not have access to government information any later than the corporate lobbyist inside the Beltway.

The Paperwork Reduction act that soon followed proclaimed that government information should be available in a cost-effective manner, that equitable access be provided, and that this was a priority for every agency. The bill, unlike other planks of the contract, passed unanimously and with the enthusiastic support of the Clinton Administration. Nowhere did the bill mandate free Internet access, but we claimed that no other method satisfied the law.

To build up our case, we also posted our estimate of the annual cost of running the service ($175,000), statistics on who actually used the system, and the source code for processing the database on a daily basis. We even allowed users to click to send mail to the Speaker or the vice president. The reaction from the public was swift and definite; memos and email started flying in Washington.

A public meeting had already been scheduled for the retail information industry and EDGAR users to comment on subjects like how their electronic filing was going. Various industry executives and SEC officials had been formed into a series of panels. We had not been invited, nor had Jamie Love from Nader's Taxpayer Assets Project. We both decided to crash the party.

The meeting was interesting, to say the least. At the first mention of EDGAR in the year 2000, Jamie Love rushed the microphone and launched into a tirade about how there were more important matters at hand, specifically the imminent death of EDGAR. An industry official interrupted Jamie to explain how the EDGAR system really wasn't used by many people, so I grabbed another microphone and gave a full statistical report on our user base and the cost for running the system.

David Lytel, a White House official, got up and theatrically turned to look around the room. He then introduced himself and said that his comments might not necessarily reflect the views of his employers, but that if one added up the hourly rates of all the lawyers in the room for the length of the meeting,

The Internet has to be the greatest invention since the zipper. The biggest Encyclopedia … Freedom, a window to the world, the leap into the future of communicating!

—**Lothar W. Goesch**
Cottonwood, AZ, USA
lothar@sedona.net

perhaps enough money would have accumulated to pay for the cost of running the silly service. He commented that he was very pleased they were paying attention to issues a few years away, but that perhaps the termination of EDGAR on the Internet in less than 60 days should receive some consideration.

We managed to catch the attention of the two commissioners of the SEC. Neither had been very aware of the issue, EDGAR having been relegated to the back offices of the bureaucracy as a computer problem. The SEC called Luther Brown and me into a meeting with Commissioner Steven Waldman and Michael Schlein, the SEC's chief of staff. Also attending was Mike Bartell, the newly appointed director of the computing section, who turned out to be a real live wire with infinitely more progressive views than his predecessors. All of them felt that this was clearly something the SEC should do and they started a series of meetings with congressional officials to make sure they were allowed to do it. We offered to lend them one of our computers and configure it until they had time to bring their staff up to speed.

Only a few days later, SEC chairman Arthur Levitt announced that they would run the EDGAR service for free on the Internet. The Information Industry Association made a stab at getting the decision reversed on Capitol Hill, but the SEC staff had done their homework and the decision stuck. We sent Brad Burdick over to the SEC with a computer in the back of his car, which he installed and set up. The SEC staff did a remarkable turnaround and became enthusiastic supporters. They cleaned up our system, added much more information, and, in the first month of operation, the SEC database served 3 million documents, more than double our volume.

How can a program that was transferred to the SEC on October 1, 1995, be part of a 1996 world's fair? The answer is that only one of the databases found a new home. The patent office dug in its heels and refused to submit to pressure from the Internet community. Though our patent database had a strong following from engineers, patent attorneys, journalists, and freelance inventors, there was one big difference from the SEC database. In the case of the SEC, the senior officials were simply unaware of the issue. Once we got in the door, it was a simple matter to convince them (aided, of course by the imminent threat of catastrophe in 60 days).

In the case of the patent system, Bruce Lehman, the commissioner of patents and trademarks, was dead set against the idea. He had served most of his professional career in the cozy patent law industry, and the information retailers who sold patent data were an integral part of that community. Lehman argued that we would destroy the country's private enterprise system. The White House called him in to deal with what I learned was referred to in internal patent office memos as "the Malamud situation," but Lehman refused to budge. A friend of mine who has since left the White House described the situation to me: "Office of Management and Budget called him in, put matches between his toes, and lit them." To no avail, apparently.

We didn't view our efforts as destroying the private enterprise system. Value added should be rewarded. What the information retailers were doing was simply taking tapes and putting them on a system's disk drives. That wasn't value added; the retailers should crawl up the food chain and provide more sophisticated value to justify their profits. More important, having the government sell the raw data meant that the barriers to entry in the industry were high. By 1995, the SEC data were costing the Internet Multicasting Service over $110,000 per year to buy the daily tape feeds. Building a proper patent database would cost close to $250,000.

Keeping the initial cost of the data high meant that a graduate student at a university couldn't come up with some new way of accessing information, say neural network-based searches of patent information, and set him- or herself up in the retail information business. High costs for the initial data kept the retail providers as a small oligarchy, not the most stimulating economic structure for a rapidly changing market.

Even more dangerous, in our view, was treating the basic data as a product. The purpose of our patent system is to stimulate the arts and sciences by giving inventors rights to their works. If an engineer can't find a patent and read it, he or she has no idea how intellectual property has been defined in a particular field. Intellectual property is an asset, there is a multi-billion-dollar market in licensing of that intellectual property, and the patent database is the basic database that makes that market function. Likewise, the SEC database is not a product, but the way that investors are informed of the status of public corporations so they may direct their investment dollars to the proper place.

Large government databases are not products; they are the very fuel that makes an information economy function properly. Pictures of the commissioner are nice to have on line, but it is in the meat and potatoes of the large databases that government can play the most important role. The Internet Multicasting Service considered our successful transfer of the SEC database as an important example of a pavilion in a world's fair and, more important, we wanted to keep the issue alive because the patent database had been removed from the Internet as we had promised. We wanted somebody, preferably the patent office, to cry uncle and start running the service.

In my world's fair speeches, I always mentioned our on-line government database project, if only in passing. When the occasion was right, indeed with any excuse, I'd launch into stories about the SEC and patent office wars. Near the end of 1996, somebody finally listened.

I was asked to address a group of executives who ran the Intellectual Property Licensing division at IBM. These lawyers and engineers were in a big

A wonderful idea, I hope that many of the world's people will be able to visit and learn about each other, and the things that are of value.

—**Tony & Marleen O'Donovan**
Dallas, TX, USA
tonyo@us.ibm.com

Great Concept!

One Common Language for the world!!! Why are WE fighting amongst ourselves when the whole universe is OURS to conquer and civilize????

—**Mark Kocak**
Amherst, OH, USA
mkocak@kellnet.com

The first "new media" press credentials to the U.S. Congress.

business unit for IBM, the leading filer of patents in the United States and a company that receives hundreds of millions of dollars per year licensing its patent portfolio. The occasion was a year-end retreat, where the division executives could reflect on the past year, agree on goals for the next year, and step back to look at the changing nature of their marketplace.

IBM had asked three speakers to come in. First was the chief scientist of IBM, who explained how the world was changing. The world had been populated by elephants, big corporations that could exert lots of muscle on situations such as getting a bank on line. But the world now had mice, small groups that could quickly deploy services on the Internet or pop a new computer model off of the assembly line. The nature of the intellectual property market was changing, he argued, and IBM needed to look at these changing markets.

Since I was speaker number three, I knew there was one more outside speaker scheduled, but I wasn't aware of who it was. It turned out to be the deputy assistant commissioner in charge of the day-to-day operations of the patent office, who gave a little speech about how he was pleased to come and talk to IBM, which by filing the most patents was their largest customer. He explained a series of procedural changes his office was implementing for the next year and discussed technicalities of the patent filing system.

I was then introduced as the "Internet person," a by-now mandatory slot on any well-appointed agenda for such functions. I was going to talk about the world's fair, but decided the reinventing government speech was more appropriate. I made the case that the lack of patent information on line was hurting the IBM bottom line because those new customers that the chief scientist had warned them about had no way of browsing IBM's vast portfolio of intellectual property. It was as if you opened a department store but hid the merchandise behind a wall. If IBM's revenue from its patent portfolio was going to increase, getting the full text of the patents on line was not only good for the intellectual property division, it would be a great demonstration project for the Internet business units and might just make the company folk heroes on the Internet for rescuing such a valuable archive.

As I flamed on, the deputy assistant commissioner sat in front of me, a studiously neutral look on his face. The IBM people liked the idea, however. A few months later, IBM announced that it was posting the full text of all patents on the Internet, 20 years of data including over 20 million patent documents. IBM did it because it was good for the company, but the move was certainly a PR coup with the Internet community. Even the patent office, relieved that a respectable player had taken the by-then considerable public pressure off them, supported the move.

Can nagging government agencies to make their information available be considered a world's fair pavilion? Just what was a pavilion in the Internet

1996 World Exposition? At first, the definition seemed obvious, that it was a web page. We quickly found that pavilions in our world's fair were a much more subtle creature, one that could not be associated with a single concept. Web pages were certainly important, but if that was all that a pavilion was, we were no different from any other collection of links, such as those maintained by Yahoo or the Cool Site of the Day.

Some of our pavilions were indeed simply links to collections of materials. In other cases, groups of people around the world worked to put together web pages specifically for the fair, in many cases funded by fair sponsors and hosted on Central Park computers. Our best pavilions, however, were much more than just the html text and images in a web page. Underneath any web page there has to be some substance. A page that exists only on the net and has no relationship to some place in the world is an empty page, nothing more than a meaningless digital billboard.

A site like the Congressional Memory Project demonstrated how deep a pavilion can go. The audio from the U.S. Congress was visible on the web, but it also was a nonstop stream of broadcast data that people could tune into live. In the real world, the pavilion was about convincing the U.S. Congress to issue its first-ever "new media" press credentials, as well as using our activities as a way of showing people in the press some of the potential of the medium.

An on-line pavilion in this world's fair could go beyond simply providing a window into the events happening at some place in the real world. We used our pavilions as a way of pushing the Internet into places where we thought it should be, no different from using a world's fair in the last century to demonstrate that electrical lighting had a place in the home. With on-line government databases, the Internet component of the pavilion was important, but so were the fights conducted in the press and in public meetings. Web pages were important, but liberating the raw stuff needed to fuel our information economy was more valuable still.

Two Million Patent Filings to Be Made Available Free: Giant I.B.M. Data Base Placed on Internet.

—***New York Times***
January 9, 1997

OFFICIAL SOUVENIR
WORLD'S FAIR– ST. LOUIS 1904

Palace of Transportation.

H. Wunderlich

1904 ST. LOUIS WORLD'S FAIR

Ropes of Sand

7

Just before announcing the fair in March 1995, I received voicemail from an Al Cohen at NBC. Thinking that this was a call from a reporter, and knowing that reporters tend to call about eight minutes before deadline, I returned the call from an outrageously priced British Telecom credit-card phone at London's Heathrow airport.

Mr. Cohen was in a meeting and could not be disturbed, but I insisted that because I was about to be on a plane, if he wanted the interview then this was his chance. A few minutes later Cohen came on the line. He started asking questions about the fair, but something didn't seem right. The questions were different from the usual reporter ones and were focusing instead on issues such as our PR plans, staffing, and sponsor relations.

At the Internet Multicasting Service, we had learned to sort out calls from the "real" media into two categories. Sometimes a reporter would call and we'd be as charming as possible. Often, however, the call would come from executives of the New Media section of the company, which was charged with "doing something about the Internet," and usually what these people were fishing for was whether we'd build their web site under contract. We built lots of web sites, but the feeling was that groups such as NBC didn't really need our help; we concentrated our meager resources on places such as the City Lights Bookstore in San Francisco or establishments that weren't represented on the web, such as the Red Sage Restaurant or the National Press Club.

"Hold on a second here, Mr. Cohen," I interrupted rudely, "just what exactly is it you *do* at NBC?"

After a pause during which it sounded like somebody was chuckling he answered. "I'm executive vice president of NBC," he replied, "and we'd like to be the media partner for your world's fair."

This was a little higher in the food chain than I was used to. I was taken aback, but not so much that we were unable to negotiate a deal. NBC would be our media partner, give us half the normal sponsor fee, and market the fair to their existing sponsors. We would get access to the NBC studios, and they'd be the fair's exclusive media partner.

We'd hit the big time! After three years of running a cyberstation I was acutely aware of how tough production is. There is a feeling with Internet

The spacious Internet Multicasting Service studios, located atop the Young Chow Chinese Restaurant.

NBC headquarters in
Rockefeller Center.

pundits that content is king. We had never had a problem getting content. Talk is cheap; it's the microphones that are expensive.

Everybody involved in the fair was excited and NBC started popping up in all our speeches. Luther Brown, our vice president of programs and a former producer for NBC News, was assigned to work with NBC and made numerous trips up to the 40th floor of NBC's Rockefeller Center. The meetings were upbeat bordering on peppy. We were glad and honored to be there. They were glad and honored that we had come.

At the first meeting, Al assigned us a point of contact among his marketing minions. We started sending email to follow up but received no answers. A month or so later, we learned that our contact had taken a job at another company. We went back to New York. The cycle repeated itself three times. Each time our contact person would go into an email hermitage and end up with a new job. Then Al Cohen left for another network.

Meanwhile, NBC had negotiated a megadeal with Microsoft for the MSNBC network. At $170 million per year invested for four years, this deal was huge and all-consuming. A new vice president of marketing was assigned and, after numerous email messages, phone calls, and faxes, he gave us the straight scoop. NBC just didn't see why this fair was interesting and would not honor its contract. No studios. No marketing help. No more money.

It was thus with some amusement that we watched the MSNBC network struggle through its Internet debut. Their web servers couldn't handle the load, their domain name got pulled accidently by the Network Information Center, and the cable systems were lukewarm on the channel. The web site, fueled by hundreds of staff members working feverishly, struggled along with tepid reviews and even more tepid hit rates. The site wasn't bad, but for $170 million, you kind of expect a bit more than that.

The Future of Media

Meanwhile, in a cramped studio in a bad part of London, three people were putting a system together called the World Radio Network; the brainchild of Jeff Cohen and Karl Miosga. Cohen and Miosga started by gathering U.S. rights for the English-language news broadcasts of many European radio stations, such as Radio France International, Radio Netherlands, and the BBC. Each hour was a different broadcast, which was uploaded via satellite to the United States and broadcast back down to radio stations.

Internet connections in England were quite expensive in 1994 and World Radio Network only had a small PC and a dialup modem, but they very much wanted to put their service on the Internet. As part of the world's fair, the Internet Multicasting Service worked with them through 1995 and 1996. We began in

Thank you for providing this web site to the olympics. It is an excellent alternative to NBC's noisy coverage. Thank you.

—**Ron Aylward**
Cincinnati, OH, USA
aylward@aol.com

January 1995 by installing a satellite dish on the roof of the Young Chow Chinese Restaurant in Washington, DC, our network control center. World Radio Network was carried on an audio sideband of the Turner Broadcasting System, so we subscribed to a satellite TV package in order to be able to descramble the signals.

The audio from World Radio Network was fed into a mixing board, processed, and routed over to a Sun workstation where it was broadcast live on the Internet. This 24-hour feed was the first nonstop live audio feed on the Internet. A web site was put together with the schedule of broadcasts. The service proved popular with users who were connected to the multicast backbone and was used not only as background sound for engineers but as a test stream to assess the health of the underlying network.

After the first bootstrap, the people at World Radio Network started working to improve the service. The web pages became better and began to be produced on a PC in London, then pushed over the network into the big web servers in Central Park. In addition to the 7,500 bit per second audio on the multicast backbone, techniques such as Real Audio were used to improve accessibility for PC users with slow Internet connections.

An even more sophisticated technology for broadcasting sound was installed in January 1996. Called Streamworks and manufactured by Xing Technology, the system allows audio streams to be sent from World Radio Network's main audio servers to other large servers, such as one operated in Finland. The end user connects to the audio server closest to his or her PC, providing better audio performance much in the same way as Central Park provides better web performance by being "close" to the end user.

Each live daily feed was also recorded, so that users who could not tune in during the live performance could use a RealAudio server to play back the file, or use the File Transfer Protocol to transfer the file locally and listen to it there. Many of the stations that World Radio Network served, such as Radio Sweden and the Voice of Russia, featured their own email addresses and web sites.

There is a remarkable difference between operations like MSNBC, with hundreds of staff members and hundreds of millions of dollars to spend, and shoestring operations like the World Radio Network, with fewer than half a dozen people and a meager operating budget. Yet one can make a strong case that it is groups like the World Radio Network that really represent the future of media, not the current big giants. It is unusual, as a new infrastructure gets introduced, for the giants in the older technologies to win the race and become the market leaders in the new one. Though articles about new media (which invariably appear in the traditional media) trumpet the efforts of the big operations, on the Internet it appears that the smaller operations have an early lead.

Karl Miosga, cofounder of World Radio Network.

World Radio Network produced the first
nonstop audio stream on the Internet.

According to one train of thought, the Internet means everybody and anybody can and will become a publisher. That train is dangerously close to derailing. While anybody can publish, not anybody can publish well. It takes time and money to produce quality material in any new medium, particularly the time and money it takes to learn how to use it effectively. It does not, however, necessarily take millions of dollars to use the medium effectively. A laptop computer with MPEG video compression hardware, MIDI wave table support, Adobe Premiere video editing software, and all the other building blocks of a sophisticated computing environment mean that individuals with creativity and the willingness to work hard will be able to produce work up to the highest professional standards.

Groups like MSNBC are attacking the rock-and-roll business with a symphony orchestra. While MSNBC might find its niche, the organization is trying to run a small, creative enterprise with a cast of thousands. The smaller operations, the ones with a few people working hard to create new things, can often move much more quickly when it comes to creating meaningful content for this new medium.

Real World

A big TV network can be thought of as both a content producer and a distribution mechanism. The TV networks as a distribution medium have come under severe attack, first from satellite broadcasters like Ted Turner, then by cable networks, and most recently by digital satellite systems. World Radio Network shows how the huge distribution infrastructures of the TV networks and other established media such as newspapers are vulnerable to attack from the Internet. The Internet will certainly not replace TV, just as TV did not replace radio. However, TV carved out a large niche from radio's hide and the Internet is doing the same thing to the established electronic and print media.

While some of the growth of the Internet will come from providing an alternative distribution outlet for established media, the real growth will come from producers designing specifically for the medium. Any form of media is highly technical. Producing a newspaper starts with reporters who understand how their questions will go through the process of writing, editing, layout, copyfitting, production, and distribution. Television has its own unique production stream, as does radio. If you're going to put together a program that is meaningful in one medium, it can't simply be a rehash of material that was produced specifically for another.

A good example of the search for what makes the medium unique is the Real World Studios, located in the village of Box near Bath, England. Real World Studios was built in a converted mill by musician Peter Gabriel, who

I invite to everyone at the net to join the expo—is the best idea since the tv's invention!

—Jaime Mercado
Humacao, Puerto Rico
JAIME5224@cuh.upr.edu.cl.com

REAL WORLD STUDIOS

Visitors to Real World Studios can read biographies of the artists, order Real World products, look around the studios, and even learn to cook from one of the best artists on the campus, cook Tony Chivers.

http://realworld.on.net

Xploral

Xploral was Real World's first CD-ROM project. It contains 100 minutes of video, over 30 minutes of audio, hundreds of full-colour still images and the equivalent of a book's worth of text.

The four main sections of Xploral cover a glimpse into Peter's personal life, a world music area with information on Womad, Real World Records, the musicians and their instruments, an US sampler with videos and samples of the tracks, plus a lot of background information, and a chance to take the official Real World tour and find out what goes on behind closed doors

Xploral was originally designed for Macintosh, with later versions being developed for PC and CDi platforms.

AFRO CELT SOUND SYSTEM

The Afro Celt Sound System deftly illustrate how to mix African and European music without destroying their essence. Its instruments may belong to history but its music sits proudly at the forefront of club culture. Its beats and rhythms have resonance today: jungle nestles next to jigs and reels; African jazz flows into Gaelic eulogies.

Producer Simon Emmerson, aided by visualiser and co-conspirator Jamie Reid, maintains it was always thus.

"What we've definitely shown is that the deeper you go into European musical traditions the further you get into African tradition, and probably vice versa as well.

I personally believe there was a neolithic culture that was far more sophisticated than we give it credit for. The stone masons, builders and musicians were living the same lifestyle experiencing the world in the same way in the Northern

Womad Weekend, Barbican Centre, London
6-8 December 1996

The spirit of WOMAD comes to London! This is one global fusion that I'm really looking forward to. Hosted in the Barbican Centre - generally a reserve of relatively cerebral pleasures - it will be interesting to see how the urbanite audience respond to the challenge of The Workshop! The comfortable distance from the performer dissolving to the hideously embarrassing level where you are actually expected to do something and not be particularly bothered about looking relaxed and confident whilst doing it. Hopefully a few brave souls will start it off and then the group dynamic will make it acceptable to take part - standing casually at the back of course!

But what temptation there is in store for those brave enough. Where else on the planet will you be able to find someone to teach you, hands-on style, about:

White Chocolate and Raspberry Cake

(Serves four normal humans)
(Gas mark 4, 180 C/ 350 F)

INGREDIENTS

110 grammes/ 4 ounces white chocolate
225 grammes/ 8 ounces self raising flour
170 grammes/ 6 ounces butter
110 grammes/ 4 ounces caster sugar
4 tablespoons milk 340 grammes/ 12 ounces fresh or frozen (but not thawed) raspberries (buy 450 grammes/ 1 pound and save rest for topping)
55 grammes/ 2 ounces ground almonds
2 eggs
1 teaspoon vanilla essence
Large pinch of salt

The Edible World

People come to Real World to work in an atmosphere of quiet serenity, technological brilliance, creative inspiration and privacy. They also come for the food. Lovingly prepared by Real World's jealously guarded superchef, Tony Chivers, every meal is a veritable feast.

Here, on Radio Real World's Studio Site, with the organic carrot of international culinary stardom dangled before him, Tony has agreed to divulge his innermost secrets. Those of you who have not experienced the delights of dining, Real World style, may now create Tony Chivers' masterpieces in the comfort of your own kitchen..

Real World Upside Down Pineapple Tarte

Piquant Veggie Stuffed Mushrooms

Real World Tomato Pasta Sauce

Introduction

WOMAD is a group of people who devise delightful environments to invite people to. These events are used to showcase a glimpse of the musical and artistic talents that exist in the different regions of our planet. They take place in different countries at different times of the year; you can find out where the next one is, have a look at what the last one was like, or you can slip into another slinky paragraph of seductive description of what makes a WOMAD festival unique.

WOMAD also runs an educational Foundation, supported by the Friends of WOMAD, releases records of the artists who have played at the festivals and produces some delightful clothing.

Virtual visit

If you have the necessary QTVR software, you can select the ground or first floor plans of Real World Studios. From these plans you can choose a number of QTVR panoramas taken from

Real World **Notes** # 2

Ground floor
First floor, balconies and roof

Radio Real World is produced and directed by Lisa Howe & York Tillyer, Real World Multimedia Ltd.

VRML/York Tillyer

lives in another converted mill a short walk down the river. In addition to being Gabriel's recording home, the studio is the host to numerous other recording artists. Real World is also the home of the leading world music festival, known as WOMAD for "World of Music Art and Dance." Every year, WOMAD collects dozens of world music artists and takes them on tour. After the tour is finished, the musicians go back to Real World for "Recording Week," an intensive recording marathon that provides the raw material for many of the records issued during the rest of the year.

Despite its rustic setting, Real World boasts a sophisticated multimedia production center featuring award-winning CDs such as Peter Gabriel's *Xplora* and the newer CD-ROM Eve. The *Xplora* disc featured a book's worth of text, 100 minutes of video, and a fascinating user interface that lets people delve into Real World Studios, Gabriel's life, and WOMAD. An accompanying book by Gabriel explored how the print media and digital media were intertwined.

While the basic product of Real World is music, it is interesting to see how that music is applied to each medium. Real World is quite fastidious about its products. The concerts, audio CDs, and CD-ROMs are all thought about intently and produced very carefully. A community of close to 100 works regularly at Real World, and the sprawling complex has lots of little projects and enterprises all coexisting.

The world's fair participated in the development of an Internet presence for Real World Studios by contributing Simon Hackett, a leading Internet engineer and the manager of the Australia Central Park systems. After some preliminary visits to talk about the world's fair and Real World's participation, Simon and I showed up with a Sun workstation, disk drives, network hubs, and miscellaneous other equipment.

We were installed in one of the old mill buildings with the rest of the new media group. The building was right behind the garbage dump for the complex and the huge open doors let swarms of wasps fly and buzz in circles around anything that moved. Between swatting away wasps and an occasional mass evacuation when a particularly aggressive contingent mounted a full attack, we surveyed a situation that was an artist's dream and an engineer's nightmare.

The Real World complex has a dozen buildings and had close to 100 Macintosh systems. There was, however, only a single system with a modem connected to a dialup Internet account. A few web pages had been developed, but the beautiful graphics were so big that dialup access would be impossible. The work of putting the pages together was being done by one young new media person, but the entire artistic hierarchy of Real World was hovering over his shoulders to make sure that any web sites that the studio published were meaningful. Needless to say, the process wasn't going quickly.

Over the next year, Simon Hackett returned to Real World several times, gradually helping the local staff build up a network infrastructure and, more important, making sure that the people who ran the studios were comfortable with the changes. Fiber optics had already been installed, encased in a jelly-filled tube and run through the old mill streams, and this was used to connect the Macintosh systems together.

A big Macintosh system was put at RedNet, one of the new British service providers that were competing with British Telecom for a slice of the Internet market. Putting the server at the service provider meant that traffic from the Internet was not using up the scarce bandwidth into Real World. If all your bandwidth is used serving the outside world, none is left for internal users to access the Internet. The dialup modem they had been using was upgraded to a dedicated ISDN line running at 64,000 bits per second, and the Sun workstation was deployed as a cache server at Real World, caching web pages viewed by one user so that the next user didn't have to drag them off the network.

The help provided by the world's fair to Real World was really quite meager, a few pieces of equipment and a lot of free advice. What was remarkable was how quickly the spark provided by Simon Hackett was turned into internal momentum. The web pages became part of the organization and gave visitors a glimpse into Real World. The site chef's recipes, the bands currently recording in the studio, the state of Peter Gabriel, and the status of new releases all became visible via the Internet.

The Real World site is a wonderful illustration of adaptation to the medium. The graphics became very small and now load quickly, but little animated graphics sprinkled carefully throughout the pages make them glow and pulse. Virtual Reality Modeling Language (VRML) movies allow the user to tour the studio, guided by Mike Large, the technical director of the facilities.

One central theme of the world's fair has been to bring the real world into cyberspace and cyberspace into the real world. In this case, the transformations were literal.

The Sensorium

In Japan, the fair took off like a rocket. Huge contributions of bandwidth and other technical resources flowed in. Several hundred people got involved in an elaborate organizing effort of secretariats, technical working committees, and even a professional ad agency to handle the PR pizzazz. Like many large organizing efforts, this one had many impressive pieces, but the whole was still missing some meaning. There were dozens of events being scheduled, showrooms were being planned, and stacks of routers were piled in Jun Murai's office waiting to be staged in locations throughout Japan.

What a great concept … I will be visiting this page for some time! Peter Gabriel is on of my favorites! Good luck to all participants from this small Village outside of Chicago, Illinois.

—William Pedroza
Streamwood, IL, USA
usarail@ix.netcom.com

What was missing, however, was a theme. There were no unifying concepts to bring together this huge effort. For the global fair, we had a series of themes, such as "building a public park for the global village," or "bringing the real world into cyberspace and cyberspace into the real world." Such rhetoric can be quite empty, the kind of thing you hear at countless industry trade shows and conferences on future this or future that. Sometimes, however, broad and simple themes, such as "a public park for the global village," can serve as a very useful way to guide many projects in a similar direction. As with herding cats, if your instructions get too detailed, your effectiveness tends to be limited.

Just as themes were important in organizing the overall fair, agreeing in some detail on what exactly the fair was about was a useful exercise. In some cases, this became the province of a committee of people who developed things like license agreements. In the successful examples, however, the organizers turned to people who could produce that elusive product referred to in our industry as *content*. Such content providers are people who take all the equipment and other resources and actually do something with them.

The content providers that the Japanese committee turned to were an inspired choice. They first approached Shin'ichi Takemura, a cultural anthropologist at the Touhoku University of Art and Design and the son of one of the country's most famous economists. Takemura called in Yoshiaki Nishimura, a long-time associate who had worked with him on projects such as a concept design for 21st-century vehicles and designing and building an ecological park (a real one).

Starting with a clean slate, the group wanted to do something that showed the unique capabilities of the Internet, a way to broaden sense and sensibility instead of just sending email or putting magazines on the net. Takemura and Nishimura, who engage in recreational activities like swimming with dolphins, wanted to develop a place on the Internet that broadened a sense of the earth as an interconnected place.

Two more people were then drafted. Tetsuya Ozaki was was the editor of a monthly magazine for young people, a "transcultural" publication that devoted each issue to helping children understand what it might be like to live in a different city. He was joined by Sohichi Ueda, an assistant director on films. Together, the four started planning the web site, drafting other volunteers as they went along.

At first, the Sensorium was going to be a world divided into seven pieces, including fire, water, and earth. They were going to draft famous artists and writers and have them contribute material. They went down this road for a while, but the group decided that it wanted the project to make "content that could only be realized on the Internet," and what was emerging was just another on-line magazine. So the project headed off in a very different direction, and what emerged ended up surprising everybody—a set of ways of using the Internet that none of us had really imagined before. Though the effort worked somewhat like a magazine, with updates every two weeks or so on a schedule that synchronized with lunar cycles, it certainly didn't look like a magazine.

The Sensorium features a series of ways of looking at the world. One of the most impressive is Net Sound. Professor Hiroyuki Ohno, at the Tokyo Institute of Technology, runs the kind of laboratory that is teeming with bright graduate students and has all sorts of projects lying around. One such project was the network stethoscope, a network management tool. Ohno is part of WIDE, a group of Japanese researchers who run the national backbone in their country. This is a huge operation, and people like Ohno frequently get stuck with jobs such as monitoring the status of routers, computers, and other components of the network.

Ohno turned to Tetsuya Narita, one of his doctoral students, and they developed the stethoscope, a computer you could place on a particular part of your network, such as a busy Ethernet that has lots of big servers and key routers. The stethoscope monitors the network and turns each kind of network packet into a distinct sound, so you can listen to your network. A telephone interface was then put on the back of the system, and Ohno was able to dial into various parts of his network using a cell phone and listen to see if it was behaving properly. Another system was put into Ohno's reception room and the secretarial staff was all trained to listen for the sounds of a network gone awry.

The Sensorium group persuaded Narita to come over and work with them to turn the stethoscope from something used by technical staff into Net Sound, a more general instrument that would let people hear what the Internet sounds like. The original stethoscope used very strong sounds for each kind of packet, trumpets blaring and pianos banging away. As music it wasn't very interesting and, more important, there was too much of it. There were so many notes that it was hard to understand what was happening on the network.

Working with professional sound designers, Net Sound first came out sounding like a jungle, with birds chirping in the background as the network hummed along, and lions roaring when momentous events such as the start of a big file transfer occurred. This first version worked too well. You didn't feel that you were listening to some new kind of sound for the first time, you felt that you were in the middle of very realistic-sounding jungle.

The group went back into the studio. They spent days with a real stethoscope, going around listening to walls, bodies, trees, computers—anything that moved or didn't. What emerged was a very original set of sounds, eerie pings and clicks that let you understand that you are listening to an entity that is breathing and moving all the time. Narita and his colleagues in the Sensorium group speak enthusiastically of the potential of the Net Sound stethoscope. They

Hi world! ;-)

Carles Xavier Torres
Barcelona, Spain
c910544@alumnes.esade.es

sensorium

http://park.org/Japan/Theme/

THE SENSORIUM

Below: The Sensorium's Web Hopper allows a user
see the requests going from a user to servers located
throughout the world. Right: The Breathing Earth is an
innovative visualization of seismic activity throughout
the world.

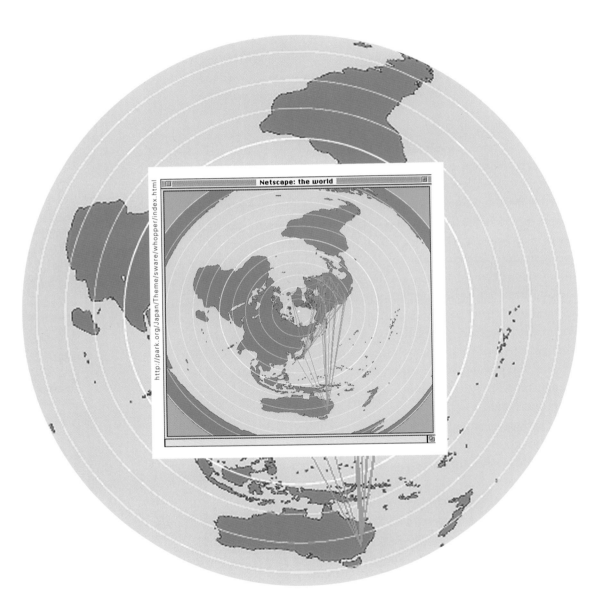

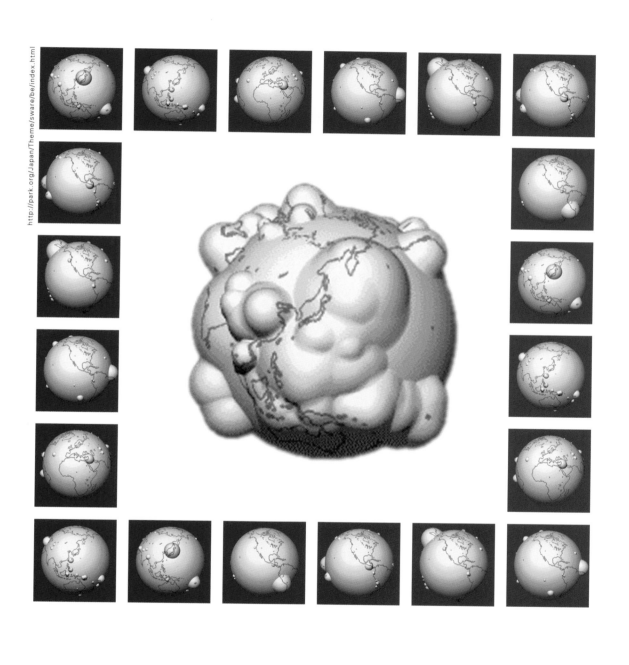

http://park.org/Japan/Theme/sware/be/index.html

Sensorium producer Shin'ichi Takemura demonstrates the Net Sound project, which allows users to listen to the Internet.

I met Earthquake last year in KOBE before, I met los angeles Earthquake in L.A. too. I dont wanna meet Earthquake 1996. Anyway Great Happy New Year on the Earth.

—**Toshiaka Kanda**
Kobe, Hyogo, Japan
PFB00566@niftyserve.or.jp

pointed out that African drummers such as Milford Graves had long talked of the therapeutic effect of drums in African culture, used in the healing process by tuning up the heartbeat of an individual. Was it possible, Narita wanted to know, that Net Sound could be used the same way?

Other projects also used the Internet as a way of listening to the world. The Sensorium team discovered that the Internet contained a series of databases detailing seismic activity all over the world. The number of small earthquakes that occur is strikingly large, and the team set out to find a way to visualize this information, to give people the sense of a breathing earth. Takuya Shimada, one fan of the initial Sensorium released in January, had sent enthusiastic email offering to help. They drafted Shimada, a systems researcher at GK Tech, to work on the Breathing Earth project.

Like Net Sound, Breathing Earth went through several iterations, but what emerged was an application that would show you the earth breathing over a two-week period. You could spin the globe around and see it swelling as earthquakes hit high seismic areas such as Japan or California. Other people joined up and developed a way that people could walk the World Wide Web, a visual representation of the globe that shows you where the servers that you access with your browser are located. Shoichi Ueda, an artist, produced a site called Star Place that let people track the position of the earth in the cosmos.

The entire project was anchored by a team of artists and writers that packaged all this material into a beautifully designed web site, under the careful watch of Ichirou Higashiizum, the art director. Instead of a magazine, they

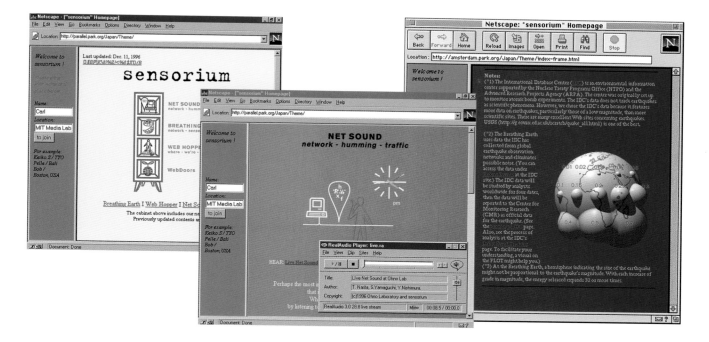

created a way of seeing the web as a live medium. The ability to see beyond the established metaphors and invent new ways of treating the Internet is what made the Sensorium so special.

As Nishimura, the director of the project, explained it, "The World Wide Web is a book. We were more interested in how to read the book than adding more pages." Nishimura and the producer Takemura were intent on creating a public space on the Internet, the antithesis of a shopping mall. As Takemura puts it, "there are many government and commercial efforts on the Internet, but there are also many things that need to be public. More than just public libraries and databases, we need to use the Internet as a public sensory platform to allow people to see better."

Windows to the World

The Sensorium took general marching orders—build a pavilion—and created something new. There was another example of this type of innovative thinking that was just as original.

As part of his world's fair fundraising, Jun Murai had procured a donation of 200 cameras from Sony, a new model that had just come out of the labs and was not yet available on the market. These remarkable little cameras were computer controlled and were mounted on a motor. They could be instructed to move right or left, up or down, to change focus, and even to fix on a target and track its movement.

There are two kinds of people in the world. Those who are creative, who take the risk, and get into new and crazy things, they are like the saints, always against the common. We are able to have a 1,000 Silicon Valleys in the mind. Those are who push history, and create, those are artists of mankind. And there are those who follow the sheep, wolves, chicken, pigs, and more sheep. You choose. Be a Steven Spielberg, Sting, Subcommandante Marcos, el Che, Steven Jobs, Bill Gates or Angel Spotorno, la Fuerza Creativa de América latina!!! Or be an insect, pushed by media, consume and trivial life. You choose.

—**Angel Spotorno**
Santiago, Chile
creativ@inet.macland.cl

In Windows to the World, François Bérard of the IMAG Institute in France and Nuria Oliver of the MIT Media Lab created an interface that allows a user to look around a room on the other side of the net.

wow! there is real soul here! i can sense the workings of great imagination and see the attention to detail … thank you all very much for being there … virtually yours …

—**Paul Searle**
Sacramento, CA, USA
drpaul@midtown.net

Jun Murai sent 20 of these cameras over to me and I wandered down with a couple to the Vision and Modeling group at the MIT Media Lab. The graduate students in this group are specialists at processing video and have developed some remarkable programs that do things like analyze facial expressions to guess if a person is happy or sad.

The cameras came with a remote control device and I had in the back of my mind the idea that a graduate student might be persuaded to build a replica of the remote control on a computer screen, allowing a user on one side of the network to control a camera on the other side.

Tucked away in a corner of the lab behind a stack of computers and cameras, I found François Bérard, a visiting researcher from the Institut d'Informatique et de Mathématiques Appliquées de Grenoble (IMAG) in France. Bérard was working with Nuria Oliver, a Media Lab doctoral candidate from Spain.

I offered a trade. They could have a couple of cameras to play with if they came up with a computer screen version of the remote control.

François and Nuria really wanted the cameras to play with, as they would want any new toy that came out in their field, but they demurred on the idea of replicating a remote control. "Don't you think we can do something a bit more interesting?" François asked.

I left the cameras and came back a couple of weeks later to see how they were doing. The interface they had developed went beyond putting a piece of plastic into computer code.

They used two cameras. One camera was located someplace in the real world, say in a meeting room or a town square, or any place you might wish to view from the network.

The second camera was on top of a TV monitor, pointed at the viewer who wished to use the Internet to see the place on the other side of the network. The camera on the monitor was connected to a computer program that analyzed

the head position and mouth of the viewer. On the TV monitor screen was a picture from the other side of the net.

If the viewer peered into this window to the world and craned her head to the right, the computer program would tell the camera on the other side of the network to move toward the left so that the camera's field of view moves to the right. If the viewer looked down, the camera on the other end looked down. If the viewer moved forward, the camera on the other end would zoom in.

The interface was a natural way of treating an image on a TV monitor as if it were truly a window to a place in another location. No fancy remote control, no knobs, simply an intuitive way of using computers to look around a remote location.

The work was so impressive that I gave the rest of the cameras to the researchers. Over the next few months, I watched as they took these Sony cameras and started deploying them throughout the Vision and Modeling group. As the fair ended, they were taking series of cameras and linking them together, their goal being to allow a user to walk around a remote location, having one camera pick up where another's field of vision stopped.

The Windows to the World project didn't end up as a fancy set of web pages in Central Park, but to me it was what the world's fair was all about. Sony got a beautiful demonstration of what their cameras could do and some bright young researchers got some tools that allowed them to stretch their minds, building computer programs that skipped the obvious metaphors.

Very nice site. You can see thing but you can't touch it. What a pity!

—Deny Bolsee
Louvain-la-Neuve, Belgium
bolsee@bpsp.ucl.ac.be

very sensibel use electronics instead of the resource wasting transport.

—Visvanath Ratnaweera
Peradeniya, Sri Lanka
ratna@eng.pdn.ac.lk

THE 1915 PANAMA PACIFIC EXPOSITION

A Unique Assemblage

8

The Internet Multicasting Service went on the air in early 1993. By the end of the year, we were ready to put government databases on line, but there was a lull as paperwork got processed by the National Science Foundation and while Sun Microsystems assembled all the components for the large server they were donating to run the EDGAR service.

Some email arrived from England. Was Santa Claus on the Internet? Good question. I typed "whois pole.org" and received the answer "No match for pole.org" from the Network Information Center. That meant that there wasn't a computer with the domain name north.pole.org. Directory services such as Yahoo were just beginning in 1993. Yahoo was run as an extracurricular project by two Stanford undergraduates, and there were only a few keyword-based web crawlers that allowed you to search. Indeed, the web was still in a primitive state. A new browser written by a few undergraduates at the University of Illinois had just been released and was called Mosaic. Mosaic spawned a whole set of browsers, and much of the original undergraduate team in Illinois went on to found Netscape.

At the time, though, it appeared that Santa Claus did not exist. I sent back a note to the guy in London who had inquired and told him that it did not appear that Father Christmas existed on the Internet, but that we thought something could be done about it. We registered pole.org with the Network Information Center, and created an alias from north.pole.org to our poor, overworked main machine, called trystero.radio.com. Trystero, named after the underground postal service in Thomas Pynchon's *The Crying of Lot 49*, served as the main distribution system for all the Internet Talk Radio programs, and was doubling as our electronic mail server and our multicasting machine for live speeches out of the National Press Club. This old system had only 16 megabytes of random access memory and the meters that monitored the central processing unit usually read 100 percent for at least 20 hours a day.

Marty Lucas, director of audio production, who also doubled as the general counsel of the service, had a bad feeling about this. "Don't mess with Santa Claus," he warned. "People take this stuff really seriously."

I ignored his advice and sat down with Curtis Generous and Rick Dunbar, two engineers who donated a great deal of their time in the early days of our

Hi, My name is Adrianna Brown and I am 7 years old. I really have enjoyed your web site. It was a lot of fun sending mail to Santa, Rudolph, and the Elves. Thank you very much for having this here for kids to look at.

—Adrianna Brown
jimlu@clinic.net

Santa gets Christmas "spam."

—Kalamazoo Gazette
December 21, 1994

Thanks for providing this service to the Net! My son was impressed with his letter from Santa and I have enjoyed the holiday stories and the music! Merry Christmas to all of you!!! I especially appreciate the fact that you know the "true" meaning of this Season!!! God bless you ... God bless us one and all ...

—Charles Grindstaff
grinder@netscope.net

Curtis Generous

Rick Dunbar

radio station, and we set about writing an electronic mail Santa Claus. The program that emerged would answer the mailbox for Santa, Rudolph, and the elves. An administrative address, elfmaster@north.pole.org, was set up for problems and contact with a human being.

The program parsed the incoming electronic mail. First, it looked at where the message was from. If it was from a foreign country, a database would look up an appropriate greeting in that language. In the case of certain addresses in the United States, an appropriate contextual message was also added. For example, people writing from MIT were informed that the elves had all gone to MIT, proving the value of their forthcoming degrees.

Next, the content of the message was parsed. The program looked for keywords that matched expressions, then inserted an appropriate paragraph. For example, if the message contained the strings "cookie" and "Rudolph" within close proximity of each other, the response would contain:

> Rudolph says he just loves to cook. Carrots are his favorite kind of cookie, but he's really fond of green moss. He's a real taste treat, I tell you.

The service went on line right after Thanksgiving, the traditional start of the holiday season in the United States. We had no idea what we were in for. That first season, we received over 70,000 messages. We monitored the mail, and refined the computer program to respond to things we hadn't anticipated. In addition to the classrooms full of children from 70 countries, we got the occasional crank. The program was changed to recognize phrases such as "I hate Santa," usually to the great surprise of those writing the hate mail.

By 1994, the web had started to take off, so we modified the service to be visible as a series of web pages. The "talk to Santa" routine was still available by email, but we added a form that people could fill out and get instant gratification. Christmas trees were put on line and decorations photographed so people could build their own digital trees on their desktop monitors, a practice we hoped would not replace more traditional holiday rites.

Marty Lucas and Corinne Becknell went wild with sound production, producing a beautiful set of Christmas tunes and recording all of the staff playing various roles. Philippe Tabaux, who worked on the fair as a member of the International Secretariat, was drafted to play the role of the grumpy elves. Philippe speaks with a heavy French accent and is blessed with the sunny, radiant disposition of the French. He was put in front of a microphone in the studio, which was run through a Chipmunk effect, and was handed a series of lines.

A typical line that Philippe was forced to utter read: "Deck the Halls! That is easy for you to say, but look who gets stuck on the cherrypicker at three in the morning!" Another had the elves complaining: "Jingle bells, my foot! Those reindeer should read the local noise abatement regulations. How is an elf supposed to get any sleep around here with all that jingle, jingle, jingle?"

Luther Brown, who was our voice of Santa Claus, and Stephanie Faul, our editor, noticed that the classic Christmas poem *A Visit from St. Nicholas*, which begins "'Twas the night before Christmas," was past the copyright protection period, making it fair game to put on the net. They ran out and scoured bookstores until they found one that had a copy in print. Then, they sat down and underlined several key phrases in the text. For each one, Becknell and Lucas produced a little sound file that was linked into the text so the adult could read the story and the child could click on the sound effects.

The hard part was designing sound effects for some of the sounds. Some of the sounds were easy. When the text says "whistled," Marty and Corinne produced a nice whistle. But what do you do for phrases such as "had just settled our brains?" Our favorite was for "he spoke not a word," which was an empty sound file. Sure enough, it only took a week before the elfmaster received a nasty mail message from a user who informed us that this sound file had been corrupted and that we should get our act together.

For some reason, the end of each year was when the Internet Multicasting Service was busy getting ready for a push in the New Year. At the end of 1993, we were waiting to put government databases on line. By the end of 1994, the target was putting the U.S. Congress audio up. Running the Santa Claus server was a welcome relief from the more onerous duties of acting as freelance volunteers to unwilling government agencies, so we decided there had to be a cheap stunt, some form of live celebration.

The Kennedy Center for the Performing Arts was just starting to go on line with its award-winning arts education program. We were helping to get them started by putting some of their lectures about jazz and classical music on the web. Scott Stoner, the assistant director of the arts education program, was keen on doing a live event and was able to navigate the rights obstacle course present in any national arts center.

Stoner secured rights for us to broadcast audio from the center's annual sing-along of Handel's *Messiah*, definitely the hot ticket for the rich and powerful crowd in Washington. Ambassadors, senators, and members of the cabinet would all gather once a year in an atmosphere of good cheer to sing the *Messiah* with four famous soloists and the audience as the chorus.

We called the telephone company and added one more conditioned audio line to our broadcast headquarters on top of the Young Chow Chinese Restaurant. Somehow, though, just sending out live audio to people so they could sing to their computer made the experience a bit trite. Something had to be done to spice up the pages. Luther Brown and Simon Hackett, in from Australia to write a control program for our 200-CD jukebox, were put to work.

Corinne Becknell

Marty Lucas

Your site is a lifesaver! Stuck at night with a child wanting for I read to her "Twas the Night Before Christmas" and all efforts to find the book in the house where in vain. I soon leapt upon the idea that I might find such a story on the net and that I did. I thank you, and a little girl thanks you. For without the night before Christmas, does Christmas really come?

—**Mark**
Spoogema@aol.com

"Talk to Santa Claus" received hundreds of thousands of visits from over 100 countries every Christmas season.

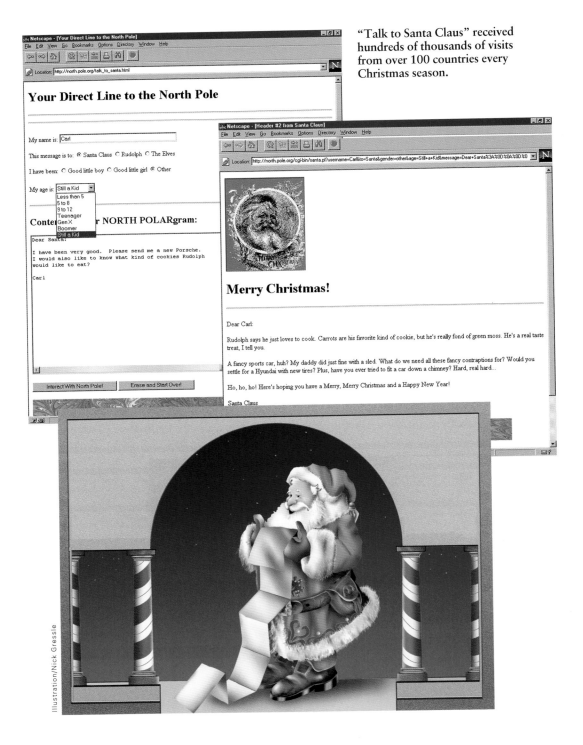

Illustration/Nick Gressle

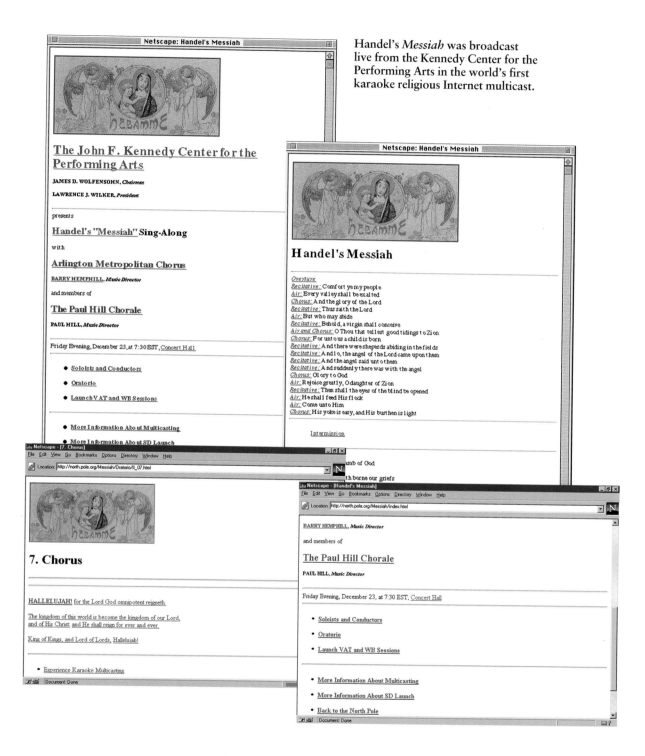

Handel's *Messiah* was broadcast live from the Kennedy Center for the Performing Arts in the world's first karaoke religious Internet multicast.

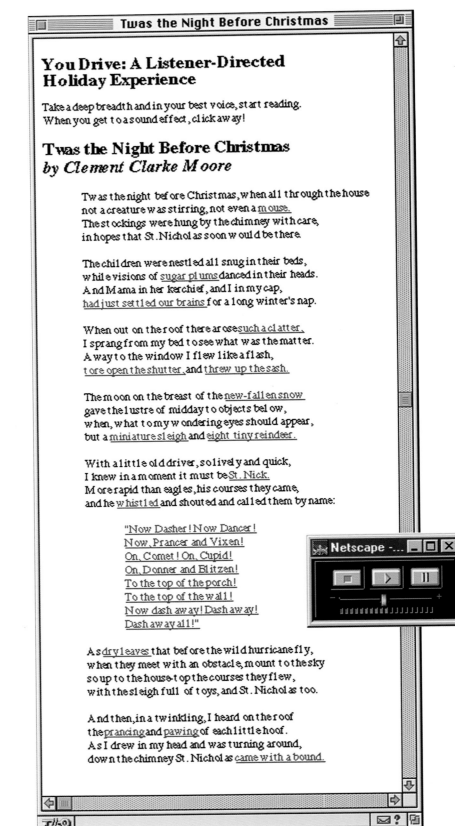

'Twas the Night Before Christmas: read the story and let your kids click on the sound effects.

The content of the browser window reads:

You Drive: A Listener-Directed Holiday Experience

Take a deep breadth and in your best voice, start reading. When you get to a sound effect, click away!

Twas the Night Before Christmas
by Clement Clarke Moore

Twas the night before Christmas, when all through the house
not a creature was stirring, not even a mouse.
The stockings were hung by the chimney with care,
in hopes that St. Nicholas soon would be there.

The children were nestled all snug in their beds,
while visions of sugar plums danced in their heads.
And Mama in her kerchief, and I in my cap,
had just settled our brains for a long winter's nap.

When out on the roof there arose such a clatter,
I sprang from my bed to see what was the matter.
Away to the window I flew like a flash,
tore open the shutter, and threw up the sash.

The moon on the breast of the new-fallen snow
gave the lustre of midday to objects below,
when, what to my wondering eyes should appear,
but a miniature sleigh and eight tiny reindeer.

With a little old driver, so lively and quick,
I knew in a moment it must be St. Nick.
More rapid than eagles, his courses they came,
and he whistled and shouted and called them by name:

"Now Dasher! Now Dancer!
Now, Prancer and Vixen!
On, Comet! On, Cupid!
On, Donner and Blitzen!
To the top of the porch!
To the top of the wall!
Now dash away! Dash away!
Dash away all!"

As dry leaves that before the wild hurricane fly,
when they meet with an obstacle, mount to the sky
so up to the house-top the courses they flew,
with the sleigh full of toys, and St. Nicholas too.

And then, in a twinkling, I heard on the roof
the prancing and pawing of each little hoof.
As I drew in my head and was turning around,
down the chimney St. Nicholas came with a bound.

The easiest task was adding background material. The libretto was keyed in, and details about the soloists, the chorus, and the orchestra were put on line. Educational material about how to listen to live sound on the Internet was added, as well as links to sites that specialized in Handel, the *Messiah*, and anything else that seemed relevant.

The day before the performance, we decided to make this truly meaningful; a unique Internet experience. A new tool had been released by Van Jacobson of the Lawrence Berkeley Laboratory, one of the most prolific researchers on the Internet. Called a *whiteboard,* this tool allowed a group of people to write on a shared writing surface on the network. The tool, like the audio and video tools that Van developed, was multicast-enabled, using a new form of the Internet Protocol that allowed a computer to be part of a group, with the data sent by one system going to all the other systems in the multicast group.

The whiteboard was a real work of art. It allowed the user to import postscript files, so diagrams and existing presentation materials could be imported into the whiteboard before the start of a meeting. The tool featured lots of different colors and pens so people could write little notes, circle the existing text from the postscript, and even doodle. A very well thought out user interface meant that you could ignore comments from people who were bothering you and could put passwords on private meetings. An innovative retransmission scheme in the case of one or more computers being temporarily unavailable minimized the potential load on the Internet.

We loaded the libretto for the *Messiah* into the whiteboard, with each section going on a different page. Luther Brown, who had long experience singing in a chorus, was put in front of a computer with the whiteboard running and told to grab a colored pen and draw a red dot over the word that was being sung, allowing people on the network to follow along. We forgot that the phrases were repeated over and over, and by the time Luther was done conducting the six people on the network, the whiteboard was a holy mess.

The Internet is the kind of medium where people are quick to claim they were the first ever to produce some technique or another. Indeed, credit for running the "first event" on the Internet has been given so many times that the claim begins to look like those of the first to "discover" the Americas. However, we feel safe in claiming the title for the first-ever religious karaoke multicast event, a feat that does not appear to have been replicated.

One of the more interesting Santa experiences, and certainly the most disastrous, was when Santa got mail-bombed. On a whim, we added a section called the Christmas Cyberspace Campaign. The idea was simple enough. Sun Microsystems put up $20,000 and adopted a local charity, the Second Harvest Food Bank. We put pages on line for the charity and whenever somebody viewed one of the pages, Sun would donate a dime, up to the $20,000 limit.

Well, colour me impressed. Howdja know I was from Oztralia? or that I asked for Peace on Earth and could respond so quickly ... I am gobsmacked. Dammed smart-arsed reindeer too. Merry Christmas to you all!

—Kate Poppelwell
Redfern, NSW, Australia
kpop@mpx.com.au

THE HANDEL'S MESSIAH WHITEBOARD

@wb:IMS: Internal Whiteboard

Activity

Handel
elbert@Mirage.SCL.AmesLab.Gov
shaas@curie

Participants

- berc@chocolate
- breslau@gratiano.parc.xerox.c
- casner@oak.isi.edu
- elbert@Mirage.SCL.AmesLab.C
- floyd@owl.ee.lbl.gov
- gjoly@muridae.cs.ucl.ac.uk
- Handel
- hpccuser@0.0.0.0
- jamin@ensenada.usc.edu
- khoward@cynic.NS

Participant Info

Network

Dest: 224.2.168.132 Port: 35677 ID: 0 TTL: 16
Name: root@also.radio.com
Key: (not encrypted)
Title: wb:IMS: Internal Whiteboard

- Point to type   Mute New Sites
- Smooth Lines   Receive Only

---

wb:IMS: Internal Whiteboard

Welcome to the Kennedy Center for the Performing Arts

Breaking up a fair bit out hee're on the west coast.

I'm a bit ignorant I'm afraid. Remind tme the tools to check? How do I interpret "Packets 12 16 72830"?

tp://north.pole.org/santa/tree.html

We had a good meetin

Sounds ok in Palo Al o, but I can't hear the speaker.   What can you do? Mics are the

No video tonight, eh?   So where is the audio feed from if not the mixing board?   Nothing.
For some reason I can't erase.   Van has broken omething else ALpha related. I'll send him a note.
at least it isn't another Alpha bug – it's easy to get paranoid

Blank Page   Import PS   Import T

---

wb:IMS: Internal Whiteboard   LBL wb 1.59

9. Chorus

For unto us a Child is born, unto us a Son is given,

and the government shall be upon his shoulder;

and His name shall be called Wonderful, Counsello

the Mighty God, the Everlasting Father, the Prince of Peace

Blank Page   Import PS   Import Text   Handel:50

Quit

---

wb:IMS: Internal Whiteboard

7. Chorus

HALLELUJAH! for the Lord God omnipotent reigneth.

The kingdom of this world is become the kingdom of our Lord,

and of His Christ: and He shall reign for ever and ever.

King of Kings, and Lord of Lords, Hallelujah!

Clap! clap!

Blank Page   Import PS   Import Text   Handel:68

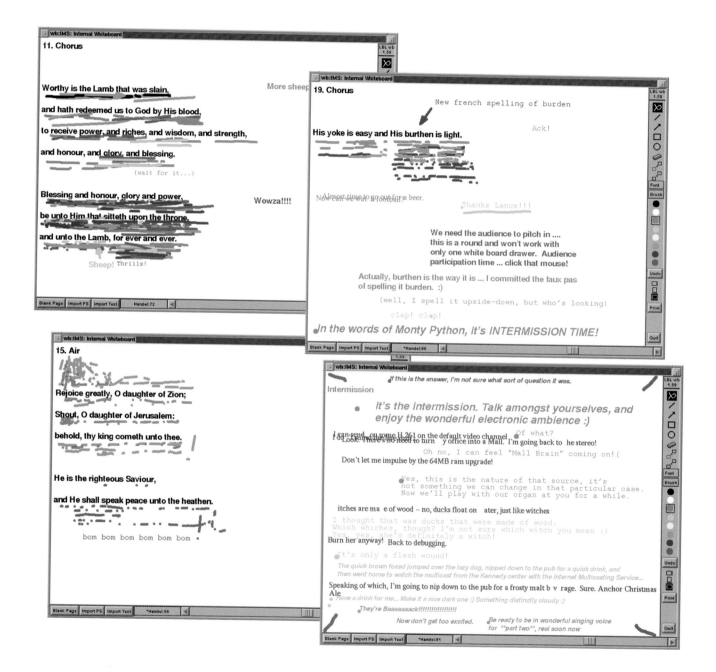

Three other corporations joined up, and a total of $45,000 was available if people came in and learned about the charities. It all seemed harmless enough, providing a little publicity for the charity and leveraging the corporation's contributions by enticing people on the net to make their own contribution. We had made the crucial mistake of underestimating the power of Santa.

We woke up one day to notice over 60,000 unprocessed mail messages in that day's queue for Santa Claus. Our system by then was a huge server that could swallow mail without even breathing hard. Days later, after the dust had cleared, we traced this to a message from a gentleman with the unusual mail address of karma-mechanic@lsd.com. He kind of got the whole concept wrong and sent out mail to everybody he could think of (an act known as *spamming*), telling them that by sending email to santa@north.pole.org, Sun Microsystems would be forced to contribute a dime to charity. No limit.

Good-hearted souls, imbued with the Christmas spirit, started carbon copying Santa and the elves on all their messages. They forwarded the message to every list they could find, urging everybody who received the message to do the same. In addition to the chain-letter effect, we found that there were approximately 100 college students spread throughout the world who felt that simply sending a carbon copy wasn't enough to help in this grand cause. They wrote programs that would go into an infinite loop, sending thousands upon thousands of blank mail messages to Santa Claus.

The *New York Times* wrote an article explaining that a few thousand individuals had been added to Santa's naughty list as the result of this mailbombing and spamming episode. At one point, the Internet Multicasting Service had a dozen powerful machines all working to do nothing but answer the 680,000 mail messages we received in a little over 48 hours.

Bah, humbug is a sentiment you can begin to appreciate when you're sitting at a workstation at 6 A.M. on Christmas day trying to figure out how to stop an unattended computer in England that is spewing out hundreds of messages and attacking your systems. Quite a few college students returned from their vacation to find an angry department head. If nothing else, Santa Claus taught many computer science students a bit about why it is considered poor form to point your computer at somebody else and have it attack.

As the fair was being built, Santa served as one of the anchor pavilions. During 1995, a series of models was put on line for people to get some idea of what the nebulous concept of a pavilion might be. Santa Claus anchored the section on world cultures and world festivals. In January 1996, when the fair opened, it was the only lonely pavilion in this section of the fair, but was quickly joined by other entries.

For the world's fair, the Netherlands contributed another Santa Claus, this one featuring realtime chat rooms with Sinterklaas, the Dutch and Belgian

http://park.org/Guests/Sint/

Sinterklaas in the Netherlands

KampungNet provides an on-line home for
Singapore's Muslim community.

version of Father Christmas, full of charming stories about how he does his work. The site, a production of the Dutch group Kindertainment, was mirrored inside of Central Park and was a big hit during the holidays at the end of the fair.

The world culture pavilions were not limited to Christmas. From Spain came the Unión Romaní, the on-line component of a nonprofit organization that provides legal aid, lobbying for Gypsy rights, and a host of other services. The on-line site, in Spanish, Romanes, and English, includes documents, such as the history of the Gypsies, that users can transfer back to their own system.

Across the world, the Singapore Pavilion entered KampungNet, a site devoted to the local Muslim community. Community announcements and information about Islam are supplemented by a series of exhibits devoted to Malay arts and to famous Singapore Muslims, including writers, artists, and scholars. By the time the fair was done at the end of 1996, we had entries on topics as diverse as Buddhism in Korea and the Jewish ghettos of Venice.

The People Pavilions

The Internet 1996 World Exposition was the first world's fair where anybody could open a pavilion. We took that rule as our cardinal guiding principle. Those who took time to write in to the fairmaster were immediately registered as a pavilion. Perhaps the most important part of our "anybody can play" rule was that individuals, not just organized groups, could open a pavilion. In late 1995, our first person signed up: Randy Walters, with his home page Randy Walters. Soon, his pages proudly flew a banner reading "first individual on the planet to open a pavilion in the Internet 1996 World Exposition."

Randyland features artwork, music, commentary on important issues, and many, many other pieces of information, all artfully intertwined in a way that make you feel like you know Randy Walters. Throughout the year, over 350,000 visitors visited the Randyland pavilion.

Other individuals used their web pages to explore the world of tenors, or ants, or to publish literature reviews. The number of pavilions got so large that even the fair's creators had a tough time keeping track of them. This was as it should be. A world's fair should be chaotic and diverse; it should contain every thing and all things.

Charlotte Brontë went to the Crystal Palace several times, and came away each time awed by what she saw: "vast, strange, new, and impossible to describe." Were she alive today, we like to think she would be equally awed by the Internet 1996 World Exposition, indeed a unique assemblage of all works known to man and web.

A great exhibition! A great idea! I hope this won't be the last effort of this kind. You bring people together in a completely new way.

—**Tom Ruess**
Munich, Germany
ruess@informatik.tu-muenchen.de

TIGER BELLS
A Gold Medal Pavilion

From the Netherlands comes one man's quest to know everything about tiger bells.

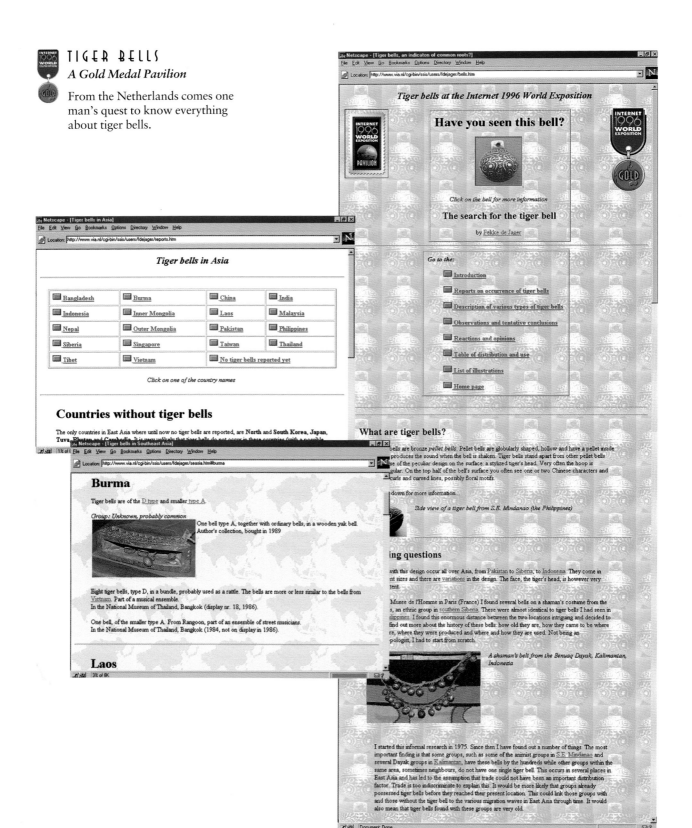

CLASSICAL MIDI ARCHIVES
A Gold Medal Pavilion

The Classical MIDI Archives boasts thousands of music files to download. For an artist such as Bach, who composed for relatively primitive instruments, MIDI is a perfect match, making this an invaluable tool for music students and fans around the world.

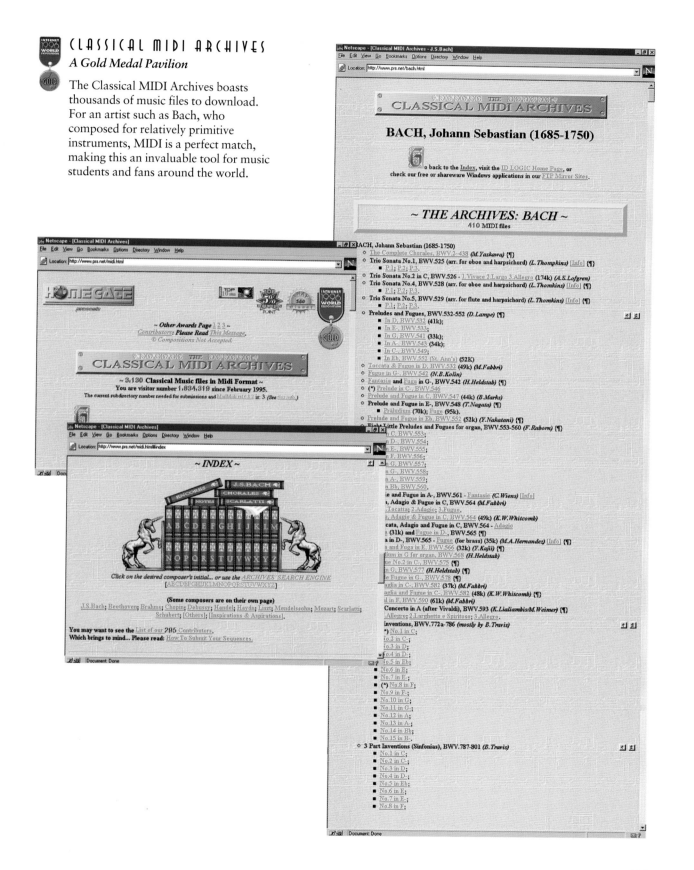

HIS VORPAL SWORD
A Gold Medal Pavilion

The personal home pages of Hart Williams, a writer interested in anything and everything, offer everything from literary criticism to reviews of football games.

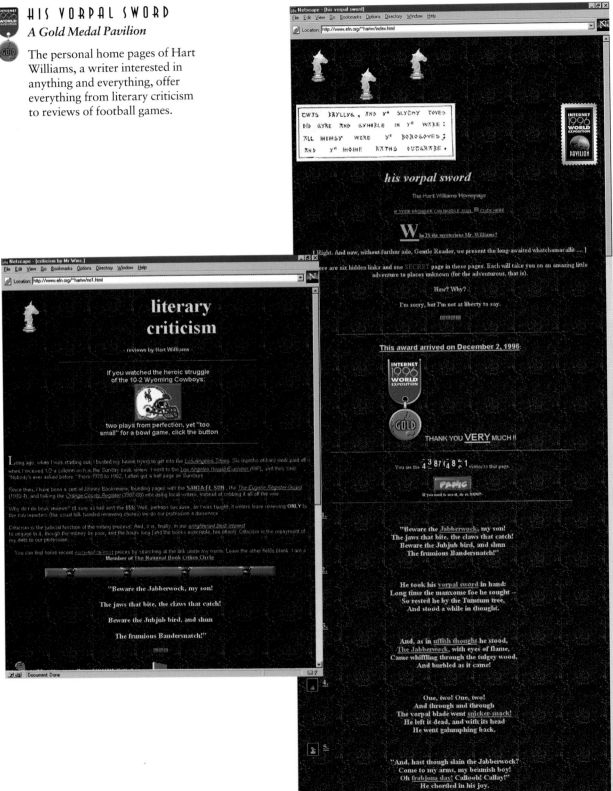

VIRTUALLY VIRTUAL ICELAND
A Silver Medal Pavilion

Gunnar Garðarsson and Garðar Jóhann keep a two-person cultural embassy for their island country, from sagas to maps, from Icelandic lessons to Icelandic recipes.

TENORLAND
A Silver Medal Pavilion

Tenorland features exhaustive information about tenors through the ages, including a place for up-and-coming singers to register themselves, their talents, and their availability.

MYRMECOLOGY
A Silver Medal Pavilion

Everything you ever wanted to know about ants!

 TRILLIUM ARTS
A Silver Medal Pavilion

An award-winning artist's cooperative located in southern Ontario in Canada.

THE GLOBAL GASTRONOMER
An Official Internet Exposition Pavilion

Susanne Hupfer's guide to food anywhere and
everywhere in the world. If you need a recipe for
Cameroon Gambosauce, this is the place to go.

 # UNION ROMANI
An Official Internet Exposition Pavilion

A nonprofit site in three languages devoted to
Gypsies the world over.

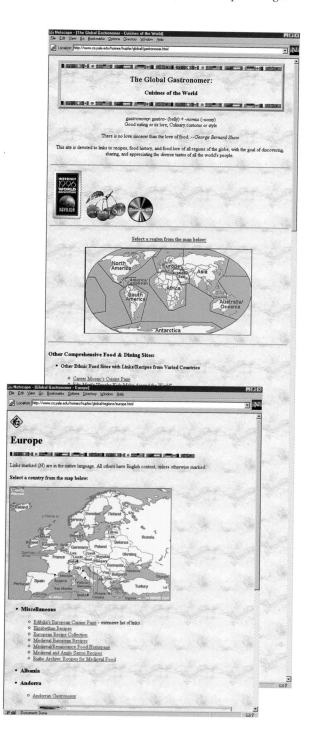

A Public Park
for the Global Village

Louisiana Purchase Exposition St. Louis 1904. Eads bridge.

Lieber Walter: Tante Emma schickt Dir ganze ihre glückwünsche und Küsse für den Geburtstag.

Published by Erker Bros. Opt. Co.

1904 LOUISIANA PURCHASE EXPOSITION

The Internet Railroad

9

Bandwidth matters. The speed of the link from the personal computer to the service provider is what obsesses people when they first join the Internet. Is your modem running at 28,800 or 14,400 bits per second? It may sound trivial, but it is the difference between a car with a top speed of 80 miles per hour and another with a maximum of only 40.

People quickly learn that even if they have a fast link, it does them no good if what's on the other end of the Internet is a slow computer than can only handle a few clients before turning into sludge. While the computer on the other side of the net may be at fault, often the problem is some intermediate link on one of the network backbones or with the routers in the path between the two computers that are trying to communicate.

The lack of backbone capacity, equivalent to having lots of access roads but not enough lanes on the main highway, is particularly felt in international networking. A link between countries requires leasing an international telecommunication circuit, a transaction that involves at least two telephone companies and often many more, and comes at a very dear price.

Though a highway metaphor seems de rigeur in describing the Internet, we chose a railroad to symbolize our own efforts. The backbones are carefully managed infrastructures that aggregate traffic from thousands of simultaneous users. These key transit links are intensely monitored and planned. The term *information highway* implies a wide-open space that people wander about in. A transit backbone is more like a train, where packets arrive at a router, queue up until a slot becomes available, and are injected into the long-distance links. If the current Internet is a set of unpaved country roads that may someday lead to the information highway, our backbones are truly the narrow-gauge rails of the beginning of the nineteenth century.

At the end of 1995, many countries had only a single 64,000-bit-per-second link to the rest of the global Internet. These lines, often based on satellite links with three-second delays, had to handle all inbound and outbound traffic, including electronic mail, news groups, file transfers, and the occasional web session. Internal national networks in the United States had backbone links at speeds of 45 to 155 million bits per second, and experimental or research networks in many other countries were beginning to run at that speed, but the day-to-day infrastructure of the Internet was not nearly as fast.

Great site—Undoubtedly one of the best currently on the WWW. And definitely the fastest in terms of image download time. I hope that all page creators take note so that we can all appreciate pages of this calibre all over the Web.

—**Steven Winer**
Johannesburg, South Africa
s.winer@global.co.za

This is a beautiful site, unfortunately it is the slowest loading site on the web.

—**Robert E. Drennan**
Gt. Barrington, MA, USA
tgo@tgo.com

I must have missed the opening! This site and the overall concept is fantastic! All we need now to tie this all together is more bandwidth. I can hardly wait!

—**Jim Lundy**
Clarke's Beach, NF, Canada
zentech@newcomm.net

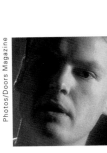

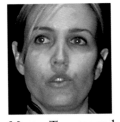

Marten Terpstra and Robin Littlefield of Bay Networks, global project managers for the Internet Railroad.

Links between countries were limited. The European Backbone Regional Network was running at speeds of 2 million bits per second. There were many links between the United States and Europe, but aggregate capacity between these two regions was under 100 million bits per second. Japan's connectivity to the rest of the world was only 14 million bits per second.

All the Internet bigots, as diehard adherents are often called, were confident that this would change eventually. Many commercial carriers were working hard on plans to install international lines that would eventually run at hundreds of megabits per second, but Internet bigots tend to want it now. The international links were so overloaded that many were losing 70 percent of all packets by trying to put the digital equivalent of a grand piano through a mail chute. Using the world's fair as an excuse, we set about trying to beg and wheedle bandwidth out of carriers.

The Center of the Universe

In the Internet, each person is at the center of the universe. What matters most is what is next to you. A computer, any computer, is connected to many things. A serial port talks to a printer, another serial port might talk to a modem. The serial port itself might be a network, with both a modem and a fax machine. As far as the computer is concerned, all traffic for modem-land and fax-land goes to the serial port. The modem, the next computer in the link, knows from the content of the transmission if the data should be delivered via modem commands to another computer or via fax commands to another fax machine. All these devices are part of the Internet.

The business of an Internet service provider is to run links between computers. Some links go directly to an end user or a web server. Other dedicated lines go to client networks, which in turn have their own links, making each service provider a network of networks. As the ring spreads out further, the service provider in turn connects to other service providers, each with its own connections to its own customer networks and to still more service providers.

The big service providers tie all this together with large backbone lines and network operating centers for regional areas. The key, though, is that much of the traffic that comes in on any one service provider is destined for a computer on some other service provider's network. An end user on InternetMCI might wish to consult the SEC's EDGAR database, which is connected to a Washington service provider called Digex, or the MIT Media Lab, which is connected to BBN Planet.

Many of the big networks have a mesh of connections between them, known as *peering points*. Peering points are where traffic from one network can cross over into another. Alternet and BBN Planet, for example, have peering

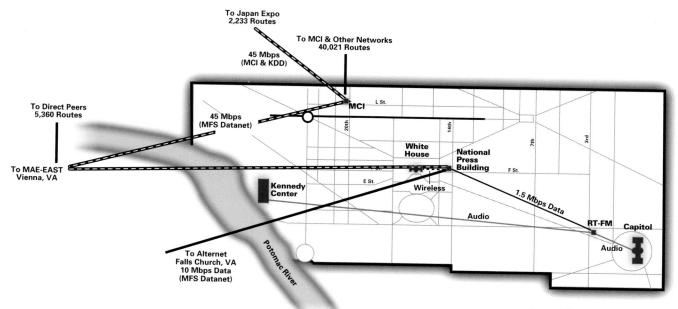

A partial map of the links installed in the Washington, DC, area for the world's fair. RT-FM was the production studio for the Internet Multicasting Service and the National Press Building held the large server systems.

points on both the west and east coasts of the United States. If traffic is destined to go from BBN Planet to Alternet, BBN Planet will attempt to route the data to the closest peering point. If one of the points is down, then all the traffic goes to the other.

Not every network can peer directly with every other network. The Internode network in Australia, for example, has direct peers with two service providers in the country, including one link with Telstra, the telephone company's Internet service. However, Internode is not directly connected to BBN Planet. Internode contracts with Telstra to be a transit provider, meaning that all data for a network that is not directly connected to Internode will be handed to Telstra for delivery. Telstra in turn uses InternetMCI to move its transit traffic to other networks.

Throughout the world, there are facilities where many networks can peer directly with each other. These peering points are known as Global Internet Exchange Points, and there are many throughout the world. The biggest exchange point is in Washington, DC, and is run by Metropolitan Fiber Systems (MFS), one of the new telecommunications companies that specialize in running fiber optic cables through regional areas, and that caters primarily to large business users. This exchange facility is known as MAE-East, for Metropolitan Area Ethernet–East Coast.

MFS provides three metropolitan-area networks that Internet service providers use to connect to each to other. The first network is a metropolitan-area Ethernet, fiber cables running at 10 million bits per second that allow all

What we need is more bandwidth. Who's paying for this funhouse, and how do you feed it more quarters? This will never die out like CB radios did, it's only going to get better and better. BTW, what's your handle?

—**Dobe Fugin Doinat**
Snohomish, WA, USA
dobe@eskimo.com

*As you can plainly see now: E is not always MC².
Thank you for introducing some future.*

—**Gijs ten Kate**
Amsterdam, Netherlands
gtenkate@solair1.inter.nl.net

the systems on the shared cables in the Washington, DC, metropolitan area to communicate with each other. MFS donated one of these lines to the Internet Multicasting Service in 1993, which we used to peer with the Alternet network, which also donated its service. These donations allowed the Internet Multicasting Service to have the fastest Internet links in DC, so fast that the White House borrowed some of our bandwidth in 1993, piggybacking onto our lines using a wireless link from the roof of the National Press Building to the White House lawn.

The other two tiers of networks that are part of the MFS Global Internet Exchange point run at faster speeds. A fiber ring uses a protocol called FDDI and runs at 100 million bits per second. The last network is a gigaswitch, which provides direct interconnections where each node runs at over 100 million bits per second (as opposed to all the nodes sharing a single 100 megabit network). Space inside MFS facilities, known as *colocation space*, allows each of the service providers to put a fast router next to the gigaswitch, then run a dedicated line back to their own facilities.

In addition to the existing line to the Internet Multicasting Service, MFS provided two 45-million-bit-per-second lines to the world's fair. The first line ran from our big server in the National Press Building over to the MFS colocation space. On either end of the line, Bay Networks placed a backbone core router, a device that weighs 300 pounds, has four redundant power supplies, and can handle dozens of simultaneous dedicated links running at hundreds of megabits per second. At this interchange point, the fair was able to exchange traffic directly with over 20 Internet service providers.

The second line ran from the gigaswitch over to MCI's network facilities, where it joined another Bay Networks router. This router, in turn, had two connections. A cable from our router to the MCI router made our connection to our default transit provider. Another dedicated line came from our router and joined our own dedicated line to Japan.

We set ourselves up as an Internet service provider, peering directly with many large networks on the gigaswitch and using MCI as our default transit provider for all other traffic. Large clusters of computers run by one group are called an autonomous system, and routing on the Internet at the backbone level is based on autonomous system numbers. The computers in the National Press Building were all put in an autonomous system assigned to the world's fair, and our routers at the gigaswitch and at MCI started announcing to other networks that we were accepting traffic for any computer in our cloud. Because the National Press Building had links directly to UUNET's Alternet, we made a special announcement to their routers, making that 10-million-bit-per-second link the preferred route for their customers. All the other traffic came in over the 45-million-bit-per-second link, with failover to the slower line.

In December 1995, the fifth transpacific cable went into service, and a team of over 50 engineers led by Nancy Berry and Serge Wernikoff of MCI and Kazunori Konishi of KDD set about putting in a 45-million-bit-per-second line between the MCI point of presence in Washington, DC, and the KDD facility in Tokyo.

First, a dedicated line had to be put in between the Washington point of presence and Los Angeles, where the cable across the Pacific terminated. Next, the line was cross connected into the cable, where it joined other lines going to Japan. The cable goes under the Pacific Ocean from Los Angeles to Hawaii to Guam, then cuts up to the cablehead outside of Tokyo. From there, KDD ran another line into downtown Tokyo, where it joined our Bay Networks router, which was waiting for it.

It sounds simple enough, but the amount of work involved was truly mind-boggling. Because our line was the first to be commissioned on this cable, an intensive testing process was conducted to make sure that the cable and our circuit overlayed on it were working. Once the low-level bits were flowing, another testing process kicked in to make sure that Internet packets would flow properly and that the routers could detect whether the underlying circuit temporarily went down.

The Japanese National Backbone

Once the Internet Railroad reached Tokyo, the challenge was to connect it to something. From the KDD international facility, a line was run to the downtown Tokyo Network Operating Center. KDD, like MFS in the Washington area, was in the interconnection business and was leasing space in its facility to service providers. Providers ran dedicated lines into the KDD point of presence, where they could peer with each other using 100-million-bit-per-second shared networks or private lines into a gigaswitch.

A set of racks was set aside for the Internet Expo computers. At the time, the room at KDD's Internet exchange point was empty, so getting space was easy. The WIDE project leased space to put in a Japanese interconnect facility. A large Central Park server was placed in one rack, and various pieces of networking equipment such as our Bay Networks router were placed in the next.

The first interconnection we made between the expo network and the Japanese infrastructure was into the WIDE national backbone, the group that serves all the universities in the country. WIDE also acts as the de facto operator of the general infrastructure for the country. A coalition of over 100 researchers from nearly every university and corporation that has a stake in the Internet, the group runs research projects, operates a production education network, and was the lead player in putting together the world's fair in Japan.

This is a great experiment to promote Internet and its various usage. I really hope that, thru this event, Internet will be substantial in Japan.

—Hideki Hirayama
Narita, Chiba, Japan
hideki@netcom.com

Chunghwa Telecom in Taiwan issued a special phone card to commemorate the world's fair in their country.

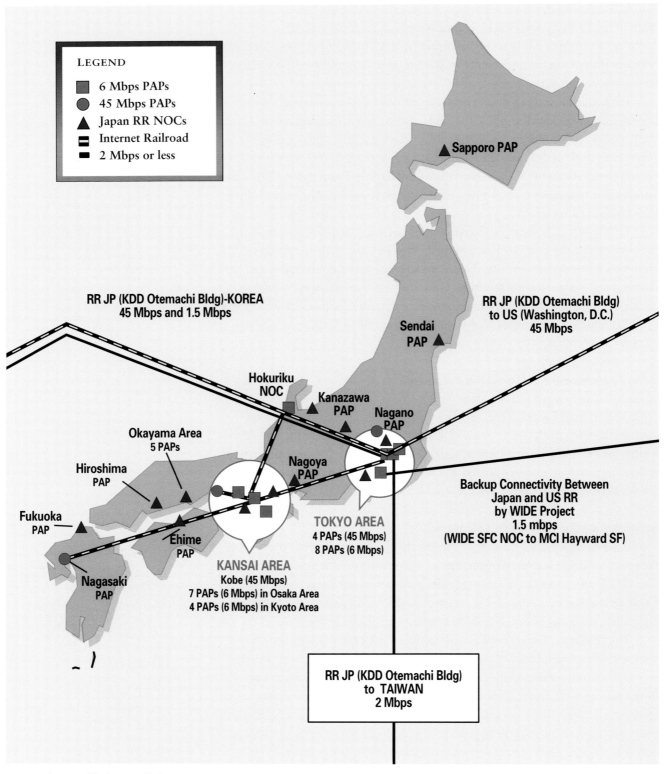

LEGEND

■ 6 Mbps PAPs
● 45 Mbps PAPs
▲ Japan RR NOCs
⊟ Internet Railroad
▬ 2 Mbps or less

Sapporo PAP

RR JP (KDD Otemachi Bldg)-KOREA
45 Mbps and 1.5 Mbps

RR JP (KDD Otemachi Bldg)
to US (Washington, D.C.)
45 Mbps

Sendai
PAP

Hokuriku
NOC

Kanazawa
PAP

Nagano
PAP

Okayama Area
5 PAPs

Hiroshima
PAP

Nagoya
PAP

Fukuoka
PAP

TOKYO AREA
4 PAPs (45 Mbps)
8 PAPs (6 Mbps)

Backup Connectivity Between
Japan and US RR
by WIDE Project
1.5 mbps
(WIDE SFC NOC to MCI Hayward SF)

Ehime
PAP

KANSAI AREA
Kobe (45 Mbps)
7 PAPs (6 Mbps) in Osaka Area
4 PAPs (6 Mbps) in Kyoto Area

Nagasaki
PAP

RR JP (KDD Otemachi Bldg)
to TAIWAN
2 Mbps

A partial map of links installed in Japan
for the Internet 1996 World Exposition.

With KDD and MCI contributing a $20 million line, other providers in Japan were not to be outdone. WIDE secured a contribution of 14 high-speed lines from NTT to upgrade their national backbone to 45-million-bits-per-second links, up substantially from their then-current system of 1.5-million-bits-per-second links. Along with a large number of routers from Cisco, the lines that were contributed connected universities to our world's fair infrastructure, giving selected components of the Japanese university system very fast access to United States Internet sites, since we were acting as the transit provider. We labeled the program the "University of Tomorrow" project, though the students in Japan didn't particularly care what the label was: they saw the speed of surfing the web instantly go from a painful crawl to a pleasant hum.

NTT also contributed a set of lower-speed lines that were used for two purposes. Over 300 lines running at 128,000 bits per second were used to connect a series of homes with dedicated lines, each one of which became a pavilion in the world's fair. Another set of 100 lines running from 1 to 6 million bits per second was used to connect special event sites for the fair, such as the Digital City of Harajuku and the Brain Opera.

All of the companies that signed up to contribute resources to the world's fair used us as a testbed, a role we willingly assumed. KDD and MCI got to break in a new cable over the Pacific. They knew they were going to sell many lines, but having the world's fair gave the engineers a trial run before the paying customers stepped up to the plate. Likewise, NTT was rolling out their network of the future, a project known as Open Computer Network (OCN), which consisted of relatively less expensive data lines for small consumers, and the world's fair was their testbed for this new product.

An Asian Backbone

One of the many projects that coexist in the cramped rooms of Jun Murai's warren of offices on the Fujisawa Campus of Keio University, about an hour south of Tokyo, is one that jumps out at you. As you drive into the futuristic-looking campus, you see a huge satellite dish with the WIDE logo painted on it. The dish is used to connect the Japanese national backbone to four transponders on satellites run by Japan Satellite Systems, a company that was working with Murai's group to develop ways to use very small satellite dishes to connect personal computers to the Internet.

Two of the transponders from Japan Satellite Systems were on the JCSAT satellite number 1 with a footprint over the Japanese islands. With a few satellite dishes, the WIDE team could descend on a site and put it on the Internet at the speed of several million bits per second without going through the bother of putting in a dedicated land line for the event. Satellite-based lines have a longer

This seems to be a grand idea! I read about it in the local paper. Sure hope the idea gets around. I see quite a bunch of folk signing in from places in Asia, Wonderful!

—John Mork
Salem, OR, USA
johne@chemek.com

I'm an Accidental Tourist, and even though I've been travelling for a while, I know the best is yet to come—especially if we can keep the traffic flowing freely. Don't forget to pick up your Blue Ribbon.

—Hilary Ostrov
Vancouver, BC, Canada
hostrov@uniserve.com

delay time than land lines because the signal has to travel all the way up to the satellite and then back down. However, for traffic such as a stream of audio, they are an ideal way to connect up a concert hall, if you don't mind climbing up on the roof to install the dish and running cables down elevator shafts to get the line to the performance.

Another two transponders were donated on a second satellite, this one with a footprint over much of the Pacific Rim. Technically, the procedure is much the same as installing a domestic link, with the notable difference that the size of the dish goes from 75 centimeters to 5 meters. The biggest problem, though, is getting permission to use those portions of the radio spectrum for data communication, permission that requires the agreement of the regulatory bodies of both countries involved.

Murai's team set out on parallel tracks. On one, the WIDE researchers worked on the data interfaces and on deploying test systems. Domestically, they broadcast concerts such as those by Ryuichi Sakamoto, a noted performing artist and the composer of the music for Bertolucci's film *The Last Emperor*. At the same time, they started working with groups abroad to clear the regulatory hurdles. During the fair, a permanent link into Indonesia at 2 million bits per second and numerous national links running at up to 6 million bits per second provided good tests of the system, which went into full production shortly after the fair.

Parallel to the satellite lines, the world's fair worked with three other providers, KDD, Korea Telecom, and Chunghwa Telecom in Taiwan. A line at 45 million bits per second, the first such Internet line inside Asia, was put between Tokyo and Korea, connecting to the Korean academic infrastructure and to a Central Park server. A line at 2 million bits per second was run into Taipei, where it connected to the Taiwan Internet Exchange Point.

What was important about our Asian backbone was not the speed, but the mere fact that it existed. Networking inside Asia was growing in each country, but each group was running a separate line straight to the United States. This was partly a tariff anomaly caused by the strange system administered by the International Telecommunication Union. Through the international price administration conventions that had come into being, it pretty much cost the same to run a line from Taiwan to Korea as it did from Taiwan to the United States. Since most of the initial traffic on the Internet runs to the place having the most data, and since the United States had set up many of the early large Internet systems, it was not a big surprise that every country had its own line to the United States and no lines to its neighbors.

This was similar to the early days of networking in Europe, before a group of network operators, including Rob Blokzijl, the fair's secretary-general, forged a consensus to install direct links to each other. Purchasing lines in Europe helped

Photo/Doors Magazine

The Japanese railroad team made extensive use of satellite links to put event sites on line during the fair.

stimulate demand for these lines, brought in competition, and has slowly started to bring tariffs down. More important, running direct links between countries with a lot of traffic is a more sensible network architecture.

Managing the Railroad

Once a network is installed, managing it is really not all that difficult, though it certainly is time consuming. It takes a group to monitor the system, and periodically a piece of equipment will fail or a line has to be tested. The hard part, though, is the initial installation and configuration. The problem is that a network is never completely installed—networks are always changing.

Just before the fair started, and for the first few months, the attention of the Network Operating Team was on getting the long lines across the Pacific and the DC infrastructure in place. Then the Japan infrastructure began to come on line. A little later, the links to Korea and Taiwan began to be installed, then the lines to other Asian countries started going up.

To make life even more interesting for railroad managers such as Marten Terpstra and his counterparts in individual countries, such as Osamu Nakamura in Japan, special events were scheduled constantly, and each of these required a line to be configured into the world's fair infrastructure. Some of these lines were fairly small and required the participation of only a few people in the area concerned. Adding a line for a Japan expo site, for example, could be done simply by working with the routers in Japan.

Other events, however, required many more people. For the Brain Opera in New York's Lincoln Center, MCI and Nynex chained together a series of four links running at 45 million bits per second to connect the Lincoln Center directly to the Washington, DC, infrastructure. This allowed us to blast full-motion video straight out of the performance site, over the railroad, and into the Interop trade show in Tokyo's Makuhari convention center.

Each of the national infrastructures in Korea, Japan, Taiwan, and the United States was monitored by a local team. Global monitoring was provided by Bay Networks, which contributed the services of ServiceLink, their 24-hour facility near Boston. ServiceLink would monitor the links and the status of routers, paging Marten Terpstra or Robin Littlefield when a problem needed to be resolved with their network. Needless to say, such pages typically come at three in the morning or minutes before a large event is about to go live on the Internet.

Management of the infrastructure for the world's fair, as for the Internet itself, was highly decentralized. The lack of a single point for decision-making was also the lack of a single point of failure. The decentralized management style goes counter to the philosophy in many large organizations, but it works.

Simon Hackett monitors a video stream out to the net.

This is what I call "JUICE!!!" what else would one want? To all the people who constitute this idea... I salute you and MORE POWER!!!!!!

— Kahlil Erwin Talledo
Bacolod City, Philippines
hinieg@durian.usc.edu.ph

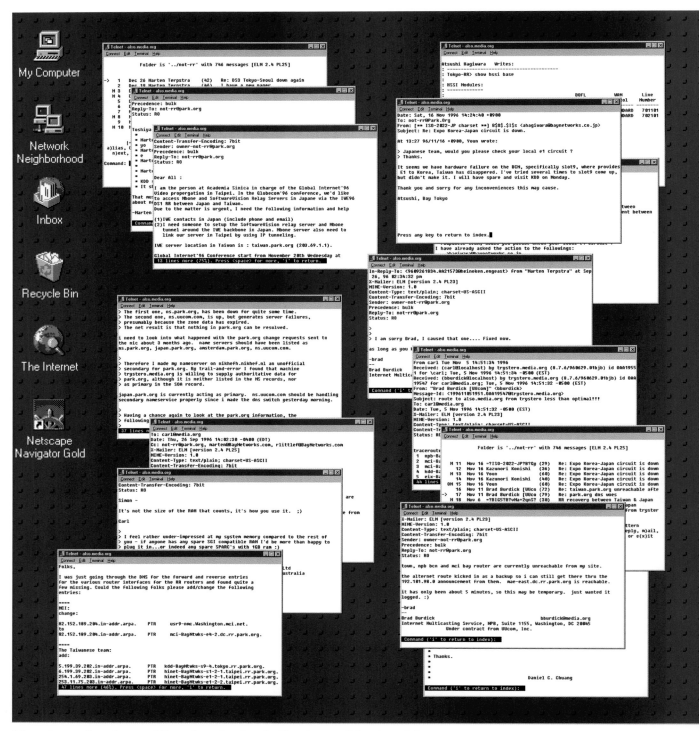

Managing a railroad or a public park can be chaotic. Here is a small fraction of the
messages that crossed the desks of the railroad engineers and park commissioners.

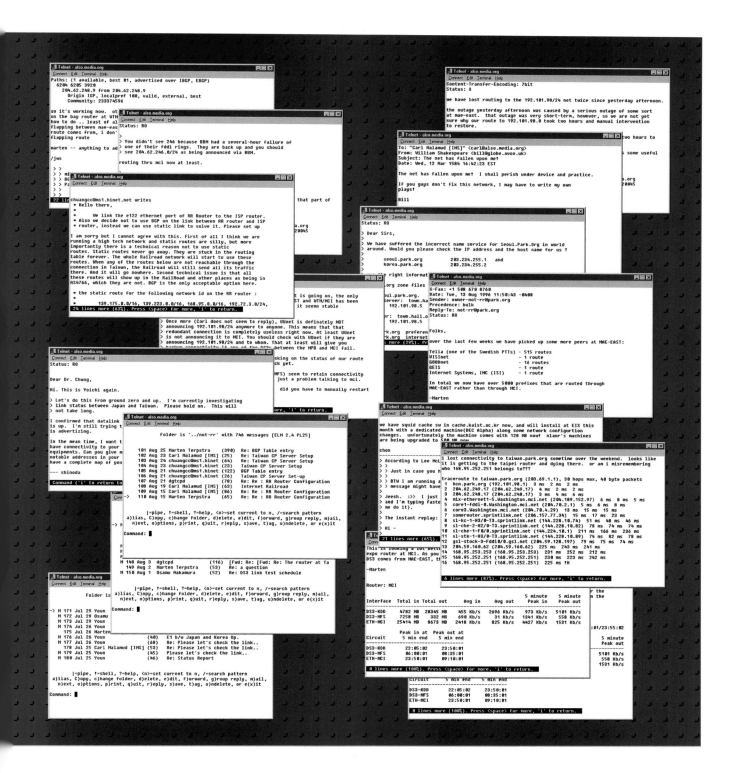

Bay Networks provided a 24-hour monitoring facility for the Internet Railroad.

Ha, finally. I did not read McLuhan for nothing some 30 years ago. Get the high bandwidth pipes in the space, air and ground and maybe we can swing this tiny planet into a hopeful 21 century.

—Jan Willem Doorenbos
Amsterdam, Netherlands
frame@euronet.nl

The Expo Effect

Just as the fair was concluding, I had dinner with Kazunori Konishi, the manager at KDD's research laboratory, who had initially stuck his head out to get his company to contribute. Konishi had spent several months convincing his company that this was a good idea and was under tremendous pressure to prove to his management that this very expensive donation was worthwhile.

Konishi took me to dinner in a very fancy French restaurant, conveniently located in the same building as his network operating center and coincidentally owned by the telephone company. You couldn't tell it by the food, which was impeccable haute cuisine, but you got a clue when you received a free telephone card along with your espresso at the end of the meal.

Konishi brought out a crumpled piece of paper that had two short columns of numbers. On the left was the list of all international Internet circuits that KDD and its competitors had in place at the end of 1995, a set of lines totaling 14 million bits per second. On the right-hand side was the same list for the end of 1996, a total of 350 million bits per second. Internet capacity in Japan had increased more than twentyfold.

My face fell when I saw these numbers. If the commercial providers had installed so much capacity, what was the point of running the world exposition lines? After all, we weren't network operators and we didn't see any point in competing with the commercial providers. The whole point of the world's fair was to go one step ahead and provide a spur to accelerate the development of the Internet. I was very disappointed.

"Oh no!" Konishi was quick to reply when I explained my distress. What had happened was a curious phenomenon that he labeled "the Expo Effect." Our 45-million-bit-per-second line to the United States had gone on line in early January; it had been announced several months before and had received tremendous press play in Japan.

When an Internet service provider goes to a sophisticated customer, the customer will ask questions about its facilities. "How fast is your backbone?" is always the first question, and in Japan the second question is always about the speed of the link to the United States. Before the Expo lines were announced, an answer of 2 million bits per second would get an appreciative nod from the customer and a little check mark on the evaluation form.

Konishi explained to me that we had upped the ante. Customers read about the line we were installing and began to realize that 2 million bits per second was not really all that fast. Six service providers in Japan were major players in the market, and all six rushed to accelerate their plans to install new lines. The lines would have sold eventually, but only by a miracle could capacity increase over twentyfold in one year. KDD booked enough revenue off these sales to be quite pleased with the Expo Effect.

The Internet connections between Japan and the United States at the close of the exposition totaled 350 million bits per second. Telephone company officials found this a remarkable number. Konishi estimated that total voice and fax capacity between Japan and the United States was only 300 million bits per second. It was a real eye opener to many people that Internet traffic had surpassed traditional telephony applications.

For one year, the Internet Railroad was an international service provider with operations in a half-dozen countries, 24-hour network operating centers, and a host of users at universities, special event sites, and Central Park sites. The railroad provided an ideal customer story for the contributing companies because everything we did was out in the open; most commercial customers would prefer not to have the topology and details of their key systems revealed to competitors. More important, the regional backbones, national backbones, and special event sites provided ideal training for the engineers participating.

But the bottom line for us was that we were able to build the infrastructure for our world's fair, just as engineers in Chicago in 1893 installed lights and trains and the other networks that they used for theirs. Getting the toys to be able to do fun projects, be it in a corporate or academic setting, is never easy. The world's fair provided the perfect excuse for all the engineers involved to convince their organizations to let us build a railroad for one year.

A prodigious undertaking and ... so far ... a most excellent site!

—**M.R. Smith**
Dededo, Guam
mrsmith@iftech.net

Chris Liljenstolpe of SSDS monitors a video transmission out to the Internet.

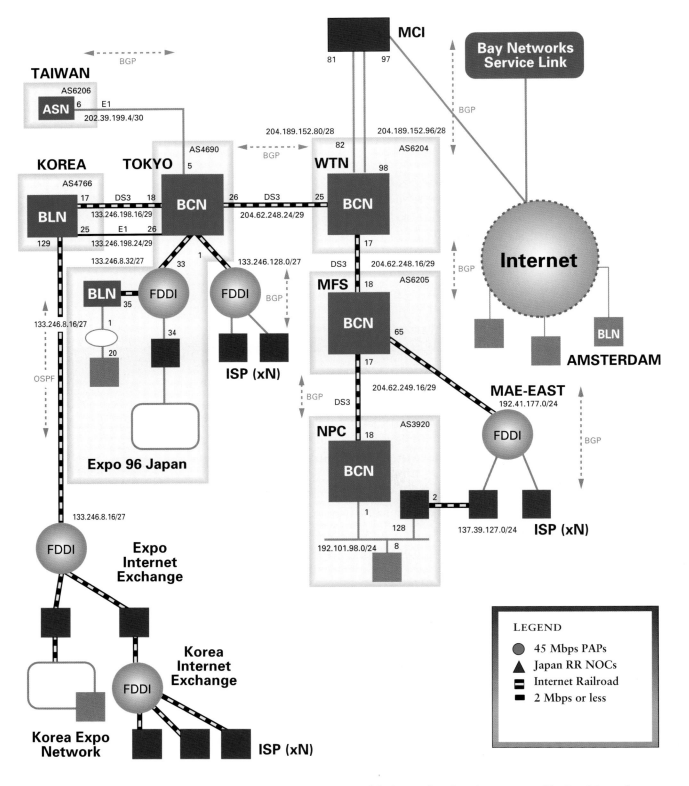

One of the internal engineering maps used by Bay Networks
engineers to construct the Internet Railroad management system.

The key to the growth of global backbones is to continue these efforts. While a 45-million-bit-per-second line from the United States to Japan is no longer a scarce commodity, there are many other parts of the global grid that need to be put into place. Government and industry must work together to build these essential public infrastructures.

Hoping that somebody else will do the job is not enough: key infrastructures are a vital part of our societies. Governments looking to promote a Global Information Infrastructure should look beyond the white papers and the conferences that are all too often the only product that they produce. The world has enough paper and no amount of words can substitute for working directly with the telecommunications providers to build the railroads that will move information around the world.

The most accessible Exposition around the world. I Enjoyed My Visit. I Will Be Back. Saludos desde Caracas a Todos.

—**Humberto Albano Moret**
Caracas, Venezuela
halbano@dino.conicit.ve

157

1904 LOUISIANA PURCHASE EXPOSITION

Central Park

10

The Internet can bear an uncanny resemblance to the suburbs, with lots of roads but no place to go. Internet service providers put in lots of modem servers and modems and routers, but often the only computers on their network come from the customers. The problem is one of scale. Private citizens can provide a host of businesses in a city, on-line convenience stores, personal home pages, or digital museums. But cities that are worth living in are not just made up of a few 7-Eleven stores in strip malls neighboring vast homogeneous bedroom communities, all connected by miles of clean blacktop roads and parking lots.

In a city, in a livable city, a public infrastructure grows in parallel with the private infrastructures. Businesses and housing are an important part of the equation, but we also build city halls, firehouses, art centers, libraries, schools, and, at least as important, public parks. What we do in the public infrastructure is usually the subject of our attention. How shall we teach our children in our schools? What kind of books shall we stock in our library? Who should get the corner office in city hall?

As any teacher will tell you, the debate on the fine points of educational methodology pales in comparison with the more fundamental question of the mere existence of proper facilities. Deciding whether or not to teach the phonetic method or Darwin is an interesting fine point, but the more important issues in most schools around the world are overcrowded buildings, poor equipment, and insufficient money to pay people to properly staff a school facility.

The Internet has suffered from the same public infrastructure problems as the rest of the real world. Some things are simply too big for one well-meaning corporation to provide as a public service. Public infrastructure is a group enterprise, something that we all do together because none of us can do it alone. At a physical level, there is the simple question of scale. Public infrastructure, because it serves us all, tends to be big and expensive.

On the Internet, the piece that is often missing is the large, well-managed computer complex that can serve as an anchor for a region of the Internet. Many people can design web pages on a simple PC, but that personal computer is not going to have the muscle needed to serve those pages up to an eager world. Providing disk space for public organizations is an example of a function that a large computer can provide, but the issue goes beyond mere space.

Have yet to explore the park, but what a wonderful idea …

—**Paul Rossy**
Montreal, Canada
rospau@cycor.ca

Central Park ... Yahoo !!!
I Love It !

—**Fu-Chien Wu**
Taipei, Taiwan
wfc@iiidns.iii.org.tw

Brad Burdick, global project manager for Central Park.

Running an Internet server capable of handling several hundred thousand hits per hour requires attention to numerous matters, including routing, disk space, scheduling of CPU capacity, and load-balancing over many different machines. Keeping systems secure and performing well is a day-to-day operation. Security, for example, arises daily as new bugs are found in protocols such as mail handling systems and those bugs are patched.

To stage a world's fair, we obviously had to have computer capacity to serve our data to the world, but we wanted to do something more permanent than act as system administrators for the year. Thus arose the idea for building Central Park, a public park for the global village. The idea is simple, though the implementation ended up being surprisingly complex. Large computers would be placed throughout the world, each run by a local group with the expertise to do a good job. The computers would talk to each other, mirroring data produced on one system to the other systems. The end result would be a set of computers that were synchronized with each other, providing a single view of a collection of information to our users.

The Internet Multicasting Service already had a core system in place, an 8-processor computer from Sun Microsystems with about 100 gigabytes of disk space, enough to handle the SEC and patent databases, our radio archives, and miscellaneous other pieces of information such as Santa Claus. With our donation of 1,000 more gigabytes from Quantum, we set about getting similar facilities set up in other parts of the world.

In Europe, the first to sign up was the Dutch National Institute of High Energy Physics (NIKHEF), where Dr. Rob Blokzijl was the director of networking. Physicists have been early and heavy users of Internet technology. The huge amount of data collected from experiments that must be dispersed to researchers all over the world has always pushed the edge of networking and NIKHEF had become one of the centers of computer networking for Europe. Blokzijl was the chairman of the European Internet group, and his directors had given him a lot of leeway in pursuing projects that might seem unrelated to physics but would have long-term benefits for networking.

Blokzijl volunteered a machine room and some of the best engineers in Europe and we threw in 200 gigabytes of our Quantum disks. Sun was approached again, and they donated a system with eight central processing units and one gigabyte of random access memory. For good measure, they threw in another 150 gigabytes of disk on a fault-tolerant array, bringing Rob's system up to double the capacity of ours. Figuring that we were soon going to wear out our welcome at Sun, we went and found an existing system in London, run at Imperial College as the main news feed for the country. In return for 200 gigabytes of disk, they agreed to become a Central Park mirror. A similar deal was cut in Adelaide, where Simon Hackett was running a public server.

Photo/Doors Magazine

Members of the
International Secretariat
at work in Kobe.

With Europe, the United States, and Australia covered, the systems in Asia started springing up like mushrooms. Jun Murai got IBM to donate a huge system with 32 processors, which he installed at his campus in Fujisawa. This system was used as the Japan mirror for many of the large fair events and was also an important system during the Atlanta Olympics, part of a global complex of computers that was able to swallow over 16 million hits per day. Auspex, a maker of specialized file servers that are extremely reliable and thus ideal for applications with high transaction rates, donated two 500-gigabyte servers. Not to be outdone, Nihon Sun and Fujitsu, their Japanese partner, donated an 8-processor system.

In Taiwan and Korea, they didn't mess around with getting donations. In Taiwan, Chunghwa Telecom bought an 8-processor Sun and in Korea the National Computerization Association did the same. In Germany, Siemens kicked in an 8-processor system. We had one of our old yet still powerful systems kicking around, which was traded to Boris Yeltsin's science advisor as a donation to the Moscow Central Park in return for a letter from his boss.

There was a tremendous amount of hardware in transit during the end of 1995 and in early 1996 as these systems were shipped and, in each location, eventually handed over to some poor person who had to figure out what to do with all those boxes. All told, we estimated that well over $20 million in computer equipment, routers, and other hardware was floating around for the world's fair. When you added the telecommunications lines, the time all the staff members contributed to support systems, and the cash contributions that went from official organizers to fair committees, we estimated that the cost of the fair was over $100 million.

Even at low bandwidth setting, the park looks beautiful.

—I.J. Hudson
Darnestown, MD, USA
ij.hudson@nbc.com

Hello! Everybody! The park is so beautiful!!

—James Hoe
Taipei, Taiwan
jameshoe@ms4.hinet.net

Am I in the park really?

—Gemini Lim
Seoul, Korea
lim@colt.sst.co.kr

Dr. Rob Blokzijl

Philippe Tabaux

Only a small proportion of that budget came in the form of cash contributions. The Internet Multicasting Service, for example, did all the initial organization for the fair and ran the entire operation for under $1 million. The Dutch Institute of Nuclear Physics ran the international secretariat on a staff of four people and with a budget well under $1 million. The committees in Japan and Korea raised about $6 million, but the vast majority of the money in both of those countries was spent on internally focused activities by the companies that were administering the secretariats.

Most of the investment in the fair was in the form of time. When you ask MCI to contribute a DS3 circuit to a world's fair, the issue is less one of money than of how much time it will take. The lines have internal pricings when the company makes its decision, and there are certainly costs incurred that would not be otherwise, such as for equipment. But the real cost is the time it took Vint Cerf and other executives to evaluate the proposal, the 30 people it took to install the transpacific line with KDD, putting in special event circuits, and the ongoing monitoring of the network.

In many cases, the decision to participate in the fair was up to the person who would have to do the work. Marten Terpstra and Robin Littlefield at Bay Networks, for example, wanted their company to participate in the fair. Their normal job is to install and monitor large networks at places like trade shows, and during the fair that work would continue. They spent time convincing marketing, PR, and engineering that the fair was a good thing, then spent the entire year being paged at all hours to fix some bug that had started acting up. Likewise, small businessmen like Simon Hackett in Australia, who ran the Central Park system for his region, didn't see their regular work shut down simply because a world's fair was happening.

Running the Park

When dignitaries come and visit the fair, you're supposed to treat them with the deference due their position. Traditionally, this means a special behind-the-scenes tour. For the Internet 1996 World Exposition this was tough, because our back stage was anyplace in the world we could get a few square feet of space. For special events, we usually commandeered the dressing room reserved for the stars, turning the rather austere green rooms into a chaos of wires, stacks of computers, and people sitting for 18-hour stretches staring, puzzled, at computer screens.

Our permanent network operating centers were no different. Some of the facilities, such as the international secretariat in Amsterdam or the chief network operating center in Japan, were orderly enough, but the sheer number of places that the fair was being operated from made logistics a real challenge. At the

Internet Multicasting Service, for example, it was not unusual for Deb Roy to Federal Express tapes and cartridges from Calcutta to Marty Lucas in North Judson, Indiana. Marty, operating his Big Eastern studios on the top of a hill in the mint capital of Northern Indiana, would process the audio and hammer out web pages, then transfer the data over to Becky Pranger in Enviromedia for some graphic touches. All this would then be staged at our systems in Washington, DC, and cleaned up for publication by Philippe Tabaux and Brad Burdick, then pushed into Central Park.

"Pleased to meet you" was one the most common phrases at the closing ceremony, where people who had worked together all year were meeting for the first time. Two of the chief engineers for the fair, Marten Terpstra of Bay Networks and Brad Burdick of UUCOM, have still never seen most of the people they worked with all year coordinating the railroad and Central Park.

The day-to-day operations of the fair were parceled out to people all around the world. The secretariat in Amsterdam handled the fairmaster mail, deciding which pavilions were to be accepted into the fair, and then modifying the fairgrounds to add the new entry. They developed a sophisticated database system to keep track of the over 3,000 pavilions in the fair, and managed in their spare time to build the pavilions for the Netherlands, France, and many other countries.

Getting Central Park working was Brad Burdick's responsibility. He had worked as a contractor for the Internet Multicasting Service for two years, taking the lead for keeping our large systems running and programming projects such as the SEC's EDGAR database system. Brad had to work with eight different systems around the world, each configured differently and many running on different brands of equipment.

The challenge was much more than simply moving the web pages from one system to another. Each computer had to run web server software that was able to understand the data produced on another system. When the Japanese pavilions started making active use of the virtual reality markup language (VRML), the servers in the other sites all had to be modified so that they recognized this as a valid type of web object.

Security was extremely difficult in such a loose-knit configuration. Many of our web sites were active, so that instead of pulling up a static page of data the user would have the page built for him or her on the fly. Each page consisted of a program running on the server computer. When a program runs, things happen, and a whole host of security holes can develop.

For example, one utility that was part of the standard distribution for one of the web server packages we used had an escape command, which allowed the programmer to use common system calls. An example might be using the escape command in a program to keep track of the number of web hits to a certain page

I will enjoy good time at this Park, thank you very match.

—**Takeshi Matsuhira**
Kasiwara, Osaka, Japan
JAB02046@niftyserve.or.jp

Photos/Doors Magazine

Network Operating Centers for world's
fair events tend to be a fairly chaotic,
toy-intensive environment.

CYBERFAIR '94

Many of the people who played a key role in the world's fair first worked together in 1994 at the world's first cyberstation, set up for three days in the Las Vegas Hilton ballroom. The Interop Cyberstation featured nonstop programming, including live talk shows, interviews over the network to government officials such as Secretary Ron Brown, radio programs from France and Australia beamed in via a satellite dish anchored in the parking lot and then shipped out to the net, and even our own house rock-and-roll band to play during the shows. Four 14-foot trucks crammed with over 50 computers, a ton of audio-video gear, and a special space-age situation room from ARPA were set up to make this the first sustained live programming on the network.

or the current time and then dynamically inserting the current value of the counter into the web page. A few hackers found a way to exploit that call and, in certain circumstances, take over a user account. When the security coordinating bodies on the Internet sent out a warning about the bug and instructions on how to work around it and close the loophole we had to insert a new utility on each Central Park server that scanned for any occurrences of the offending program that might have crept back in from one of our servers.

Each time something like this would be found, as occurred daily, a blizzard of email from around the world would result. Things got even more chaotic during special events, when teams would be dispatched to descend on some festival or concert. For events like the Sakamoto concert or the Brain Opera, special lines were run into the facility, new computers were configured to join Central Park, and mirroring and monitoring activities had to be stepped up to keep pace with the increased flow of data.

When journalists come to interview people working on the fair, they invariably want to snap a photograph of the engineer in charge in action. It is sometimes unclear how the journalistic mind works, but these people come to interviews with an image of frenetic activity, and somehow the chief engineer should be a whirlwind of motion. "Do what you usually do, act natural," the photographer will urge. When the engineer sits down at the computer and starts to read through a folder of 300 email messages, the photographer is inevitably disappointed. At the Internet Multicasting Service, we always kept a supply of microphones, mixing boards, and power tools next to the computer so that the photographers could get their action shot.

Beyond the Mirror

Running a data warehouse was a necessary operation to support our fair, but we wanted to use this infrastructure for more than a large web site. Several Internet research projects were given space on the systems in order to allow them to deploy new research. Perhaps the most successful was a project called Squid (which is not an acronym), a caching system originally developed under the leadership of Professor Mike Schwartz at the University of Colorado in collaboration with a task force of researchers working on a broad set of tools for efficiently distributing information between servers.

Many of those tools were aimed at making distributed indexing of sites more efficient and effective, a technique used in web crawlers. The collection of tools was called Harvest (which is also not an acronym). Many of the techniques pioneered by the Harvest group have become incorporated into commercial systems. The cache work was originally led by Professor Peter Danzig, one of the Harvest researchers.

the theme behind central park seems cool. i can't wait to see more.

—**Damaria**
Wilmington, DE, USA
damaria@friends.wilmington.de.us

The Squid cache attacks the problem of duplicate transfers of popular files on the network. When a big system, say an event such as Kasparov versus Deep Blue, produces new pages, many users go in to see the same page. Mirroring is one way to solve this problem, but it requires a coordinated set of systems and a way of redirecting users to the proper server for their location. Mirroring also sends large collections of information around the network, some of which is never accessed.

Another approach is to store temporary copies of information in regional caches. Users set up their web browsers to point to what is called a *proxy server*. All requests from the web browser to the Internet stop first at the proxy server. There are several uses for such a proxy, and security is one of the more prevalent. The outside world talks to the proxy server, which is very tightly configured to let in only certain types of data. Web data are allowed in to the end user, but unknown Internet ports are filtered out.

Another use of proxies is for censorship. Users in Singapore are required to configure their web browser to use the national proxy server, which will filter out URLs of banned sites so the user cannot see them. In addition to security and censorship, however, there is another use for a system like this. Since all the users inside of a network go through the proxy server, it makes sense to cache any information brought in, saving it in case a future user wants to see the same page. This reduces the amount of data that has to be dragged in from across the network and reduces latency for users because the data are closer.

Big Internet systems like America Online all run proxy servers, both for security and for caching. The Internet sees one, two, or perhaps a dozen systems, which interact with the rest of the internal network on behalf of the outside world. Danzig, Schwartz, and a research assistant, Duane Wessels, set out to build software to allow caches that can be arranged hierachically, working on behalf of a larger population than a single network, such as a country.

The code that Wessels helped develop went with him when the Harvest project concluded and he moved over to an innovative set of projects funded by the National Science Foundation under the label of the National Laboratory for Applied Network Research (NLANR). NLANR doesn't exist in any one place, but is a coalition of researchers in various locations. Wessels went to work for two of the more innovative researchers in the NLANR system, Dr K. C. Claffy of the University of San Diego, and Dr. Hans-Werner Braun, who at the time was on the staff of the San Diego Supercomputer Center and was the principle architect of the original NSFnet.

Wessels set out to put together a hierarchy of international and regional caches that would systematically begin caching data from one region to another. With a grant from NSF and an equipment discount from Digital he set up systems in various locations in the United States that acted as parent caches. Regional caches in other countries were configured to serve data from their own areas.

What a great park to go surfing through! Remember, confidence is the companion of success.

—David Berndt
Dearborn, MI, USA
usfmcpst@ibmmail.com

http://www.nlanr.net/Cache/

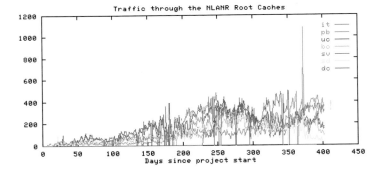

Top: Visualization of access patterns to and from Squid caches in Europe. Bottom: hit rates through the major global caches. The brown line is the Washington, DC, Central Park server.

The caches were then configured in a set of relationships as parents and siblings. As pages of data flowed around the world, they would be kept in different computers. A user in Korea, for example, would contact a local cache. If the local cache had the information, it would give it to the user. If not, the local cache would send a request to siblings for local data and up the hierarchy for more remote data, asking all the other caches if they had the page. If none of the caches had the page, it would be fetched from the server that had it, and then all the caches in the chain would update their logs to indicate that they now had a copy of that page. There are many details in configuring these systems, ranging from figuring out what is "local" to a particular cache to adding new national and regional caches into the hierarchy.

The world's fair gave Wessels space on Central Park systems, allowing NLANR to supplement their dedicated caches. On the main Central Park server in Washington, DC, a Squid cache was established that had 500 megabytes of dedicated random access memory and 50 gigabytes of disk space. This system was a regional hub and was receiving over 250 transactions per minute, transactions that were requests from national caches throughout the world.

A project such as the global deployment of lots of Squids seems like a no-brainer. Bandwidth is money and Squid caches help networks make more effective use of that bandwidth. Building a global backbone of caches seems like a highly desirable goal for the Internet, but project directors Claffy and Wessels have a tough time getting funded, as do any of the other nonprofit public infrastructure projects on the net. Groups such as the National Science Foundation, Digital Equipment Corporation, and some research centers have all supported their work, but large infrastructure projects are beyond the reach of ad hoc efforts and deserve serious attention from the Internet industry.

Other examples of ugly stepchildren of the Internet infrastructure are key software modules used to help keep the network running. Internet servers and routers have dozens of core modules in common. These modules, programs such as mail handlers or multicast routing systems, typically are developed at one or two sites and then placed in the public domain or otherwise made publicly available. These key implementations of vital pieces of software are known as *reference implementations*.

Often, vendors will take the reference implementation and put it directly into their own product. Other times, they use the reference software as a model on which they can test the operation of their own software. Many of these pieces of software come out of corporate, university, or government research laboratories and they are often supported for a time by the institution that started them. Washington University, for example, started a project to develop a sophisticated server for the file transfer protocol and has continued to support that system over the years.

Happy New Year and may 1996 find this park a peaceful place to visit all year long.

—**Bruce Tadd**
Orlando, FL, USA
btadd@mci.newscorp.com

Visual representation of traffic among root-level Squid caches.

*The Park is a great idea.
I'm looking forward to
my next visit!*

—**Larry Miller**
London, Ontario, Canada
larry.miller@sympatico.ca

Often, though, the software becomes an orphan. The programmer who started the system and spent a few years supporting thousands or sometimes millions of users will move on to another project. The group that supported the work in the first place will grow tired of that role. Meanwhile, however, the software has become a vital part of operations all over the world.

The Internet Software Consortium was founded to try and match vital pieces of Internet software with programmers who were willing to spend their time working on reference implementations instead of trying to strike it rich selling software. The consortium was founded by Rick Adams, the chairman and founder of UUNET Technologies, the first commercial Internet provider. Rick took a nonprofit fund he chaired and applied the money to supporting key reference implementations.

The project was administered by UUNET for several years and deployed several hundred thousand dollars to support some of the most talented freelance programmers on the network. As Rick's business started exploding with the growth of the Internet, he turned over the administrative burdens of the Internet Software Consortium, along with two years of operating funds, to the Internet Multicasting Service, which made it part of the fair.

Supervision, and some of the key programming, comes from Paul Vixie, technical director of the consortium. Vixie works out of his house, perched high up in the hills with a view of the San Francisco Bay and the Pacific Ocean. A 1.5-million-bit-per-second dedicated line has been run up the mountain to his house, with a diesel generator installed in case of power outages.

Vixie has an incredibly thorough knowledge of the Internet protocols, and could easily spend all his time serving as a very high priced corporate consultant. Like several of his colleagues who have been involved in keeping the Internet going, Vixie spends half his time doing corporate consulting and donates the other half back to the community doing various public service projects.

The Internet Software Consortium administered four key programs in 1996. The most important was Vixie's implementation of the software that is used on almost every Domain Name System server. Every computer on the Internet issues requests for the current location of a domain name, such as park.org. The servers that coordinate that namespace, mapping names into the current Internet address, are located on tens of thousands of computers. If this protocol breaks, the Internet is gone.

The three other projects were all examples of orphans that needed help. The software used for transfer of network news, for example, had been foundering and was in need of an updated reference implementation. The original software that most large news servers used was written by Rich Salz, but after a few years of keeping the software going he had moved on. It is important to understand that creating a key piece of software like this is not a trivial

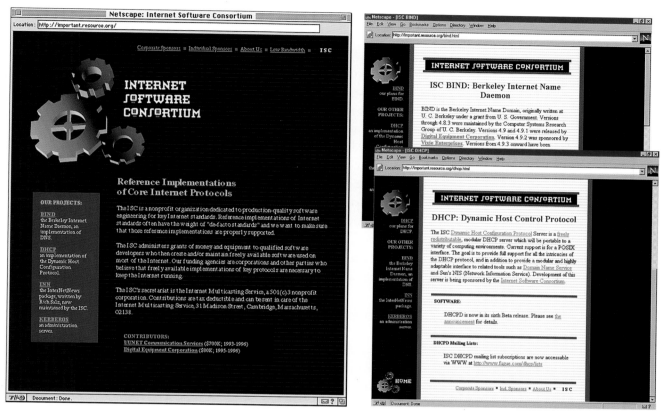

The Internet Software Consortium supports freely available implementations of key portions of the Internet infrastructure.

undertaking. The code is revised almost constantly as bugs are found on different operating platforms or ambiguities are uncovered in the protocol definition. Thousands of email messages per month come into the program developer of such a system. The Internet Software Consortium issued a grant to take Salz's code and have James Brister, a talented programmer, modernize it.

There are quite a few programmers who are willing to work on public service projects, working for a fraction of what they are worth on the market, but who don't have the temperament or desire for a permanent, full-time job in a government research laboratory. These freelance programmers and engineers played a crucial role in the development of the Internet. Thousands of such people around the world spend their time wiring their local school or administering Internet mailing lists to hash out the details of a particular protocol.

Keeping the key software going is more than a hobby, though. Rescuing complex pieces of software takes an intensive investment of time. But getting these kinds of projects funded is not easy. After all, at the end of 1996 the Domain Name System software was in its fourth major revision. In Version 4 alone there were nine minor releases, and the last minor release had a total of five different patches applied to it, making the current release number 4.9.5.

I like very much what I have seen so far, and I hope the park lives up to expectations. I wish you all the very best of luck.

—**Jack Holt**
Nottingham, UK
jackholt@innotts.co.uk

Approaching the marketing people at a computer company to try and convince them to fund version 4.9.6 of some software is not what you would call a sexy project. The industry consortium approach works well for large chunks of protocols, such as that covered by the World Wide Web consortium. Lots of little pieces, however, continue to fall through the cracks.

Projects like the Internet Software Consortium proceed on a hand-to-mouth basis. Many engineers know that this is key software for their operations, and a few of them are lucky enough to be able to convince their bosses that something as plain-sounding as "fixing the bugs in a security module" is actually important. John Curran, the chief technical officer of BBN Planet, convinced his company to donate Internet service, an engineer at IBM convinced his company to pitch in $50,000 of funds, and Usenix, an association of Unix programmers, matched that contribution. There is not, however, any systematic way to keep these projects going and programmers like Paul Vixie must try to do long-term planning for key software on a short-term budget.

Did Anybody Come?

What was impressive about the old world's fairs were the numbers. When one reads about 28 million people going to Chicago in 1893, a year in which the population of the United States was well under 100 million, it makes one stop and think. The numbers don't capture the real meaning of the event, but they do give an idea of the scale. Today, if you go to any trade show or watch a network broadcast, the suits are sitting back anxiously waiting for the numbers to come in. How many people watched the show?

For an Internet world's fair, this is an exceedingly difficult question to answer. The log files for just the main Central Park servers take up 16 gigabytes of disk space and require two weeks of computing time on the Amsterdam server just to get a first pass at the statistics. Events such as Kasparov, Sakamoto, and the Brain Opera all ran on their own systems. A huge amount of data was housed inside Central Park, but we estimated that over five times as many pavilions resided outside the park and were outside our direct control.

Two of the lead Central Park engineers teamed up to try and develop an official estimate, preferably one with some basis in fact. Yoichi Shinoda is a professor of computer science at the Japan Advanced Institute of Science and Technology and served as Central Park commissioner for Japan. Philippe Tabaux was a long-time employee of the Internet Multicasting Service who managed the Central Park services for the international secretariat with his colleague Herman van Dompseler.

The starting point for an analysis is the number of hits. A hit is an object on the web server, perhaps an html file containing text and layout instructions,

It's wonderful !

Let us contribute to make Internet a clean & beautiful place for our future generation.

—**Donald Wee**
Singapore
donjenwe@po.pacific.net.sg

or images such as icons, or photographs, or other objects such as a java program. A single web page may be made up of many components, particularly if lots of icons are used. A more revealing figure is the number of page views, but even this figure does not tell the whole story. For Central Park, we had approximately 55 million hits and 12 million page views. Several of the event sites racked up 30 million hits each, so we felt safe in saying that 100 million hits had been received in the center of Central Park.

How many hits did the fair receive in total? That was hard to tell since we didn't have the logs; even if we did they would be too big and in too many formats to process in less than a few months. Using the scientific technique of making up a number (supplemented by an analysis of the number of pavilions we hosted in the park versus those outside), a multiplier of five was assigned for the ratio of things inside Central Park to things outside the park. With 100 million hits inside the park, and another 500 million outside, that made total hits of roughly 600 million.

Total hits don't really reveal much about the number of people, because of caches, proxies, and other systems that keep copies of pages or hide the numbers of users. Caches and proxies also obscure another important number, the total number of unique computers. For Central Park, roughly 740,000 unique computers from 132 countries visited the fair. It was safe to say that the event sites such as the Kasparov match made this a significantly larger number, so the number was rounded up to an even million.

Turning a million unique computers into an attendance estimate is tough. America Online is represented in the statistics logs as a set of a few dozen proxy computers. Caches such as Squid were also doing a lot of business. An accepted multiplier in the industry for the average number of users per unique computer is five, averaging the massive number of users on a proxy like AOL and the large number of individuals with their own Internet addresses.

One million computers and a multiplier of five led us to an official estimate of 5 million unique individuals who visited the fair. It is highly likely that this number is wrong, but it is certainly within the right order of magnitude. Perhaps the correct answer is really that two million unique individuals visited the fair, perhaps it is as many as 50 million, but it is certainly in the millions.

Working backward from the estimate of the total number of hits yields similar results. Shinoda extracted samples of the Japanese logs for more extensive analysis and determined that, inside Central Park, there were an average of 3.7 hits per page and that the average number of pages viewed inside Central Park during a single session was 9.5. A session was counted as a visit to the fair. That meant that with 600 million total hits, the fair was visited over fifty million times, a number that seems reasonable if five million unique individuals visited the fair.

The Idea and Site are great. I have Bookmarked the Park and will return often.

—**Gary Miller**
Underwood, IA, USA
garyone@ix.netcom.com

LEGEND

☐ Exhibited and Visited
■ Exhibited Only
■ Visited Only
○ Central Park Site
▬ High-Speed Link
▬ 2 mbps or less

People from 130 countries visisted the fair, and people from 80
countries and regions opened pavilions.

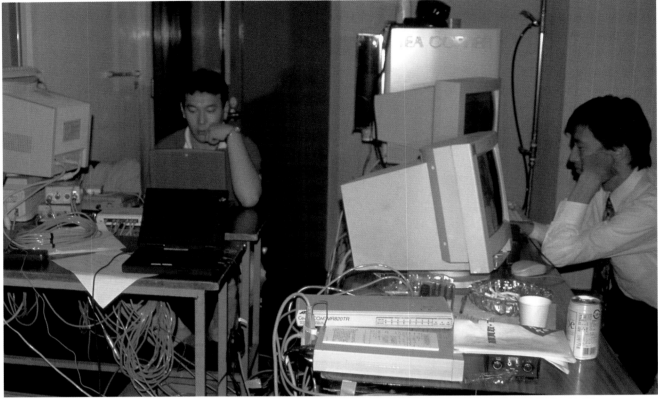

Photo/Doors Magazine

Tucked backstage at a concern, a member of the Network Operating Team tries to determine why the network is behaving like a notwork.

Hi, I just come across this Guestbook. I have enjoyed walking around this park.

—**Yuichi Iwamoto**
Yokohama, Japan
FWGD0738@mb.infoweb.or.jp

Public Parks for the Global Village

World's fairs leave us with memories and history, but sometimes there is a more tangible legacy. Like the Olympics, the infrastructure built for such a massive number of visitors is often converted into public facilities for the permanent residents of the city. Some fairs leave us only their ancient ruins, as in the eerie empty buildings of Flushing Meadows, home of the 1964 New York World's Fair. Sometimes, the grounds of a world's fair are enduring monuments, icons like the Eiffel Tower in Paris.

Some, like the Crystal Palace Exposition, leave us their space. After the 1859 show, the Crystal Palace itself was moved to another location, where it ultimately burned. The original grounds, however, were dedicated in perpetuity for public uses. Among the tenants of the site is Imperial College, which served as the Central Park site for England.

There is still an official commission left from the 1859 exposition, a commission that will probably live as long as the perpetual trust it administers. This obscure body is housed on a dusty upper floor of Imperial College. In addition to its primary business of issuing an annual report, it maintains the archives from the Crystal Palace. We approached the commission with the idea of building a virtual reality fly-through of the Crystal Palace, based on archival material, but the idea was not taken to kindly. As custodians of the granddaddy of all world fairs, it somehow seemed trivial to them for a few engineers from computer science to claim to be mounting an event that deemed itself in the same class as this historic one.

Whether a public facility will prove useful is often hard to tell, but we were determined that this world's fair would leave behind at least one permanent piece of infrastructure. The Internet Railroad was a temporary measure, an attempt to convince the world that fast, dedicated, international lines make sense as regional backbones. It succeeded very well in that respect, helping spur the growth of the network just as the big lighting demonstrations at the end of the last century were an essential tool in the growth of the electric utilities.

Central Park, though, is meant to last. After housing the fair for a year, the park shrunk on New Year's Day, losing a few of the mirroring servers. The key machines in Tokyo and Amsterdam remained in place, as did several of the mirror servers in locations such as Australia and Germany. A Public Park Commission was formed and charged with coming up with a long-term plan to keep the park alive as a global piece of infrastructure, and particularly as a testbed for global deployment of innovative new systems such as the Squid caches.

The goal of many Internet protocols is to construct a service that is distributed and robust. A news feed, or a mail handler, or a domain name system must be able to adapt to large numbers of users and frequent failures. With Central Park, we designed the system in a similar manner. Each part of the park is run by a group that volunteers to perform local work and to cooperate as part of a global community of Central Park servers. The details of how the park are run can be worked out, but the sense of community is the first requirement, the threshold condition.

One of the systems in Central Park did not survive, however. The Internet Multicasting Service was founded in April 1993 and survived hand-to-mouth for three years. Huge donations of servers and bandwidth were coupled with a nonstop race to bring in corporate sponsors who would make cash contributions to help us pay the bills. Like any other small nonprofit group, money was always an issue and the world's fair pretty much broke the bank.

On April 1, 1996, the Internet Multicasting Service went off the air. We made over $2 million in donations of equipment from vendors such as Sun and IBM to different world's fair sites, and to special events such as the Brain Opera. We transferred administrative responsibility for the fair to Secretary-General Rob Blokzijl, who built up a true international secretariat. Philippe Tabaux went off to the international secretariat, and the rest of us dispersed into our former lives of freelance work.

Brilliant initiative, easy to use interface, perfect balance of graphics and speed for low-band-users, staggering graphics and sounds exhibits on the high-band-end. I wonder what you will leave as a reminder, what the first CyberEiffel will look like to be as impressive to users now as to users in 20 years.

—Kees de Vos
Groningen, Netherlands
cwadevos@pi.net

Photo/Doors Magazine

The main Tokyo Network Operating Center.

*time has come let's play
those network mind game
together!*

—Toyofuku Tsuyoshi
Tokyo, Japan
rf6t-tyfk@asahi-net.or.jp

Since the Internet Multicasting Service was pretty much a virtual corporation, not much changed. People like Marty Lucas, Brad Burdick, and Becky Pranger scouted around for various contract jobs, but all managed to stay involved in the fair. Nicholas Negroponte offered me a post at the MIT Media Lab to give me an institutional home to work out of so I could stay involved in the fair. By donating our computers to other sites, we provided an infusion of equipment to the rest of Central Park. This infusion meant that many of the other Central Park sites had the equipment they needed to convince their managers to let them keep working on the project.

The Internet Multicasting Service set out to build a radio station. Marty Lucas and I created the Geek of the Week program with two people and a borrowed workstation. The radio station kept morphing, into Santa Claus, into the face of the SEC and the patent office, and finally into a world's fair. At the end, all that was left was a park.

I GOT THE IMPRESSION OF A MAN WHO HAD
ENTERED THIS SECRET WORLD BY THE BACK
DOOR, WHO HAD HAD THE VISION OF A
MENTAL CONSTRUCTION MORE MARVELLOUS
AND INTRICATE THAN ANYTHING ON EARTH,
A CONSTRUCTION TO MAKE MAN'S MATERIAL
ACHIEVEMENTS SEEM LIKE SO MUCH DROSS—
YET WHICH SOMEHOW EVADED DESCRIPTION.

BRUCE CHATWIN
THE SONGLINES

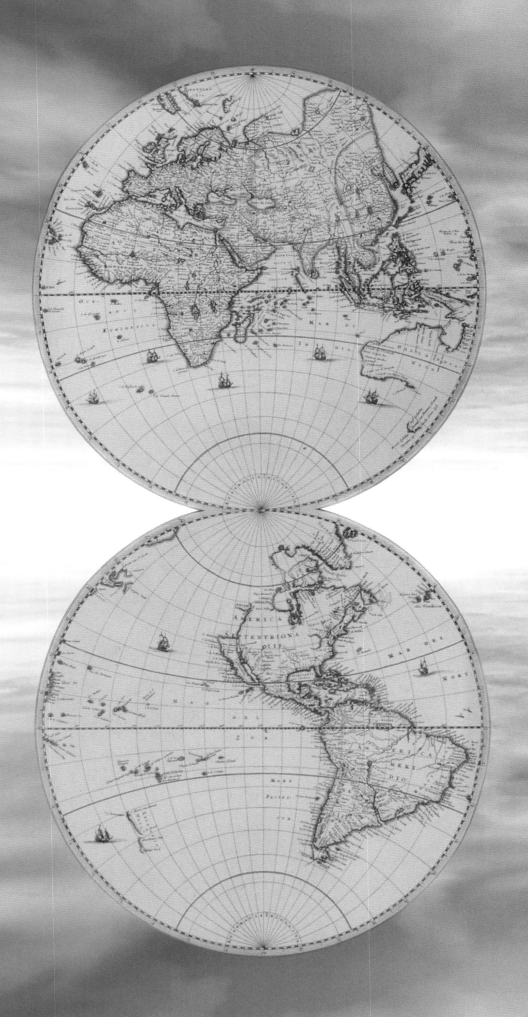

Nowhere and Everywhere

U. S. NAVAL EXHIBIT.   BATTLE SHIP "ILLINOIS."

OFFICIAL SOUVENIR POSTAL
WORLD'S COLUMBIAN
EXPOSITION.

1893 WORLD'S COLUMBIAN EXPOSITION

The Americas

11

I first met Marty Lucas in 1977 when, as a freshman at Indiana University, I opened my dormitory room window and heard the strains of a Neil Young song wafting by on the wind. It was a nice day and my academic responsibilities at the university didn't seem very pressing, so I went in search of the music. I walked through the endless hall of the big housing complex, following the music as it got stronger, stopping periodically to catch the direction at a hallway window.

At the end of the last building in the quadrangle, there was a terrace where five people had set up amplifiers, guitars, microphones, and drums, and were playing through the folk-rock anthems of the day. I became firm friends with all the players. One went on to do sound for bands like the Grateful Dead, another is a professional blues singer in Chicago, a third teaches first-grade children in the south.

Marty was studying the archeology of North America, with special emphasis on Indian sites. He worked his way through school doing archeological reconnaissance, searching for potential dig sites. This not considerable income was supplemented by odd jobs such as playing in punk rock bands, or working as a contract surveyor. He went on to law school at Indiana University, then moved back to the north of Indiana to North Judson, where his family farm was located. There, he practiced law, continued his music, and supervised contractors on the land who grew crops such as mint. North Judson, as is well known, is the mint capital of Indiana and hosts an annual Mint Festival.

Marty and I had stayed in touch, and when in early 1993 I started work on Geek of the Week, I called him up and asked him if he could compose a theme for this radio program. After a few weeks, he sent me a two-minute piece, put together on his home recording system of a few keyboards, synthesizers, and tape recorders.

Marty quickly got sucked deeper into the project. I had bought a spiffy new DAT recorder and a few microphones, and went out to California to interview Dr. Marshall T. Rose, one of the most prolific contributors to the Internet. On the way back, I stopped in Chicago, where Tad Robinson, our friend the blues singer, was persuaded to boom phrases like "this is Internet Talk Radio, flame

Congratulations to the Internet Multicasting Service on the announcement of the Internet 1996 World Exposition—the first global fair of its kind for the Information Age. Just as world's fairs in earlier days popularized the electric light, the telephone, and other technologies that dramatically reshaped our lives, this Exposition will help people everywhere to realize the promise of the future.

—President Bill Clinton
The United States

Marty Lucas plays piano on a dormitory roof in 1977. On the mike is Tad Robinson, a noted blues singer who sang lead vocals on "Distances," the fair's theme song.

183

of the Internet" into my microphone. These corny phrases would serve as our audio logos for the next two years.

I drove down to North Judson, and we tore apart Marty's studio trying to put together a radio program. By the time we were done, the second floor of his house was a sea of cables, and keyboards perched precariously on top of speakers were threatening to spill over onto a forest of microphone stands. I brought the tape back to my house near Washington, DC, and somehow managed to get the digital audio tape digitized and transformed into the only audio format that the network then supported.

For the next three years, the Big Eastern Studios in North Judson expanded at the same rate as corporate headquarters in Washington. Marty flew out to Washington numerous times to help set up our sound studios, or go through marathon three-day sessions of producing ten 30-minute radio programs so I'd have a stack of Geek of the Weeks we could queue up for the weekly release.

The real creative audio production though, was all done at Big Eastern. Marty worked with his partner, Corinne Becknell, a talented singer who had been in rock-and-roll bands since the age of 15 and was the minister of music of her local Methodist church. Most of the original work that was done for the United States pavilions in the world's fair was done by this team of two, who expanded their original audio expertise into wide-ranging knowledge of how to produce for the World Wide Web.

Marty's family farm is several hundred acres, but most of it is not farmed. For years, he has been turning this stretch of land back over to native plants of the Eastern prairie. The ecosystem of the area near Lake Michigan is rich, with sand dunes, wetlands, and prairies all mixing together. The Lucas Farm is one of the largest private prairie restorations in the American Midwest, and restoring the native vegetation has made Marty an expert on the local plants, birds, and mammals. Keeping poachers off the land has made him an expert on the bigger mammals as well.

Being in a small town, Marty's law practice had the usual share of divorces and other family disputes. For a while, he served as the town attorney. Whenever possible, however, Marty pursues what he calls the Creek Wars, representing people in Indiana who are trying to prevent the destruction of native wildlife habitats.

One of his more famous cases, which was brought all the way up the appellate chain, involved a greenhouse owner in Northern Indiana. A local gang of beavers had built a dam on a creek running through the greenhouse property, creating a nice little lake and, more important, invigorating the surrounding wetlands with a new infusion of plants and wildlife. However, the dam the beavers built also affected a few farmers downstream, who wanted the dam

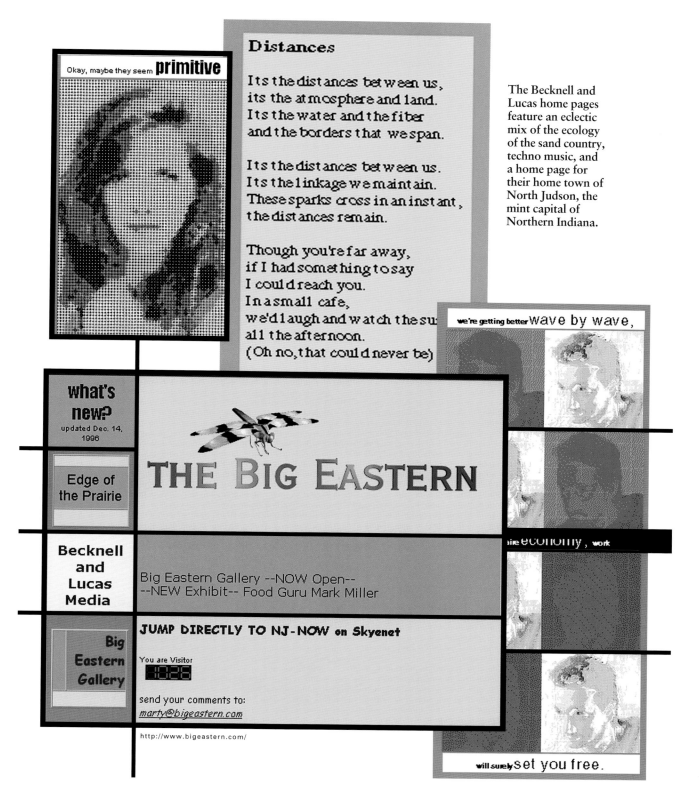

Okay, maybe they seem **primitive**

Distances

Its the distances between us,
its the atmosphere and land.
Its the water and the fiber
and the borders that we span.

Its the distances between us.
Its the linkage we maintain.
These sparks cross in an instant,
the distances remain.

Though you're far away,
if I had something to say
I could reach you.
In a small cafe,
we'd laugh and watch the su...
all the afternoon.
(Oh no, that could never be)

The Becknell and Lucas home pages feature an eclectic mix of the ecology of the sand country, techno music, and a home page for their home town of North Judson, the mint capital of Northern Indiana.

we're getting better **wave by wave,**

what's new?
updated Dec. 14, 1996

Edge of the Prairie

Becknell and Lucas Media

Big Eastern Gallery

THE BIG EASTERN

Big Eastern Gallery --NOW Open--
--NEW Exhibit-- Food Guru Mark Miller

JUMP DIRECTLY TO NJ-NOW on Skyenet

You are Visitor
1028

send your comments to:
marty@bigeastern.com

http://www.bigeastern.com/

...re economy, work

will surely **set you free.**

185

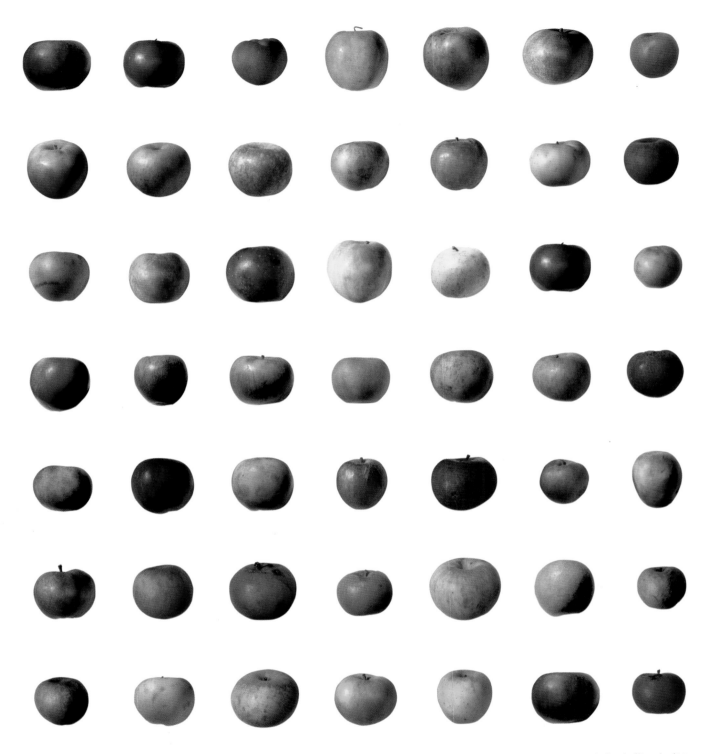

The Tree-Mendous Fruit site features
50 heirloom varieties of apples.

destroyed so they could drain the land and farm it. The greenhouse owner won the suit when Marty argued in court that it was impossible to enjoin a beaver from building a dam.

The web sites that the team of Becknell and Lucas built for the world's fair reflected these diverse interests. For the Americas, they concentrated on their own backyard and built sites that showed off the local sand country. They also scoured the region for interesting people. In Michigan, they went to Tree-Mendus Fruit, an organic apple farm. The owners of the farm had started cultivating antique apple varieties that were no longer widely farmed, replaced by the ubiquitous generic apples we see today in the supermarkets. They interviewed the owners of Tree-Mendus Fruit, took pictures of the different kinds of apples, and placed these on the network as a pavilion.

Radio on the Internet

In addition to serving as the fair headquarters in the heartland, the Becknell and Lucas studios were kept busy as the audio processing facility for the Internet Multicasting Service. They designed digital filters specifically for the audio formats in use on the network, produced a large number of the programs that came in on tape, and did a variety of original productions such as the "Ballad of Ned Ludd," a historical examination of the Luddites. They also took audio interviews and performances that were coming back from fair sites around the world and turned them into the Expo Radio program, one of the most popular pavilions in the world's fair.

In Washington, the data were staged on the Internet Multicasting Service computers, where they became the basis for much of the 12 gigabytes of audio files that we placed in the fair as part of the Future of Media Pavilion. Harper Audio contributed archival recordings from the famous Caedmon collection. This was a tremendous trove of information, featuring poets and writers reading their own work. In return for publicity for their tape sales, we got to put T.S. Eliot reading "The Waste Land," Robert Frost reading "The Road Not Taken," and dozens of other famous authors on the Internet.

Before we added a production studio on Capitol Hill, the main machine room for the Internet Multicasting Service was conveniently located in the National Press Building. In return for putting the club on line, we got the rights to broadcast all of the National Press Club Luncheons. At first, this consisted of running upstairs several times a week and watching a DAT tape recorder we put up in one of the control rooms. The tape would be rushed back downstairs, copied onto a hard disk, then compressed into Internet audio formats.

That quickly changed, however. When we moved into our studios in the building, MFS had agreed to give us a free 10-million-bit-per-second fiber circuit

Hello! I'm a girl, 19 years old. I like an apple. There are very nice apples in USA. In japan, I eat apples in Fall every year. I want eat American apples. Good-bye!

—Natsuko Yaita
Tokyo, Japan
96031090@gakushuin.ac.jp

Just a note of profound thanks for having the voice of Ernest Hemingway on the net. To hear any recordings of Hemingway has been a life long dream. I am a writer. I have always considered Hemingway a great teacher as well as writer. Certainly one of the two or three great writers of this century. Thank you. This is a real service.

—Kevin Russell
KeRus@prodigy.net

INTERNET MULTICASTING SERVICE

In four years of operation, the Internet Multicasting Service scoured the world to bring the real world into cyberspace. A few of the offerings on the world's first cyberstation included luncheons from the National Press Club, lectures by jazz authority Billy Taylor at the Kennedy Center, and chef Mark Miller from the Red Sage Restaurant.

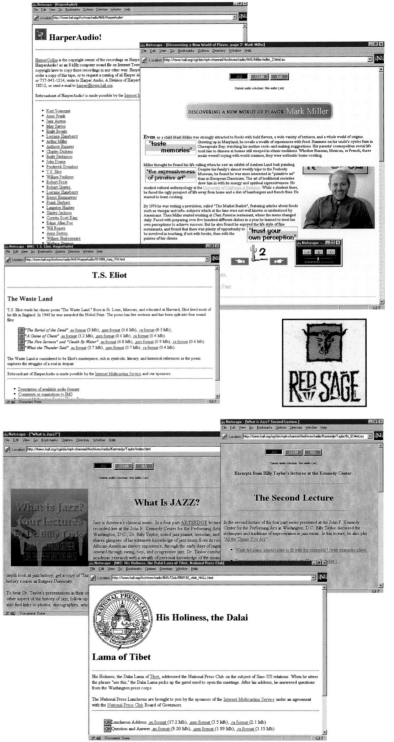

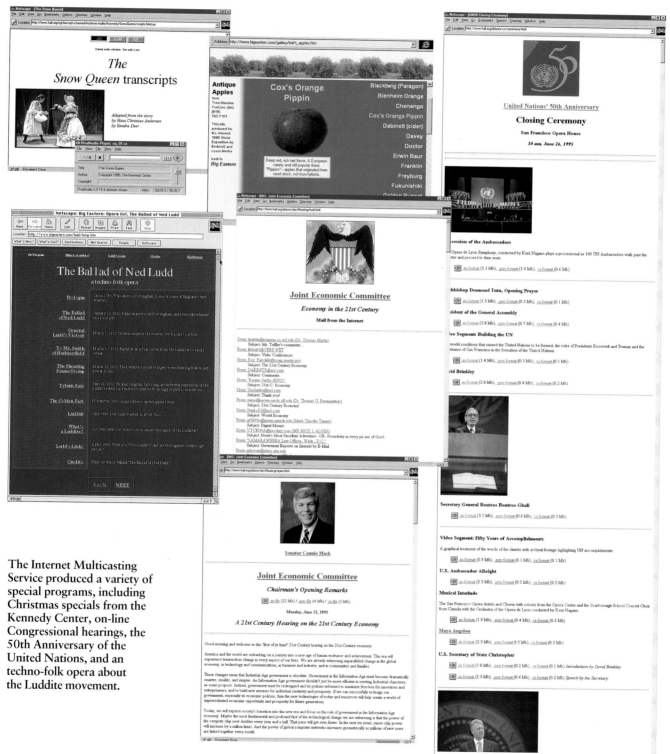

The Internet Multicasting Service produced a variety of special programs, including Christmas specials from the Kennedy Center, on-line Congressional hearings, the 50th Anniversary of the United Nations, and an techno-folk opera about the Luddite movement.

out to UUNET, our service provider on the Internet. However, we had to pay to get the fiber optics from the basement of the building to our 11th-floor office. While the people were in the building dragging fiber through elevator shafts, we asked them if they would mind continuing their run all the way up to the 13th floor, giving us fiber between the Press Club and our office. Just to be safe, we asked for two fiber runs.

The first set of fiber was used for a special kind of device called a *fiber audio modem*, which simply sends sound over the cable. The side in the club was connected straight to the house sound system; the side in our studio was connected to a mixing board and then routed over to the various computers in the office. This allowed us to record the speeches to a digital audio tape while simultaneously recording a lower-quality version on a computer disk for immediate availability.

Soon, the system got even more sophisticated, as the second fiber optic line was connected to our internal computer network and a small workstation was put up into the club and connected to the house sound system. This computer had silence suppression turned on, so nothing happened when the club was empty. When the house sound system would activate, however, as in the case of a luncheon speech, our system would start transmitting the data down to our computers on the 11th floor.

One copy of the audio stream was routed out live into the Internet. Another copy was processed and transformed into the three audio formats that we supported. An html page would then be created and linked into the National Press Club web site, letting people know that a new luncheon was available. If we had wanted to be fancy, we would have prestaged photographs of the speakers and a biography, but our small staff was usually running as flat out as a lizard, and it sometimes took a few days to go back in and change the automatically created file into one that was a bit more informative.

Other radio projects weren't really radio but were more like intensive audio programming specifically for the Internet. In conjunction with the Kennedy Center for the Performing Arts, we descended upon some of their lecture series in arts education. Philippe Tabaux, Luther Brown, and Marty Lucas set up microphones and took photos with both conventional and digital cameras. All that information was then brought back to the studios and turned into an on-line version of the lectures.

One of the most impressive series of lectures was by Dr. Billy Taylor, a noted jazz musician and educator. Putting lectures like this on line could be a trivial exercise, a long RealAudio file that lets you listen to the lecture, a few photographs of the speaker, and a bio. The producers were intent, however, on seeing if there was some way to go beyond simply projecting the live event onto the network in a straightforward manner. The audio was brought back to the

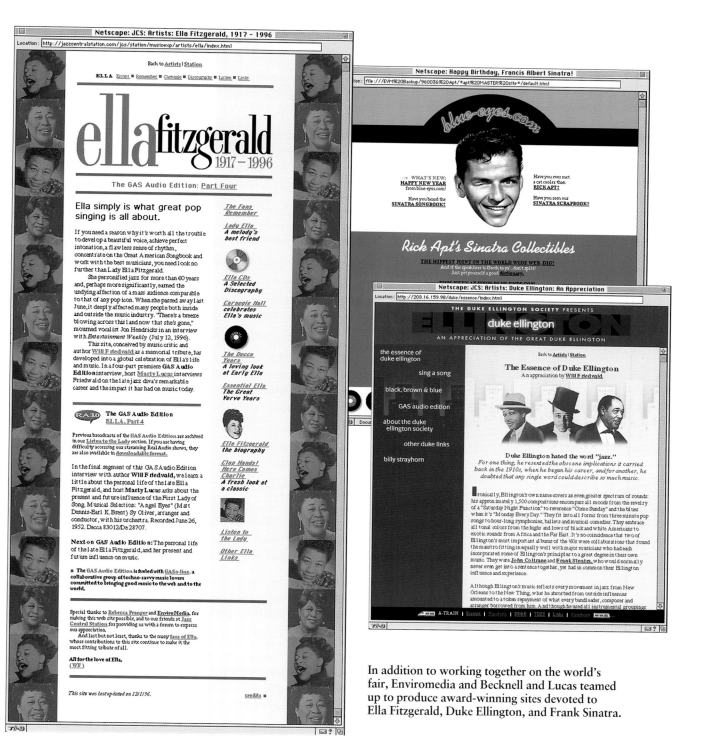

In addition to working together on the world's fair, Enviromedia and Becknell and Lucas teamed up to produce award-winning sites devoted to Ella Fitzgerald, Duke Ellington, and Frank Sinatra.

Congratulations! Your website really deserved the Cool Site of the Day. I hope we get more Expo's on line so we could participate in cyberspace, it's a lot cheaper than going to the actual place.

—John Alvin Lo
Dagupan, Philippines
jal_dag@mozcom.com

Becky Pranger

Larry Pranger

Becknell and Lucas studios and was studied carefully, then broken up into logical segments. Billy Taylor spoke in a very clear, well-organized manner and his lectures covered a wide territory.

By carefully segmenting the audio, and then indexing the material, several different paths into the material became available. One path was directly into the lectures, listening in the chronological order in which Dr. Taylor presented the original material. Another path was by topic, letting the listener hear everything that Dr. Taylor had to say about New Orleans jazz or bebop. The third path let the listener dive straight into a particular artist and hear what Dr. Taylor had to say about the artist and visit any other relevant links on that musician that we were able to dig up from search engines on the network.

Variations on this treatment of material worked very well in many other programs we put on the network. At the Kennedy Center, a performance of *The Snow Queen* was transformed by Philippe Tabaux and the staff of the ArtsEdge program. Mark Miller, a famous chef and the owner of the Red Sage Restaurant, was also interviewed and his material broken up into audio segments and then folded into a story that combined text, photos, and audio. While our association with groups like the Kennedy Center and the National Press Club garnered us prestige and quality content, the Red Sage association had the additional benefit of an occasional free dinner.

As the work at Internet Multicasting Service was winding down, the team of Becknell and Lucas continued its work on the Internet. They teamed up on several projects with another two-person team, Becky and Larry Pranger of Enviromedia, the fair's graphic designers. Together, they put sites on the network devoted to Ella Fitzgerald and Frank Sinatra. Both sites won the prestigious "Original Cool Site of the Day" award on the net. Combined with the award for the world's fair, that gave the two teams three Cool Site of the Day awards in one year, making them the Meryl Streep of the digital media.

The formal bureaucracy in charge of the United States participation in this world's fair was certainly a bit lacking. During the organizational period, the United States committee for the world's fair was minimal. A few corporate engineers worked on their projects, a few artists and web designers built pavilions. Although we had no huge committees and little luck with massive fundraising, participation from the United States started to flow once the fair was open. This was our intention.

By building a few sample pavilions, we hoped that our fair would change over the course of the year, as people saw what others were building and strove to add their own contributions. Hundreds of registrations were received during the course of the year and were sorted out by the International Secretariat into various categories, some put into the regional area of the United States, and others into the dozens of categories of thematic pavilions.

South America and Canada

South America has never been an Internet powerhouse because of the extremely high prices that the telephone company monopolies charged for international lines. Delegations from different countries' academic networks attend meetings such as the Internet Society's INET conferences, and there is a growing commercial business in countries such as Argentina and Colombia, but development was certainly not catching on as quickly as in some of the growth areas of the network such as Southeast Asia or Eastern Europe.

There were some people who saw the fair on the network and scrambled to put pavilions together to represent their country. In Colombia, for example, a college student named Jorge Lopez inquired why his country wasn't represented. He wrote "I find the Fair most interesting and challenging. On a personal basis I would like to participate in the Internet Exhibition by promoting the Exhibition among Spanish people, specially Colombians." We wrote back and told him that we'd love to have him participate and build a Colombian pavilion.

In Brazil, the fair took a strange progression, via the route of high energy physics. Physics and the Internet have always been intertwined, and Dr. Rob Blokzijl, our secretary-general for the fair, worked at the Dutch Institute of High Energy Physics. By coincidence, Rio de Janeiro had been selected as the location of the annual conference of Computing in High Energy Physics (CHEP), and Rob somehow arranged for me to keynote the conference to speak about the world's fair.

It seemed worth spending the money to fly down to Rio, and the local conference organizers promised me meetings with appropriate government officials to try and spark a world's fair effort in that country. I had to be in Almaty, Kazakhstan, only three days after the Rio conference, but after long hours on hold with the airlines, I had an itinerary that would let me fly to Rio, then direct from Rio to Almaty. Direct is one of those airline terms of art, and in this case it meant flying from Rio to Memphis to Washington to Zurich to Vienna and then on to Almaty, all in a space of about 48 hours.

The conference organizers were very gracious, but only one meeting was set up with some officials of the state government of Rio de Janeiro, along with Dr. Luiz Felipe de Moraes, a local computer science professor active in local NII politics. The meeting went well, and we discussed the way that groups in Asia and Europe were going about organizing themselves to gain local support for the fair. A month or so later, I received a vague yet formal letter indicating that some participation was being actively considered from an official who bore the grand title of the secretary of state for science and technology for the state government of Rio de Janeiro.

I am pleased to offer my congratulations to the Canadian Committee, 1996 World Internet Exposition for its efforts to create a Canadian presence for this international cyberspace showcase.

—**Prime Minister
Jean Chrétien**
Canada

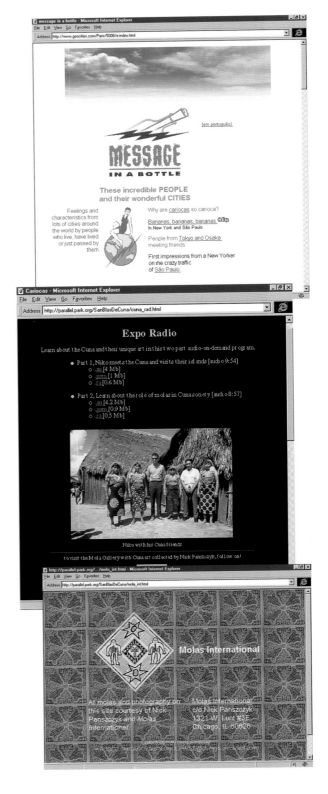

Entries from South America featured Indians in
Ecuador, a magazine from Brazil, and a site devoted
to the molas of San Blas de Cuna.

The fair started and everybody scrambled to build pavilions. Nothing had happened down in Rio, so we left Brazil blank until some email came in from a few people who wanted to put their pages up on the Internet. Needless to say, we quickly registered them as part of the Brazil pavilion.

In June 1996, the fair secretariat received mail from Dr. Luiz Felipe de Moraes. Their committee had met a few times and felt that it was time to start work. They had not built a web site, but were prepared to put one page up on the network that indicated the types of things that were going to happen. However, there was one catch. They had noticed that we already had participation from Brazil.

The good doctor had a problem with that. He stressed in repeated and increasingly strident mail messages that he was "talking about an official participation." Official meant that the other Brazil sites must be taken off of the web and he would "take charge officially." The rule that anybody can participate was our cardinal principle, and we stood our ground. The situation turned nasty and he threatened retaliation via the network and legal channels. The situation finally calmed down after we got scared by the technical threats and installed filters to block traffic from his sites, making him effectively disappear from our view of the Internet.

The Brazil pavilion ended up being quite beautiful, most notably with a site called Message in a Bottle that won a gold medal. Message in a Bottle is a magazine of sorts on the Internet, created as a hobby by four collaborators in Brazil and, as the site says, "Tadashi Naganawa, who writes to us from Tokyo and we will try to find out who he is." The site features essays and photographs on a wide range of topics, from articles about bananas to the story of traffic in São Paulo. Photographs from Brazil sit next to artwork and stories.

Message in a Bottle was a small production by a few people who wanted to create something new. Most of the sites in South America, and indeed in the fair, were also in that category. The large committees invariably failed to get enough momentum to get started, but individual efforts often had the focus and the drive to go from an idea to a finished product.

One such site featured the San Blas de Cuna Islands, a set of small islands off the coast of Panama and was, we presumed, the first time the territory had a formal representation in a world's fair. The islands are the home of the Cuna, a traditional society of indigenous people. Most of these tropical islands are very small and many are surrounded by coral reefs. The islands are part of Panama, but are primarily administered by the Cuna tribe, who are famous for their intricate and symbolic layers of hand-stiched cloth known as *molas*. The Cuna women originally tattooed intricate patterns on their bodies, but when the missionaries came in, the art was transferred to cloth and formed the basis for the blouses worn by the women of this matriarchal society.

Congrats, Guys!! This is sweeeeet! I already put it in my Bookmarks!! What about you, uh? Hey, I'd like to exchange Information about anything, however, mainly about Travelling. It's the best thing we can do during our Life-Time, isn't it?! So, please, e-mail me anytime! My house has a Guest-room ... I'm not kidding, you know! We Brazilians like to meet other people from all over our Big House, The World!! Talk to you's ... !

—Christian Schneider
Salvador, Bahia, Brazil
schneidr@svn.com.br

Es muy placentero visitar esta exposición, Me ha gustado mucho los topicos que aquí se tratan, Espero que visiten ECUADOR mi país pronto. Saludos desde ECUADOR.

—Jaime Gallardo Daste
Quito, Pichincha, Ecuador
jgallard@repycom.com.ec

I'm a student from Ecuador and I think this page is awesome!!!

—Jose Coronel
Oklahoma, OK, USA
jcoronel@frodo.okcu.edu

To produce a pavilion for the San Blas de Cuna Islands, the Internet Multicasting Service worked with Nick Panszczyk, a Chicago resident and collector of molas. He photographed the molas in his collection, and sent Marty Lucas a photo-CD full of photographs. James Nathan Post, a writer, produced a script for Nick, which was read by a professional announcer, and were combined by Becknell and Lucas with sound effects and other material into Expo Radio shows and a national pavilion for the San Blas de Cuna Islands.

Another set of pavilions came from Ecuador, where Deb Roy was dispatched with a camera and a digital audio tape recorder. He went first to the Galápagos Islands, where he joined a nature tour. Deb wrote back later that he felt embarrassed as he got on the boat for the tour as every person on board had elaborate photographic equipment with huge lenses and fancy film, while he was armed with his little Canon camera.

The highlight of his adventures in South America, though, came a little later as he visited Otavaleño weavers in the highlands of Ecuador. These weavers work at a treadle loom, producing a woolen rug of rich grays, creamy whites, and rust-reds. The Otavaleño weaving tradition stretches unbroken from before the Inca armies marched into their Andean mountain valley homeland in 1455.

The Incas introduced the llama, and llama wool was soon widely adopted by Otavaleño weavers along with the cotton upon which they had traditionally relied. Although the Incas never completely conquered the Otavaleños prior to being themselves conquered by the Spaniards, their language, Quechua, was adopted as the native tongue.

About a century later the Spanish took control of the Otavalo region and introduced the treadle loom, as well as sheep's wool. As the cash economy supplanted their traditional self-sufficiency, the weaving industry became central to the region and helped the Otavaleños retain some degree of autonomy. However, in the nineteenth century the industrial revolution allowed the mass production of cheap cloth, and the Otavaleño weaving industry was severely threatened. But rather than disappear, the Otavaleño weavers returned to their roots and today their art thrives.

Deb taped interviews with weavers in English and Quechua, but struck gold when he was invited to a *piña*. This is a place where people go to listen to folk music, dance, eat, and drink beer. It is especially popular with tourists who are interested in hearing Andean folk music. Deb Roy recorded the music with a portable DAT tape recorder, along with the sounds of the high-altitude party. Later, he interviewed a Swiss tourist who was an expert on Andean music. All this information was mixed by Becknell and Lucas into an impressive set of Expo Radio programs.

The effort in Canada was the result of insistent prodding by Wade Hong, a physicist at Carleton University in Ottawa. He saw my speech in Brazil, and

These beautiful molas formed the centerpiece
of the pavilion from San Blas de Cuna.

Deb K. Roy traveled throughout Ecuador to build pavilions featuring the Galápagos Islands and the Otavaleño weavers.

Photos/Deb K. Roy

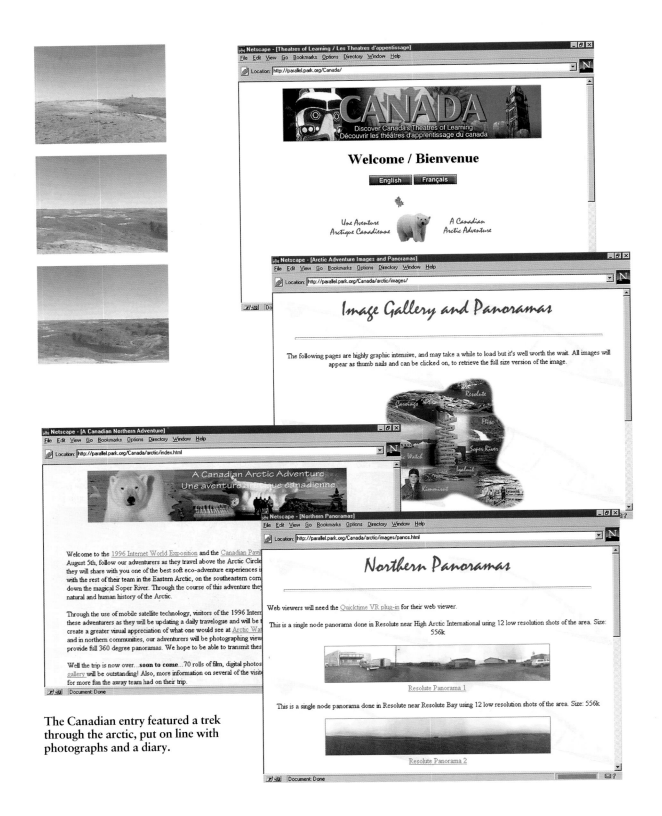

The Canadian entry featured a trek through the arctic, put on line with photographs and a diary.

promptly went home to try and organize participation for his country. The first efforts attempted to form a broad coalition of industry and government groups, but the chase for a large, formal committee got bogged down as various groups tried to control the official committee.

After several months, Wade finally gave up on the government bureaucrats, and found a corporate sponsor, Corel, a producer of graphics software. Corel agreed to give 200 copies of its software to the world's fair, which meant we could get high-end graphics software distributed around the world to pavilion makers. They also agreed to help Wade out in the graphic design of his site.

The main pavilion entry from Canada was The Great Arctic Adventure, a site that detailed a journey Wade Hong and others took up into the Canadian Arctic. As they trekked through the arctic regions, the team kept a diary and shot extensive digital photographs, materials they used to build their world's fair pavilion. After enough letters came in from other heads of state, the government groups involved in the fair managed to procure a letter of support from the Canadian prime minister, but that was as far as the government's participation went.

The last big entry from Canada was easy. The Internet Society was holding its annual INET conference in Montreal during 1996. Since officials of the Internet Society had been very supportive of the fair, we simply linked over to their web site and let them do all the work.

Canada knows how to design and produce the best World's Fairs and this one is right up there.

—Janice Kelly
Ottawa, Canada
Janice@mediabox.com

Porte Principale

EXPOSITION UNIVERSELLE DE PARIS 1900

Chocolat-Cacao
WAUTERS. Frères

1900 PARIS UNIVERSAL EXPOSITION

Europe, Africa, and the Middle East 12

I arrived in Amsterdam in the middle of 1995 to work with Rob Blokzijl, who was coordinating all of Europe for the world's fair. From my downtown hotel, I took the tram out to the complex of research institutes on the eastern part of town, right next to the old soccer stadium. The Dutch National Institute of Nuclear and High Energy Physics (NIKHEF) sits across a canal from one of the experimental farms run by the University of Amsterdam, and next to the national mathematics institute.

"Don't take off your coat," Rob said. "We're going to the other side of Holland to visit some people."

One hour later, we arrived at the headquarters of the Royal Dutch Cattle Syndicate, a nonprofit research foundation devoted to everything bovine. Rob had set up an appointment with the director to inquire if the syndicate would like to participate in the upcoming world's fair. We explained the concept of a world's fair on the Internet. Coffee was served. We chitchatted a bit more until the Royal Cow Foundation official finally got to the point. "What do you want from us?" he asked.

Rob had something very specific in mind. He wanted a mathematical model of a cow and any other background information they could provide on how cows grow. After some followup meetings, a set of cow groups in the Netherlands became official sponsors of the world's fair. In return, Rob got his cow data.

The project was then handed over to Herman van Dompseler of the international secretariat with instructions to create a cow simulator on the Internet. Herman drafted Thamon van Blokland, one of the dozens of freelance web builders who work out of Amsterdam and had volunteered to work on the fair. Together, they set about putting a cow on the Internet in a truly meaningful and interactive fashion.

The goal was to let people on the network build a cow from scratch, learning about breeding, the care and feeding of a cow, and the economics of running a small dairy farm. The mathematical model from the Royal Cow Foundation was simplified, then combined with information from champion breeding cows in the Netherlands to create a realistic gene pool.

The Cow Simulator was an instant hit, particularly with children. The system was set up as a competition, with real prizes of Dutch cheese awarded to the young farmer with the best record. These official expo cheeses were

For the last 38 days I have been visiting this site and I find it amazing, if you go to the food building you can even milk a cow. I am impressed by it all, keep it up.

—**Hank Versteeg**
Kitchener, Canada
hverst@golden.net

Holy Cow!!

—**Bjørn I. Themsen**
Århus, Denmark

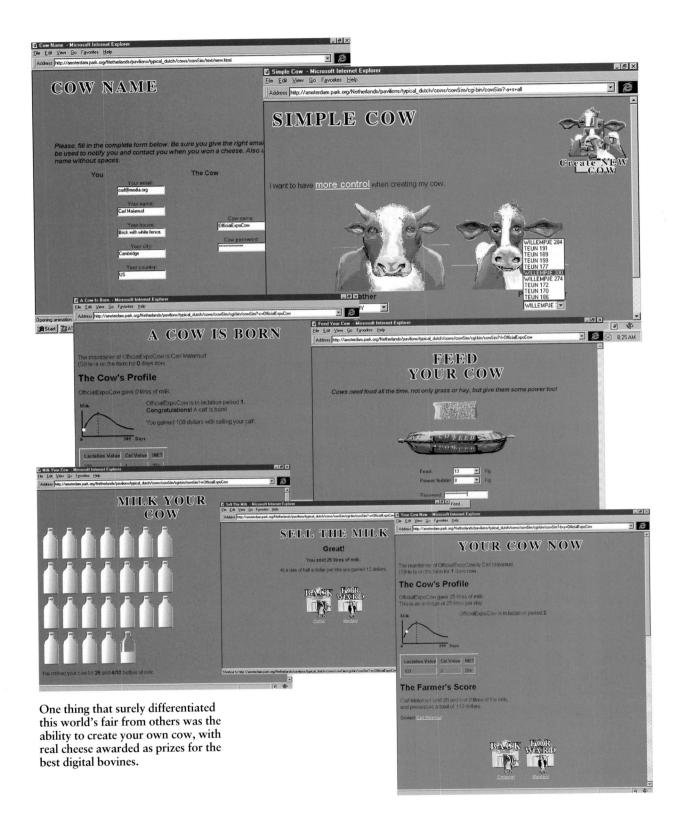

One thing that surely differentiated this world's fair from others was the ability to create your own cow, with real cheese awarded as prizes for the best digital bovines.

procured by Rob Blokzijl from the Dutch Cheese Board and were sent via express mail to anyplace in the world the winner happened to be. One young farmer even broke the bank, figuring out the parameters behind the cow simulator and then growing his herd at a maximum rate to win the cheese two weeks in a row, until he was put on the cheese blacklist and the program was changed to prevent further cow hacking.

The activity in the Netherlands was quite intense for the entire year. The first country in Europe to put up pavilions, the Dutch decided this was a project to embrace. Despite its fairly small population, the Netherlands had the third largest number of visitors to the fair, after the United States and Japan. In addition to the staff of five full-time people, the project received extensive support from the mayor of Amsterdam, the minister of economic affairs, and other government officials, unlike the committees in other European cities. Local industry also pitched in, with groups like Sun Microsystems Netherlands making large donations of equipment to support the local effort.

One of the prize-winning efforts from the Netherlands was the Rembrandt Pavilion. The starting point was the on-going work of the Rembrandt Research Project, which began its operations in 1968 with professors from the universities of Amsterdam and Utrecht and the Rijksmuseum, home of many of Rembrandt's paintings.

The project did an extensive analysis of the materials from Rembrandt's workshop, looking at panels, canvases, and the characteristics of the materials used to prepare a painting. They were able to identify characteristics of true Rembrandt paintings, characteristics that were used to spot fakes and paintings that had not been positively identified as the work of the master.

Many of the techniques used to analyze the paintings were quite high tech, and the researchers had given a talk to physicists about some of their work. Rob Blokzijl had attended the talks and pursued the researchers to convince them to come on the Internet. The world's fair team began taping lectures by the researchers, then processed that information into Multimedia Rembrandt, which allowed people on the Internet to listen to the lectures and see some of the characteristics of Rembrandt's work.

Over 70 other sites were submitted by people in the Netherlands, many of them focused on things outside the country. Numerous events, ranging from rock-and-roll concerts to the Uitmarkt theater season kept a steady stream of activities going throughout the year. What I found amazing was that building the Dutch Pavilion was basically a hobby for everybody involved. The international secretariat had its hands full simply keeping up with the stream of email and registrations from around the world and running the mirroring for Central Park, but they managed to keep several dozen volunteers active in their own country to build a pavilion.

I'm calling from a distant planet named URLBeterah. Humm ... I see that those annoying terrestrians are becoming a developed CyberWorld. URLGod help us! In a few years they will beat us and we will be eaten alive! I must stop this incredible Expo! :-) K. Selles. "The Great Netscaper" :-)

—Enrique Selles
Betera, Valencia, Spain
K.Selles@vlc.servicom.es

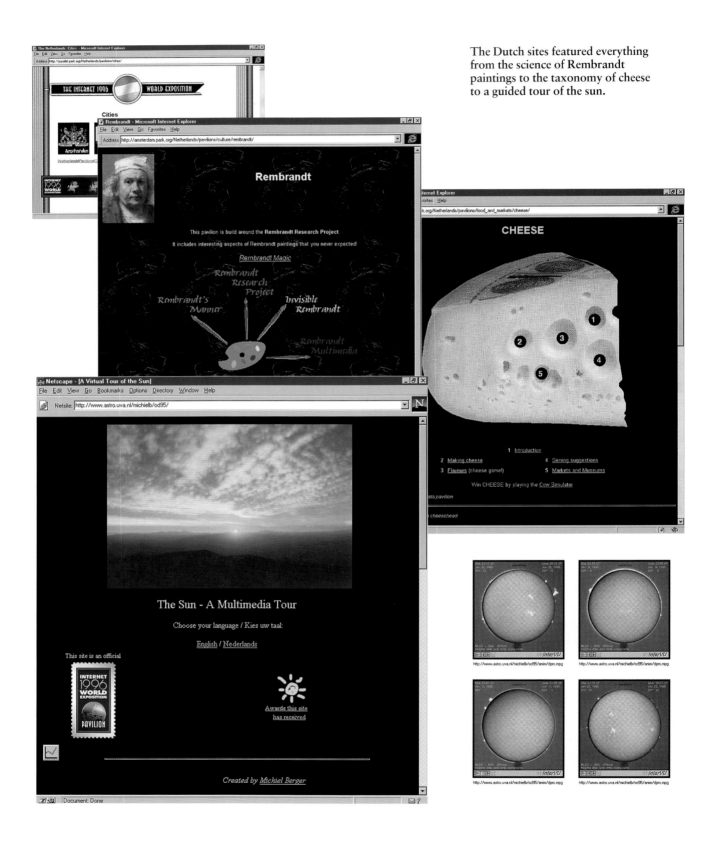

The Dutch sites featured everything from the science of Rembrandt paintings to the taxonomy of cheese to a guided tour of the sun.

The countries that we most expected to participate in such a fair, Germany, France, and England, were all very slow to get started. In England, we theorized that they were waiting for the French to do something. A formal letter of support was received from the minister of science and technology, in which he made it clear that his group would be coordinating activities in the kingdom, but nothing came of it. There were, however, three real islands of activity, all done by a few people in small organizations. World Radio Network continued its work of putting the voice of public radio on the Internet, the Real World Studios continued to put itself on line, and Imperial College continued to host a Central Park site for England.

Germany, though, was the real surprise. Germany is the site of the next "real" world's fair, Expo 2000 in Hanover, a Certified Class One world's fair. Expo 2000, a multibillion-dollar production, seemed like a natural partner for our world's fair for the information age. Rob Blokzijl went to Hanover and met with members of the board of Expo 2000, offering to host a web site for them, to make them an additional sponsor, and every other carrot in his bag. The meetings went well, memos were generated, but nothing happened.

By the middle of 1996 we had written off Germany, but there was activity going on that we hadn't seen. Dr. Hans Frese, a physicist at the German Institute of High Energy Physics (DESY) had been closely tracking the world's fair and methodically building up support inside his country. All of a sudden, he announced that the German pavilions were ready to join Central Park, and that they would host a Central Park site consisting of a large processor donated by Siemens and supported in part by Deutsche Telecom.

Pavilions started to spring up, and not just pavilions that were links to existing sites. The Central Park site got itself a staff of several people, and web designers in several locations started putting original sites on line. Most impressive, however, was that the funding for the site was not going to dry up at the end of 1996. The group had taken a while to get started, but they were in it for the long term. One of the results that we most wanted to see come out of the fair was that local groups would mobilize for it, then stay together afterward to continue their work, and this is what happened in Germany.

In France, there appeared to be some form of general strike by people who might have participated in the world's fair. Philippe Tabaux, a French citizen and a long-time employee of the Internet Multicasting Service, made numerous trips back to France, but managed to walk out with little more than a formal letter of support from the minister of telecommunications.

I must admit that Philippe's job was made a bit tougher by the fact that the Internet Multicasting Service had helped to organize the fair. In 1994, one of the places we put on line was the French embassy in Washington, the first embassy in the world to have a presence on the web. The site was, at least in

Thank you for a great work you have made so beautiful net. I have heard it about from one of ours russian computers newspapers. I like it well. I have interesting in punk music, write to me !

—**Andrew Rovenski**
Moscow, Russia
andy@kitty.sumgf.mipt.ru

In Germany, the Crown Jewels pavilion featured the history of this important collection, while in Spain dozens of pavilions were sparked by intense coverage in the magazine *Net Conexión*, edited by Josep Saldaña.

our opinion, quite progressive for the time. Maps of France directed people to the attractions of the different regions, you could download French language lessons from Radio France International, and we even put a version of the "Marseillaise" on line, triggered when people clicked the French flag.

Unfortunately, the embassy took our gift of web work very much for granted. They requested frequent changes and additions, but never took over the site. Our goal in putting groups like the embassy on line was not to put ourselves in the web design business but to have them put themselves on the Internet in a meaningful way. We donated our time and computers to them because we hoped that they would internalize the site, perhaps even spurring other embassies to get on the web.

The site languished, though it was quite popular with users. I grew more uncomfortable with the stale nature of the material and pleas to the attachés to add more material went unheeded. Then, France started nuclear testing in the South Pacific. I took the embassy site off our computers and replaced it with a note that deplored the nuclear testing and said that the Internet Multicasting Service could no longer support the pages.

Nobody noticed for several weeks, including the embassy. Then, the antinuclear groups in Australia and New Zealand noticed and started putting prominent links into their own protest pages: "French Embassy Taken Offline."

This seems to have received some attention from the French. Indeed, it rose very high in the foreign ministry; phone calls started to come in to the White House, the National Science Foundation, and any other group the increasingly desperate French officials could find.

"Can't you do anything about these guys?" one White House staffer was asked by his counterpart in the French science and technology bureaucracy. "Hell," he replied, "we can't control Malamud. Go talk to him yourself."

Finally, to stop the phone calls and email messages, which were getting more and more insistent, I took the note off of our site so that users simply got a "Not Found" error message when they connected to the embassy site. Months later, when the French were not being very enthusiastic about the Internet 1996 World Exposition, it occurred to me that perhaps they had not taken kindly to my gentle attempts at persuasion.

Most of the other countries in Western Europe ended up participating in the fair, but always with one or two individuals sparking things. In Spain, Josep Saldaña, the editor of a local Internet magazine, devoted the better part of three issues of his magazine to the world's fair, prompting a mass of registrations. In Norway, the town of Stavanger decided to go for the fair in a big way, sparked by the author Michael Holmboe Meyer and his wife Kanda, who entered a gold medal–winning pavilion devoted to their home town.

I have decided to grant sponsorship to your initiative, "1996 World Internet Exhibition," whose aim is to present the Internet to as wide an audience as possible, and to establish on the Internet a showplace for the most important cultural events taking place in France.

—**Minister François Fillon**
France

209

The Stavanger site features a rich array of information about this town in Norway, including surpising information about the links of the town's metal workers to the building of the Statue of Liberty in New York.

This really is a good idea. Bringing the whole world together can only help us all. Let's hope some of it filters down to the really information starved of the world, to help them improve their lot. We after all are so very lucky.

—Robert Chalmers
Mackay, Australia
robert@chalmers.com.au

Eastern Europe and Russia

To get participation from Eastern Europe, Russia, and the former Soviet Union, we first had to go to Asia. Rob Blokzijl's wife is Russian, and Rob speaks more than enough Russian to get through a dinner of vodka and Internet politics. Rob had spent many years leading the effort to bring together formerly warring Internet factions in Western Europe to help build regional network information centers and backbones. In Russia, he has often played a similar role, banging heads to try and get competing factions of the Internet world to work together, pointing out to them that the real enemies of their work were not each other but the various government bureaucracies that were trying to squash the newly emerging Internet in their country.

Rob was asked by NATO to organize a seminar on networking for the republics of the former Soviet Union. Almaty, Kazakhstan, was selected as the location of the seminar, and the local government appointed the State Certifying Committee to coordinate it, with Rob as the designated external organizer as required by NATO rules. Senior officials of academies of science from all the republics were invited to come hear of the wonders of the Internet.

In most countries, the Internet started in the schools and universities, then spread out to government and business. In many of the former Soviet republics, there were small commercial providers that were setting up operation, but national backbones and solid international lines were all lacking. NATO was hoping to push the development of the Internet into some of these areas by helping to get scientific institutions on line, and Rob was helping to coordinate a plan that used satellite uplinks in Germany and Amsterdam to feed 64,000 bits per second into selected institutions. The seminar in Kazakhstan was a kick-off meeting for this program.

When I arrived in Kazakhstan the day before the seminar, poor Rob was in a frenzy. He had arrived a day earlier, and found that few local arrangements had been made. The group appointed as his local partner was in charge of certifying textbooks for schools and other similar tasks and had no idea what the Internet was, other than that one of their supervising officials had told them to take care of the issue. Rob flew in technical translators from Moscow, worked with a small local service provider to get an Internet link into the Academy of Sciences, arranged meals for the 60 participants, and got airport visas for visitors from outside the former Soviet Union.

My job was considerably easier. I was instructed to give a flowery speech about world's fairs to kick off the seminar. I gave my usual talk about the history of world's fairs and the unparalleled opportunities before us, reading from a prepared text. The speech was translated simultaneously into Russian by our expert team from Moscow.

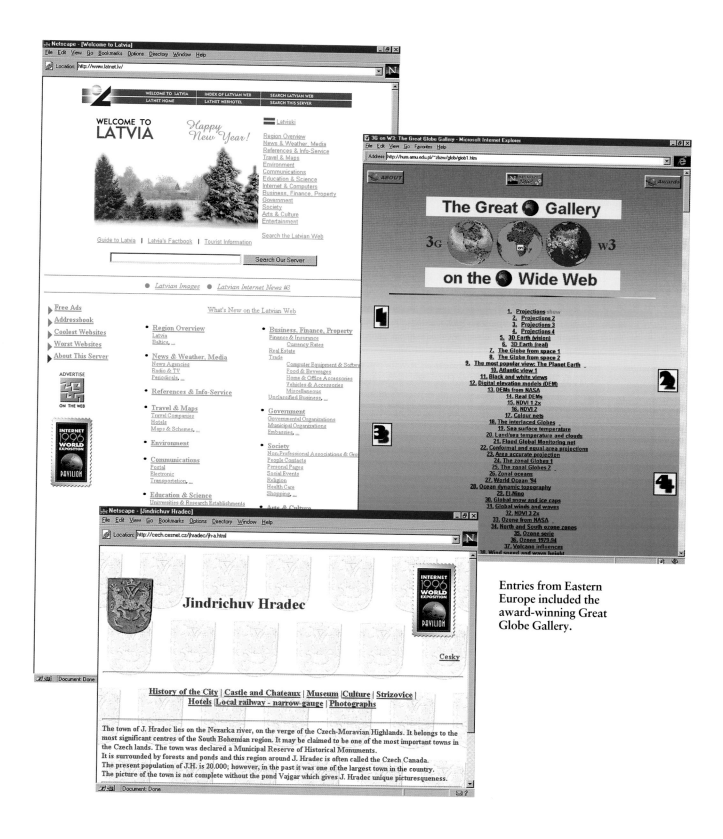

Entries from Eastern Europe included the award-winning Great Globe Gallery.

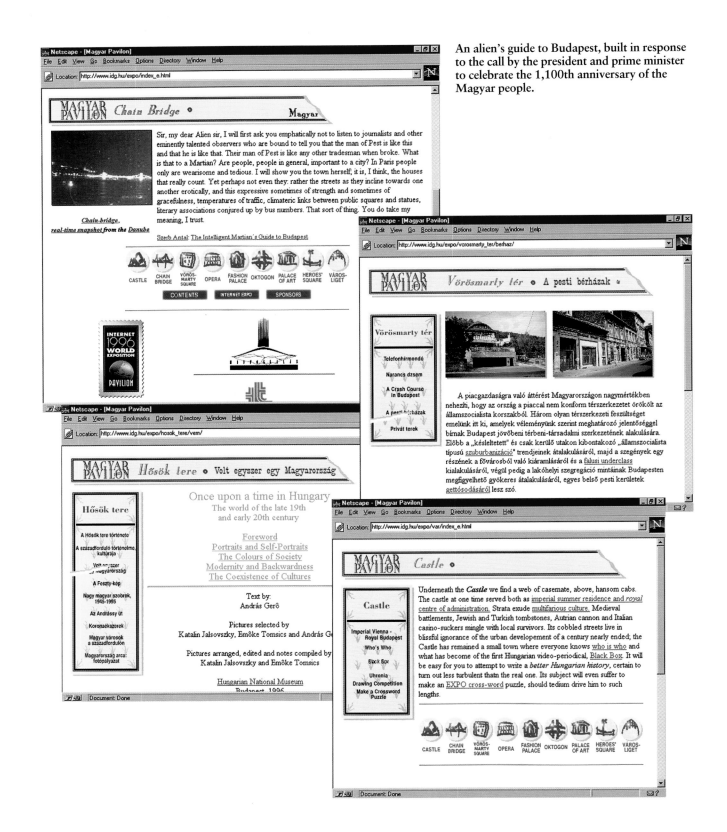

An alien's guide to Budapest, built in response to the call by the president and prime minister to celebrate the 1,100th anniversary of the Magyar people.

Later that day, Rob set up a series of private meetings with officials from various countries. We camped out in the bar of our restaurant, and met one by one with the delegations, explaining how the fair worked and what steps they could take to participate. In each meeting, we brandished our letters of support from Clinton and Gore, explaining that an easy first step would be to get a similar letter from their head of state or a government minister, officially stamping the world's fair as an approved activity.

The most interesting meeting was with Dr. Prof. Marat A. Gouriev, Boris Yeltsin's science advisor. Rumors had spread that the president was sick, and with an election looming, it seemed unlikely that we would get a formal letter of support. Still, Rob and I gave our pitch. Rob really wanted Russia to participate in a big way, so we sweetened the pot.

The Internet Multicasting Service had a 4-processor computer from Sun that had served as our original server. Sun had upgraded that with a spiffy new model; this machine was being used, but not very intensively. I offered to spark the Russian Central Park site with a donation of this machine, provided that we had some indication that Russia would take the fair seriously.

Dr. Gouriev wanted to know what "indication" I had in mind. I explained that if a letter from Mr. Yeltsin were to arrive by October 31, 1995, we would have a serious indication and, needless to say, would use Federal Express to send him his computer. If a letter from the prime minister arrived, we would also take this as a serious indication, but perhaps a bit less serious, and might leave the disk drives off the system.

Sure enough, in late October Rob Blokzijl sent me electronic mail indicating that I had received a letter from the president of Russia. The letter was addressed to me and began with the salutation "Dear Mr. President." We looked in all the web search engines on the net, but it certainly appeared that we were the first web site in the world to be endorsed by both Presidents Clinton and Yeltsin.

Over the next few months, I continued to receive letters in the mail. The president of Kyrghystan sent his felicitations, followed by a joint proclamation from the president and the prime minister of Hungary, who informed us that they would lay special emphasis "on the 1,100th anniversary of the historical date when the Hungarian (Magyar) tribes arrived in the Carpathian Basin."

Not long after the fair got started, the fairmaster account received some mail from Janez Stefanec, a small Internet service provider in Slovenia. Why wasn't his country represented? As usual, we told him to go and put something together, which he did within 24 hours. I sent him some mail congratulating him and suggested that he get some official endorsement within his country.

Two weeks later, Janez Stefanec found himself in the office of the president of the republic, receiving a formal letter of support. A press conference was arranged and was covered by all the local media, including radio and TV. His

We need some faster pipelines down here in the slow south of Africa. Your ideas are great, but we seem to be a bit (no pun) slow. Thank you—c'est cool.

—Alwyn Möller
Bellville, South Africa
leagle@iafrica.com

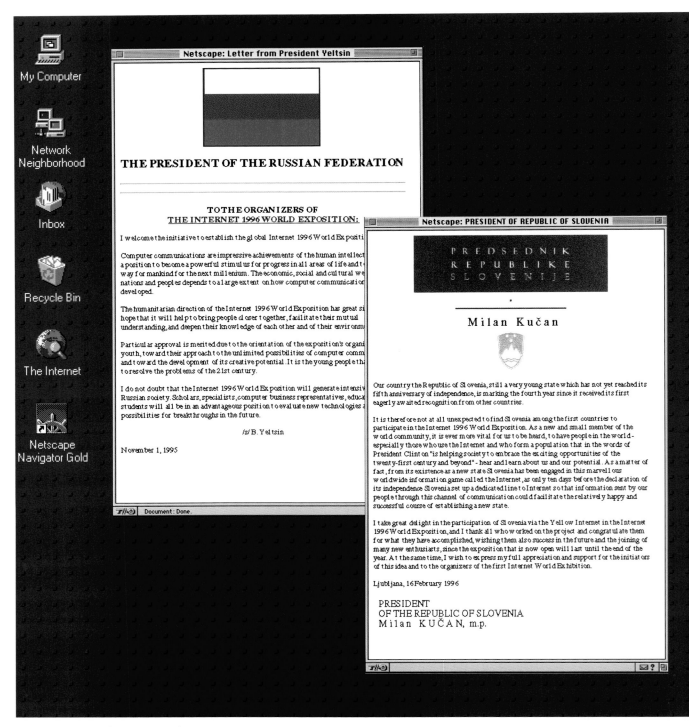

Letters of support flowed in via the Internet as
well as by the more traditional SnailMail.

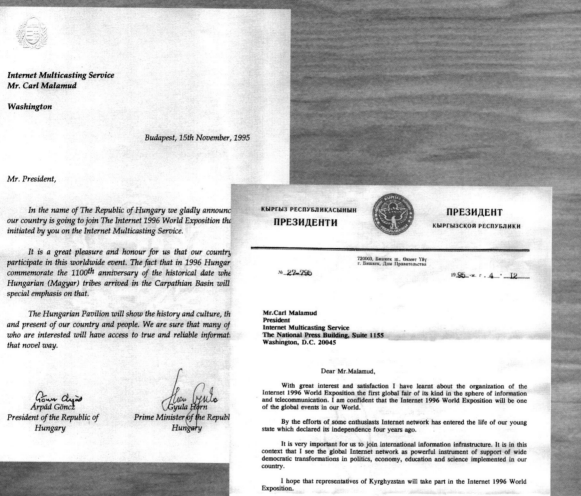

Internet Multicasting Service
Mr. Carl Malamud

Washington

Budapest, 15th November, 1995

Mr. President,

In the name of The Republic of Hungary we gladly announc[e] our country is going to join The Internet 1996 World Exposition tha[t] initiated by you on the Internet Multicasting Service.

It is a great pleasure and honour for us that our country participate in this worldwide event. The fact that in 1996 Hungar[y] commemorate the 1100th anniversary of the historical date whe[n] Hungarian (Magyar) tribes arrived in the Carpathian Basin will special emphasis on that.

The Hungarian Pavilion will show the history and culture, th[e] and present of our country and people. We are sure that many of who are interested will have access to true and reliable informati[on] that novel way.

Árpád Göncz
President of the Republic of
Hungary

Gyula Horn
Prime Minister of the Republ[ic]
Hungary

КЫРГЫЗ РЕСПУБЛИКАСЫНЫН
ПРЕЗИДЕНТИ

ПРЕЗИДЕНТ
КЫРГЫЗСКОЙ РЕСПУБЛИКИ

№ 27-795

720003, Бишкек ш., Өкмөт Үйү
г. Бишкек, Дом Правительства

19 95 -ж. г. 4 . 12

Mr.Carl Malamud
President
Internet Multicasting Service
The National Press Building, Suite 1155
Washington, D.C. 20045

Dear Mr.Malamud,

With great interest and satisfaction I have learnt about the organization of the Internet 1996 World Exposition the first global fair of its kind in the sphere of information and telecommunication. I am confident that the Internet 1996 World Exposition will be one of the global events in our World.

By the efforts of some enthusiasts Internet network has entered the life of our young state which declared its independence four years ago.

It is very important for us to join international information infrastructure. It is in this context that I see the global Internet network as powerful instrument of support of wide democratic transformations in politics, economy, education and science implemented in our country.

I hope that representatives of Kyrghyzstan will take part in the Internet 1996 World Exposition.

I wish successes to your noble endeavor to establish World Electronic Home.

Sincerely yours,

Askar Akayev
President of the Kyrghyz Republic

217

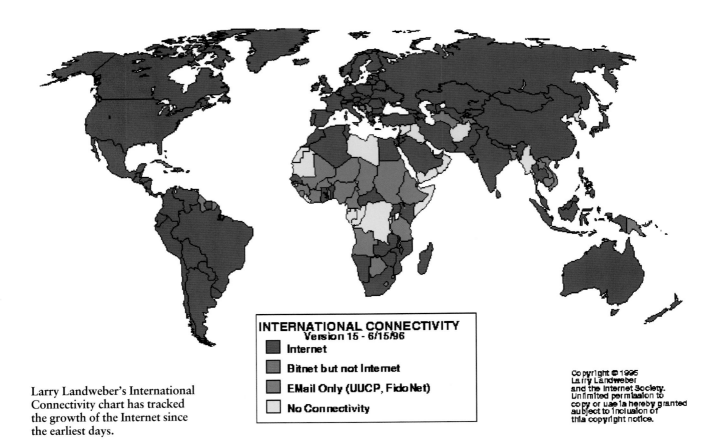

INTERNATIONAL CONNECTIVITY
Version 15 - 6/15/96

- Internet
- Bitnet but not Internet
- EMail Only (UUCP, FidoNet)
- No Connectivity

Larry Landweber's International Connectivity chart has tracked the growth of the Internet since the earliest days.

If this is a "World Fair" don't you think some representation from Africa is needed?

—Alwin Wiederhold
Johannesburg, South Africa
a87498@generation.eskom.co.za

web site had a 150 percent boost in hits, and his idea to build up a tourism site for beautiful Slovenia was suddenly taken seriously.

This was exactly the global card that we wanted to play. The fair was organized by individuals who build the Internet in their own communities. By banding together, we each got more oomph, letting us get heads of state, national arts centers, and major corporations interested.

In addition to the boost from the Kazakhstan seminar provided by all the letters of support that came flowing in, there was one additional result that we had not anticipated. The State Certifying Committee of Kazakhstan felt that it had to draw up a suitable report from the event it had hosted. Since I was the keynote speaker, my speech became fodder for this report.

Several months later, I received email from Rob Blokzijl. "You have to read this," he said. The State Certifying Committee had taken the audiotapes from the excellent Russian translation of my speech and transcribed it. The transcription was then translated back into English, having me starting off the speech with "It is the large honour for me, to attend the first working seminar in central Asia. To me it is pleasant to see here the people from several countries, which is work on Internet development."

We were so delighted with the translation that it was posted on the fair as part of the Kazakhstan pavilion. Rob Blokzijl, with his best heavy Russian accent, was asked to read the speech into a digital audio tape recorder, which was then sent over to Marty Lucas for processing as a "Dramatic Reenactment of the Translation."

Africa and the Middle East

The organizers of the Internet 1996 World Exposition were bound and determined to see that this world's fair would be for all the world. The developed countries have exclusive clubs such as the OECD and the European Commission in world capitals such as Brussels, but we wanted this fair to be one where anybody could (and would) open a pavilion.

In many areas of the world, this did happen. In Asia, the world's fair produced the first web pages for many countries in Southeast Asia. From Central Asia to South America, we saw pavilions sprout up. Often, the efforts were the result of one or two people working, but nevertheless, those regions were represented. In Africa, however, we failed miserably in this goal.

There were a few pavilions in places such as Ghana, South Africa, and, on the Arabic Peninsula, Yemen, but these were simply links to existing web pages, sometimes on servers run from the United States and Canada by expatriates or by visitors who had fallen in love with the country. An excellent pavilion for Sierra Leone, for example, is run by Paul Vreugdenhil, who first went to Sierra Leone with his family when he was four and lived there for 11 years. Now, as a researcher in the Department of Surgery at the University of Wisconsin at Madison, he maintains an extensive set of pages about the country.

There were some participants in the fair from Africa and the Middle East. One in particular stood out, winning a gold medal. Established as the official site for Egypt's Information Highway project, it was started in 1995 and is run by Egypt's Information and Decision Support Center. The site is huge, featuring five clusters focusing on health, tourism, the environment, culture, and government. The government section has statistics for each of the sections of Egypt; the tourism section has information about local tourism and companies. A Cairo Café allows the user to translate English phrases into hieroglyphics.

What didn't happen in Africa was a large set of unique activities spurred by the world's fair, partly due to the development of the Internet in general. Most of the countries in Africa do have some Internet activity, however, and the

Egypt's award-winning site includes the ability to translate simple phrases into hieroglyphics.

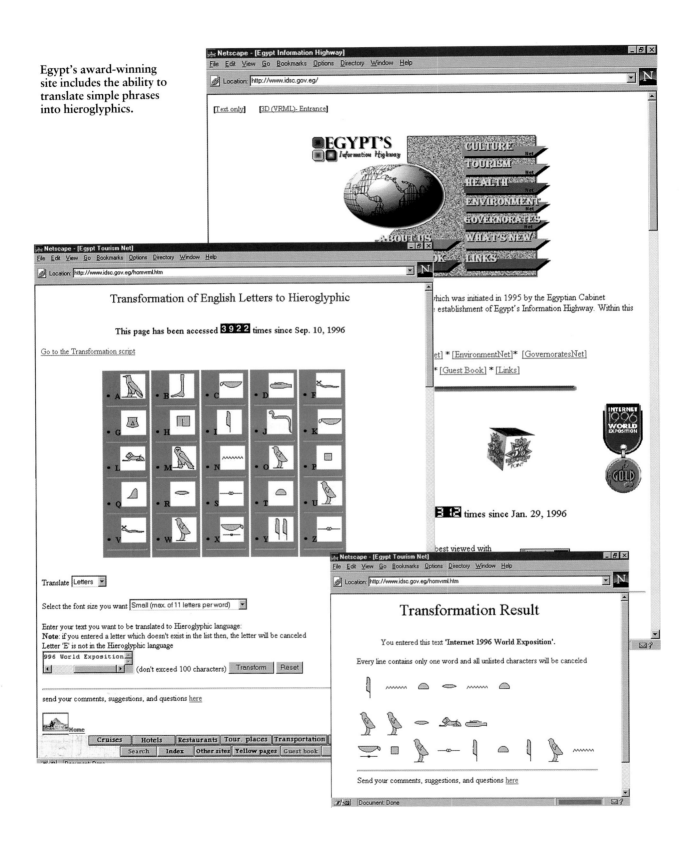

level of activity is no different than in many of the areas where the fair did have a large impact.

We tried a variety of tactics to increase participation. At the meeting of the Internet Society, we looked for delegates from Africa and tried to interest them. We approached the International Telecommunication Union in Geneva to sponsor a pavilion for countries with a newly developing infrastructure. They were interested, but large treaty organizations like the ITU have trouble moving at the speed that we were moving. Work in these bureaucracies is done in biennial or quadrennial cycles, and the Internet 1996 World Exposition was put together in less than a year, scarcely a blink of an eye by their standards.

Some people argued that an Internet world's fair, indeed the Internet itself, was frivolous, given the more pressing needs of many of the poorer countries of Africa, but that is not an argument that stands up to reason. Putting the Internet into every home in a poor country makes no sense. Putting a few Internet connections in strategic places does make sense, if those locations include places such as universities, nonprofit aid groups, or a few government agencies. Even the poorest countries invest in some infrastructure, no matter how meager, building airports, roads, electrical systems, and water treatment facilities.

The Internet has not taken off yet, however, in most of Africa. Professor Larry Landweber, a founder and chairman of the board of the Internet Society, publishes a biannual study that shows how far the Internet has spread. At the end of 1996, in a large swath of Africa, only email connectivity was known to exist, and in many others there was no known Internet activity except for a very few dedicated hobbyists who called out on bulletin boards.

One can argue that a nurse in the remote Sahara has much more need to access Internet medical archives than a colleague in a major teaching hospital in the capital city. A professor in any one of the obscure specialties practiced in academia has much more need to access electronic mail and web sites than a colleague located in an established center. Engineers building bridges, telephone systems, or waterworks have a need to keep up with their profession.

Perhaps it is a biased perspective of of those who build the Internet, but to us this is clearly an essential infrastructure, one of a series of tools we use to try to modernize our cities or our farms. However, if political leaders do not view the Internet as an essential infrastructure, it is hard to make the case for the expenditures necessary.

While the world's fair was unable to do anything in most of Africa, one group has had several years of experience with wonderful results. Under the auspices of the Internet Society, volunteers have been holding an annual workshop of one week of intensive hands-on training for people from developing countries. The workshops are coordinated by George Sadowsky, director of the Academic Computing Facility at New York University, with help from volunteers such as

This is THE site of the year, it must be !!

—**Carlos Campos**
Johannesburg, South Africa
carlos.campos@mail.liberty.co.za

Your Exposition will help further broaden the base of users hence enhancing the Internet's usefulness to all. I wholeheartedly welcome your initiative and look forward to UK organisations and individuals playing a full and active part in ensuring its success. We are happy to act as a focal point within the UK to stimulate and coordinate the effort of industry in participating in your exhibition.

—**Minister Ian Taylor**
The United Kingdom

Setting up a portable office, Randy Bush (front) works during a meeting of the Internet Engineering Task Force.

network guru Randy Bush. Over 750 engineers from 100 countries have received training each year on the basics of configuring a computer and a router and installing Internet services. In 1996, because the Internet Society meeting was held in Montreal, a special workshop was held for French-speaking West Africa.

Many of the graduates of these seminars have gone on to run the national networks in their countries, starting up Internet connections from nothing. Randy Bush, the outspoken, hands-on teacher for many of these seminars, claims that the graduates of these workshops were responsible for every new country that joined the Internet between 1993 and 1996, with the exception of a single one that was aided by France Telecom in Francophone West Africa. While people like Randy Bush and George Sadowsky travel the world hosting technical workshops for a few dozen people in places such as Nairobi, Trieste, and Ifrane, they receive very little formal support for their efforts.

The United Nations Development Programme helps, but for the most part the foreign aid bureaucrats are busy with much more grandiose projects. In the United States, a $15 million program called the Leland Initiative has been run by USAID with a goal of connecting 20 countries, but the results have been less than stellar, in part because the program ran into substantial resistance from Republican members of the Senate. There have been some exceptions, mostly in Eastern Europe and Central Asia, where the Soros Foundation and NATO have been very active in boosting Internet connectivity, both internationally and within the countries.

Meanwhile, people like Nii Quaynor in Ghana, a graduate of the Sadowsky-Bush seminars, are making the difference. Quaynor started the first Internet connection in Ghana with a 14,400-bit-per-second modem. When the telephone company could not provide him with a 64,000-bit-per-second local loop, he petitioned for and received permission to install his own 128,000-bit-per-second satellite link straight to Virginia. With the connections in place, a set of Ghanan programmers started providing off-shore services to U.S. corporations needing development work.

Nii Quaynor is not an international diplomat or aid worker; he is a quiet, gentle programmer. Randy Bush, likewise, is not an international diplomat, he is a gruff, outspoken, highly focused trainer who only deals with people who really want to learn how to make routers work properly. It is people like Quaynor and Bush, however, who have made the Internet grow and it is a pity that organizations such as USAID don't pay more attention to their advice. The world would be a better place if they did.

SO OZ FINALLY *BECAME* HOME; THE IMAGINED
WORLD BECAME THE ACTUAL WORLD, AS IT
DOES FOR US ALL ... THERE IS NO LONGER ANY
SUCH PLACE *AS* HOME: EXCEPT, OF COURSE,
FOR THE HOME WE MAKE, OR THE HOMES
THAT ARE MADE FOR US, IN OZ: WHICH IS
ANYWHERE, AND EVERYWHERE, EXCEPT THE
PLACE FROM WHICH WE BEGAN.

SALMAN RUSHDIE
THE WIZARD OF OZ

THE 1915 PANAMA PACIFIC EXPOSITION

Asia and Pacifica

13

The Internet 1996 World Exposition was not intended to be a geographic event, but it was inevitable that geography would be important. Large international gatherings invariably end up not only being in one place but also using location as the way to organize themselves. At the World Cup or the Olympics, slots are assigned by country.

We also use countries to organize meetings in areas outside of sports. From the global GATT negotiations to membership in regional groups such as the Asia Pacific Economic Forum, seats at the table are assigned to national delegations. Even in such an amorphous entity as our telecommunications infrastructure, work is done along national lines. Monopoly control over running copper cables was allocated like feudal estates in cozy clubs such as the International Telecommunication Union.

The desire to be the official representative of a country is a powerful draw for people all over the world. Gatherings such as the International Organization for Standardization (which is officially known by the dyslexic acronym ISO) or the Consultative Committee for International Telephone and Telegraph have long drawn huge numbers of people from the engineering community, though more often a professional cadre of standards bureaucrats staff these meetings rather than working engineers.

In the late 1980s, it was not clear that the Internet would succeed. A large number of people were working on a rival set of standards that would go far beyond the ad hoc nature of the Internet, which was cobbled together from a suite of independently developed protocols and services. This rival standard was called the Open System Interconnection model, and at one point the host organization boasted that each day saw an average of nine meetings on the subject, spread throughout the world in a massive structure of general committees, subcommittees, plenary committees, and ad hoc committees.

The Open System Interconnection effort became an instrument of policy, receiving strong backing from the U.S. State Department and the European Commission. It became the official international way that computers would be connected together. Thousands of people were producing paper at an astonishing rate, all translated into the multiple official languages of the Geneva secretariats that staffed the effort. At one point, I had four file cabinets full of these standards. But very few people were writing computer programs or designing hardware that would implement the standards they had invented.

Participation of Nepal in the Internet 1996 World Exposition will be a starting point in our strategy to promote free information exchange characterised by the Internet. The electronic global village is making the world a smaller place in which we live. Nepal's inclusion and active participation in the electronic global village affairs will benefit our nation.

—**Prime Minister Sher Bahadur Deuba**
Nepal

Meanwhile, a different group was stitching together the Internet. As a new technology would develop, say, a new way to do compression for modems or a way of labeling a mail message to signify the date that it was sent, various groups would start experimenting with the technology in their own networks. Several competing ways would often develop for any given task, and these differences would be hashed out in electronic mail.

The Internet was built with a very informal structure. A few coordinating meetings sprang up, such as the triannual meetings of the Internet Engineering Task Force, which is more like a workshop than a meeting. Anybody can attend, and most of the time is split up into 80 or so different working groups. There is no voting, and standards emerge through a poorly defined but well-implemented consensus process.

However, even in the Internet, national politics would intrude. One of the most common problems was control of the Domain Name System. The group that controls a top-level domain decides who gets to use the next level. The institution that owns the "org" name decides who gets to be "park.org." The person who owns park.org decides who gets to be amsterdam.park.org. Most of the world uses geographic Internet domain names, such as nikhef.nl for the NIKHEF research institute in the Netherlands. Periodically, nasty fights would break out on the Internet over who got to control which top-level country domain. Rob Blokzijl helped to broker a consensus on some of the nastier fights, such as the one for control of the Russian domain, using the simple strategy of forcing the combatants to reach a consensus among themselves.

With a world's fair, we knew we would be faced with the question of who got to represent which country. Many groups, faced with the requirement to do something about the information revolution, saw a world's fair as the perfect vehicle for getting some bullets on their annual report. Some groups took the idea of a world's fair and ran far with it, but others were dragged down by it.

There was a risk that the whole idea of a world's fair would sink. Jun Murai in Asia, Rob Blokzijl in Europe, and I in the Americas were acting as overall coordinators, but three people can't organize a world's fair. Indeed, it wasn't very clear to us that even a few thousand people could pull this off, but it was clearly necessary to delegate control. We simply didn't have the budget to put together a world's fair as a single monolithic project, but as a loose cooperative of like-minded groups, we stood a chance.

When the question of delegation came up for a particular group, one of the most frequent requests we encountered was the group's desire to be an official representative of one sort or another. Sponsors were official sponsors, we had official coordinators for pavilions, and we even developed a set of official titles for the people involved. Rob Blokzijl and I, for example, periodically traded the titles of secretary-general and general-secretary.

The titles and the designations could get out of hand, however. In particular, groups that wanted to control all activity in their country were regarded as dangerous. We adopted a policy that there would be no official country representatives in our world's fair, and that a given area might have several groups working. In Russia, it was unlikely that a single consensus effort would develop, but independent efforts came about in St. Petersburg and Moscow.

It was up to people to organize themselves. If there was a consensus, as among all the groups working on the fair in Spain, then the page was given to them to maintain. If there were warring groups, as in Andorra where one service provider got very upset because another provider had beat him to the punch and put up an Andorran pavilion, then we kept control of the pages in Amsterdam and listed all the groups involved.

"Anybody can participate" and "there is no official representative for a country" seemed like easy enough rules, but even they broke down very quickly. As a grass-roots distributed project, the fair naturally organized along geographic lines. The people in Korea all worked together to organize an extensive local infrastructure, complete with committees, a large secretariat, and detailed event schedules. More informal groups met in Germany, the Netherlands, Japan, and many other countries.

In December 1995, this mass of activity all funneled into one location, our master web construction facility in Washington, DC. It was if a world's fair had been started by first constructing all the buildings, then trucking the prefabricated structures to an undeveloped location. What would the fair look like? What would be the infrastructure that tied all this material together?

We developed two ways to look at the fair. Theme pavilions let us group material by subject matter, and the country pavilions were the geographic path through the fairgrounds. This led us straight into a basic philosophical question we had not anticipated. What was a country?

Tibet

The first test came when Deb Roy, finished with his journeys in South America, traveled to Calcutta to help build a pavilion for India. Deb was from the Bengal area to the west of Calcutta, and he had enlisted his family in Canada to write back to the old country to help him find places to go. Deb had timed his visit to coincide with the Durga Puja, a massive religious festival which takes place in the streets of Calcutta. He arrived a few weeks early, though, and decided to travel around India to look for other material.

In Agra, while photographing the Taj Mahal, he met an interesting American woman. She was going up to Dharamsala, the headquarters for the Dalai Lama and Tibet's government in exile, and Deb decided to travel with her.

Hallo, I would like to receive mails from Bhutanese people. Thanks to park.org for the hospitality. Ciao.

—Antonio Giliberto
Turin, Italy
tpsline@mbox.vol.it

227

Tibetan monks gather in
Dharamsala.

Photo/Deb Roy

Deb had full control of his schedule and could adjust his itinerary to follow stories (or pretty Americans) around the country, but he was traveling on the world's fair budget, no matter how meager that budget was. He knew I would skin him alive if he returned without something to show for his efforts. When he called me from Delhi to tell me he was on his way to Dharamsala, I asked him to see what he could find about Tibet and, if possible, to try and interview the Dalai Lama or his staff.

Deb's family had moved to Canada before he was born, but he had good knowledge of his heritage, being familiar with Bengali music, food, and the language. He had a passing familiarity with the region but certainly was no expert on Tibet, located so far from Calcutta. The day after his arrival, he introduced himself to the Department of Information and International Relations of the Central Tibetan Administration of His Holiness the Dalai Lama.

The introduction was a mite unusual. He said he was a journalist representing the Internet Multicasting Service from Washington, and was there to build the Tibet Pavilion for the Internet 1996 World Exposition. Some confusion resulted, Deb continued to explain his purpose, and within 30 minutes found himself in the office of the secretary of the department, Tempa Tsering.

The secretary listened carefully to Deb's spiel, asking several intelligent questions about the World Exposition, and then request that he leave some materials explaining the project. Deb left his kit of news clips and letters from presidents and returned to the hotel. Twenty-four hours later someone showed up at his door, explaining that she would be Deb's guide, translating interviews and showing him Tibetan culture.

The next two weeks were a whirlwind. Armed with a battery-operated digital audio tape recorder, a little stereo microphone, and a camera, he met with the heads of various cultural and political institutions and with members of the Dalai Lama's family. He learned about the art, religion, and tumultuous history of the Tibetan people. At the Norbulingka Institute, he interviewed master craftsmen who shaped metal and wood into traditional art. He also met with three recent escapees from Tibet and talked to the Dalai Lama's younger brother and nephew.

The highlight of the trip was a visit to the Tibetan Institute for the Performing Arts. Formed in the late 1960s, the institute was dedicated to preserving the performing arts, including theater and opera, as well as other live music. The institute had scheduled a performance for that evening, and, in addition to receiving tickets to the performance, Deb attended the rehearsal. He photographed the rehearsal, where he was allowed to intrude on the stage, then spent the evening recording the performance.

When Deb came back to the United States a few weeks later, he went straight from the plane to the Internet Multicasting Service studios in Washington. A first cut was made at the material, and then it was sent to Indiana, where Becknell and Lucas assembled it into web pages and an expo radio show. In Deb's notes from his two weeks in Dharamsala, he tried to sum up his experience for the producers who would build the pavilion.

Despite his interest in the arts and culture, Deb is the canonical example of the hard-nosed scientist. He writes low-level computer code that attacks fundamental issues such as how to process audio streams to recognize different speakers and what they say. "I had the chance," he wrote, "to read some of the Dalai Lama's writings on Buddhism and found his explanations both accessible and compatible with my own scientific beliefs. I also came away with a sense of peace which I truly believe the residents of Dharamsala maintain even in the face of the difficulties they face."

In December 1995, I was putting the main fair pages together. Some things were easy. The CyberFair for kids, for example, was an obvious candidate for the Global Schoolhouse Pavilion. Japan had a huge organized effort and was clearly a candidate for the country area. Where should I put Tibet? Was it a country?

A great site and a great idea! I particularly enjoyed the India site on Durga Puja. When I am not working on Objects, Relational Databases and the WWW, I am planning Web Services for the Unitarian Universalist Association. This site will be very useful to promote global understanding.

—Dr. Jeff Sutherland
Winchester, MA, USA
jsutherland@vmark.com

Photo/Deb Roy

Children learning their culture and language at a school for Tibetan refugee children.

Traditional arts and crafts thrive at the Tibetan
Institute for the Performing Arts and other
Dharamsala institutions.

A Tibetan opera was featured on Expo
Radio as part of the world's fair.

Photo/Deb Roy

People await the return
the Dalai Lama from
an overseas trip.

*I major in history course
in my university. I am
interested in India. So I
enjoyed reading Durga
Puja, A Demon King in
heaven. In Japan, we also
have myth. Its name is
Kojiki. We can know a
variety of the ancients
and the ancients I want
to go to India.*

—Aki Mukouyama
Tokyo, Japan
96032072@gakushuin,ac.jp

The square in Lhasa is occupied by troops and tourists, the monasteries
are carefully circumscribed in size and function, and the Panchen Lama was
appointed by the Chinese authorities. Clearly, China did not regard Tibet as a
country, but how could such a distinct culture not be listed as a separate entity
in a real world's fair?

I listed Tibet. The question had come up earlier when Taiwan became an
early and extremely strong supporter of the world's fair. Should Taiwan not be
granted equal status because China might protest? How could a few engineers
even begin to arbitrate such disputes? We let everybody participate, and to save
face for a few fair groups worried that it might cause problems, changed the
name of the area in the geographic area of the fair from "Country Pavilions"
to the less politically charged "Regional Pavilions."

We did receive one protest from China. A university had been named by the
government to coordinate that country's participation. When the representative
saw that Taiwan was listed, not only as a participant in the fair but with a seat
on the International Executive Committee, we received some email:

> If Taiwan should participate in the Expo as a founding country instead
> of a representative of China's Taipei district, we are afraid the Chinese
> Government would not only refuse participation in the Expo, but would
> take opposing measures.

We replied that China was free to participate and that we welcomed any concrete measures the Chinese would take to build a pavilion. However, we were not in the business of destroying pavilions and if people had put the time into building something real, we were ready to welcome all such efforts.

India

The Durga Puja is by far the biggest annual event that takes place in the state of West Bengal. Just about everyone takes part in some way. Schools and most businesses declare a holiday for at least three days. Family and friends exchange gifts, usually clothing, and take the opportunity to visit one another, not unlike Christmas in the Western world. Although Deb grew up in Canada, the puja has significance for him since the Bengali community in Winnipeg has always had some celebrations for it, and his most vivid memories of childhood visits to Calcutta are those of the puja.

The most striking aspect of the celebration is the huge *pandels,* bamboo frames decorated by the best available local artists and designers. Each neighborhood in Calcutta will raise money and build its own pandels, holding competitions for the best ones. Every evening during the celebration, families with young children, bands of kids, and young couples will stroll the streets, looking at the maze of multicolored lights arranged into geometric patterns and into the shapes of deities from Hindu mythology.

For two weeks, Deb went around Calcutta to learn about the people building the pandels and about the puja's significance. The first ritual of the puja is the bathing of brides-to-be, who take the form of a young banana tree, in the holy Ganges river. At dawn, a constant stream of banana trees was brought down to the river, bathed, and then returned to their pandels so that the rest of the rituals could begin.

After the Durga Puja, Deb went to Ecuador to interview the Otavaleño weavers, but came back to Calcutta a few weeks later to gather more material. He met musician Uma Guha, a former student of the maestro Ali Akbar Khan. Uma Guha gathered fourteen amateur and professional musicians from the Calcutta area and brought them to a recording studio. The musicians jammed for over seven hours just for Deb Roy and his trusty tape recorder, producing several hours of beautiful classical music including an amazing performance on the sarod by Uma Guha herself.

Other entries soon came in from India and Tibet, but I was quite proud of the job that Deb Roy, together with Philippe Tabaux in Washington and Becknell and Lucas in Indiana, had done. Having these pavilions built when the fair opened made it very clear that this was a fair for all the world, not just the Internet powerhouses.

I feel Indian religion custom is very interesting. i think their belief for Hory tree come from their thankful feeling. I would like go to India.

—**Megumi Mura**
Tokyo, Japan
Keiko.Kimura@gakushuin.ac.jp

Photos/Deb Roy

Photos/Deb Roy

The Durga Puja in Calcutta.

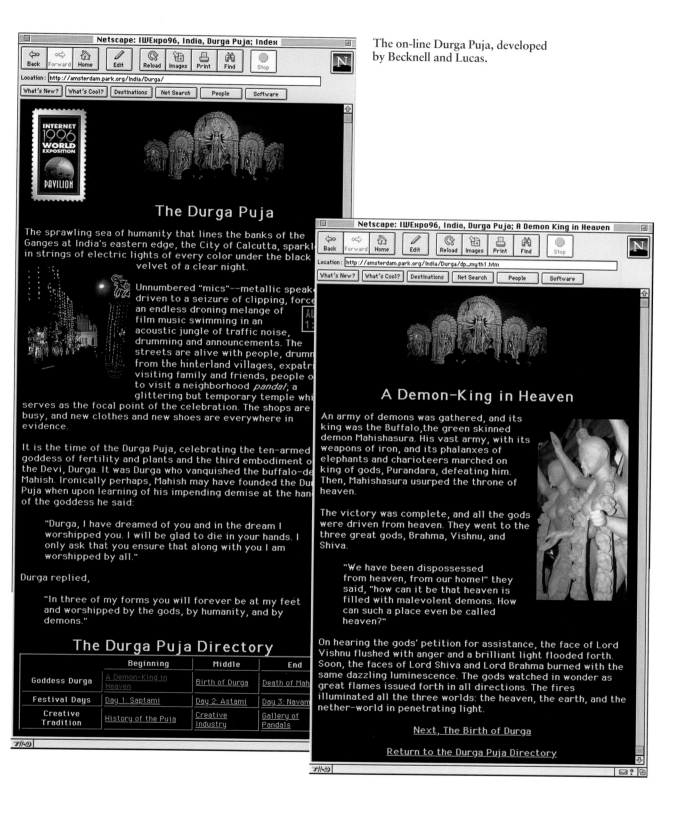

The on-line Durga Puja, developed by Becknell and Lucas.

Thailand

I first met Bob Halliday in 1986 on what was supposed to be a brief stopover in Bangkok on my way to enter Rangoon. At the time, the government of Burma was only issuing visas from Thailand for the mandatory seven-day maximum tours. Bob had lived in Washington, DC, briefly in the 1970s, his only stint in the United States since he moved to Bangkok in 1968.

In Washington, he worked in a small book store, spending most of his time reading and listening to music, the rest chitchatting with the diverse clientele that frequented the small but well-chosen shelves of the book shop. In Washington, he struck up a firm friendship with a freelance writer named Stephanie Faul, who was editing one of my first books. When she heard I was going through Bangkok, she insisted that I meet Bob Halliday, and the next thing I knew he was waiting for me at the Bangkok airport.

Bob has an encyclopedic knowledge of literature. He's the kind of person who rereads Proust, and does a page-by-page examination of *Finnegans Wake*. He had reviewed literature for publications such as the *Washington Post* and the *New York Times*, and was currently employed as the critic for the *Bangkok Post*. In addition to his love for literature, he indulged his passion for food by doubling as the restaurant critic.

In 1987, when Bob met me at the airport late that night, he brought me straight to one of the night markets where he fed me fruits I had never seen, from airy mangosteens to fresh rambutans and lychees. We even tried the mythic durian, a potent-smelling fruit that is much sought after in Asia and reviled in much of the West. The durian has a very ripe banana smell, with pungent hints of Limburger cheese. The taste, however, is heavenly. One Englishman described it as "eating strawberries and cream in the public lavatory."

The next day, Bob and I went to the market and purchased some more durian and went back to his house to whip up a durian cheesecake, the first such marriage of East and West that is known to have happened in Thailand. Bob wrote it up for his food column and the recipe was a huge hit. To celebrate, we went to Chatuchak, the largest market in Thailand, on the outskirts of the city. To the side of the Chatuchak is a special food market, Aw Taw Kaw, a cooperative that boasts the best that Thailand has to offer, an incredible place with rows and rows of small stands selling fruits, curries, grilled shrimp the size of your arm, and mounds of sweets, peppers, and flowers.

By 1995, when I was organizing the world's fair, I had stopped in Thailand dozens of times. On each visit, Bob would come to my hotel armed with a list of several dozen little restaurants he had discovered, and we would set out to do research. Every trip to Thailand included at least one visit to the Aw Taw Kaw market, and I would buy an armful of plastic baggies full of delicacies and

The Aw Taw Kaw pavilion featured mouth-watering pictures of Thai food.

Photo/Somkid Chaijitvanit

bring them back to my hotel room, emptying the minibar to hold my own private buffet.

For years, on every visit I had described what I was working on, and Bob always took a keen interest in the Internet. It took a while, however, before nonresearch Internet accounts became available in Thailand and it was only in early 1995 that Bob had connected to a local commercial provider. He became an avid amateur Internet hobbyist. When I told Bob I was organizing a world's fair, he had recently been induced to write a web column for the Sunday magazine of the *Bangkok Post,* adding to his other duties writing about literature, food, and music.

Halliday immediately decided that Thailand had to be represented. He loved the idea that anybody could open a pavilion and that the whole process was free of bureaucratic regulations or commercial overtones. The pavilion he entered was Aw Taw Kaw, putting the market on line as a window on the glories of Thai food, but also a window on Thai culture.

The world's fair shipped over an IBM Thinkpad computer, from which he wrote tantalizing descriptions of Thai food. He dispatched a young photographer from the *Bangkok Post,* Somkid Chaijitvanit. An extremely talented feature

Just a few of the delicacies at the
Aw Taw Kaw market.

239

photographer, she spent two weeks at the market, photographing the food from every angle. All the material from the market was turned into photo CDs, then shipped to Washington and Cincinnati, where it was cobbled together through a steady stream of email messages from Thailand to the United States.

I had assumed that the Aw Taw Kaw market would be the extent of Thailand's participation in the fair, but then I was introduced to Kanchana Kanchanasut, a professor at the Asian Institute of Technology. The Asian Institute brings students from over 40 countries to Bangkok to study technology, an effort for which the institute won the prestigious Magsaysay award for international understanding in 1989. Dr. Kanchana is a very effective computer scientist who works with young engineers from all over the world, but she is an oddity in the male-dominated worlds of both Thai academics and the Internet.

The world's fair ended up supporting Dr. Kanchana's efforts, with contributions of equipment from Korea, which sent 15 computers, and with other help contributed by the U.S. and Japanese teams. In return, Kanchana's students set about creating an Asian pavilion. The effort was remarkable because it involved students from many of the countries of Asia, all working together to build web pages for their countries. Kanchana's students succeeded in putting together the first-ever World Wide Web presence for several countries.

Taiwan

In Taiwan, the effort was jump-started with strong support from Admiral Hsia, the minister in charge of national information infrastructure policies. The Admiral called in powerful colleagues, including General Kuo, the CEO of the Institute for the Information Industry. They in turn called in their colleagues in the private sector, and a massive coalition of the PC and Internet industry groups with government bodies resulted.

Being an American Internet bigot, I'm by nature suspicious of large, formal committees, but in Taiwan the results were spectacular. Rather than an unwieldy structure, what emerged was a large coalition of people agreeing to work on the same things. Over 1,500 free Internet accounts were provided to almost every retail computer outlet in the country. The outlets provided the computer, the telephone company provided the Internet access, and together they provided fair viewing points.

Twenty companies were asked to submit designs for home pages, and the winners were given a contract to develop their proposal. Hundreds of web pages were put on line, and a massive campaign was launched to show people the fair. Kiosks for viewing the fair were even put in locations such as the Sun Yat Sen memorial and the central train station, right in the heart of downtown Taipei.

Transcending national boundaries as well as racial, religious, and cultural differences, the Internet enables all individuals in the world to freely exchange messages, share thoughts, and make friends with one another. The Republic of China is therefore pleased to participate in the Internet 1996 World Exposition.

—President Lee Teng-hui
Taiwan, Republic of China

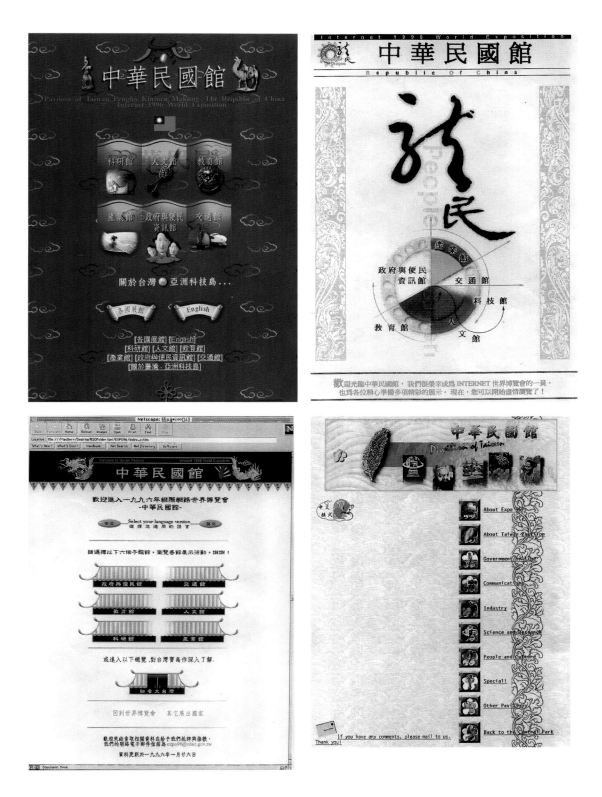

Taiwan hosted a competition for their pavilion home page design. Shown here are the four finalists, with the winner shown top left.

COOL! I saw my home-country (Taiwan) here! Soon or later I think everyone is going to fall in love with this internet!

—**Maggie Liu**
Warrensburg, MO, USA
jl5998@cmsuvmb.cmsu.edu

Perhaps the most impressive location that the world's fair entered was the National Palace Museum. This mammoth institution on the outskirts of Taipei features a collection of materials from Beijing's Forbidden Palace, supplemented by a trove of other materials collected from all over the world. The collection is so extensive that much of it is hidden in special warehouses, built into and under the mountain that is behind the museum.

The Taiwan group took seriously the fair's motto of bringing the real world into cyberspace and cyberspace into the real world. To achieve the latter, they installed a half-dozen personal computers in the reading room of the National Palace Museum, a quiet scholarly enclave where researchers examine rare scrolls and precious manuscripts. This facility was used to teach children and scholars alike how to use the Internet, using the world's fair as a guide.

To bring the real world into cyberspace, the National Palace Museum partnered with researchers at the Industrial Technology Research Institute, the home of Dr. James Lee, chief spark plug for the Taiwan effort. In an unprecedented agreement, the museum let the researchers photograph from every angle 200 priceless objects.

The photographs were brought back into the laboratory, where a team of three engineers and artists worked to put the museum on line. They developed two interfaces. One, optimized for the World Wide Web, was the main feature of the cultural pavilion of Taiwan. These web pages were very popular, allowing the user to see the objects twirl on the screen and read commentary from art experts.

It was only when I went to Taiwan near the end of the fair that I saw what lay beneath the tip of the iceberg. The same photographs had been scanned at very high resolution and were being viewed on a high-definition television screen with 1800 by 900 pixels and a high-fidelity sound system. They were packaged with beautiful music and commentary by art historians into a Macromedia Director movie that took my breath away. When I poked inside the code, I saw that some of the background images were 4000 by 2000 32-bit pixels, an image that uses 32 megabytes of random access memory to display.

Eyewitness Ancient China, as the exhibit was called, is an excellent example of an important principle on which the Internet is based. There is no one single technology that works for everybody, and the Internet has always been a mix of very low tech and very high tech. The web-visible version of Eyewitness Ancient China worked well on a slow modem.

Eventually, however, lines will become very fast. The second version of the Eyewitness Ancient China project was an experiment, a way to see what we'll be able to do with these fast lines. By developing on both tracks at once, this team was able to create different ways of presenting a national treasure such as the National Palace Museum to an on-line world.

Photo/Taiwan NII Task Force

Taiwan world's fair organizers gather for a group portrait with the author.

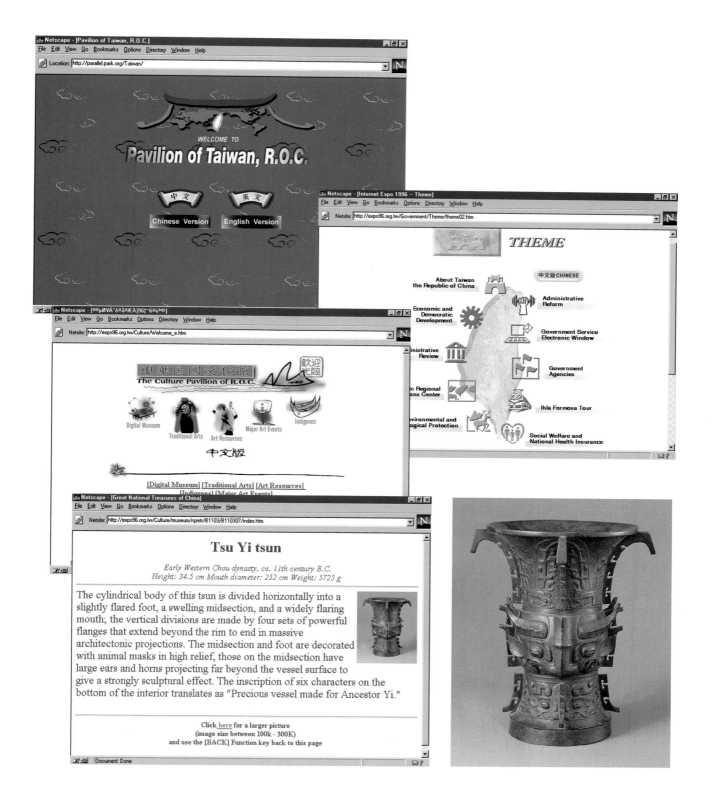

Tsu Yi tsun

Early Western Chou dynasty, ca. 11th century B.C.
Height: 34.5 cm Mouth diameter: 252 cm Weight: 5725 g

The cylindrical body of this tsun is divided horizontally into a slightly flared foot, a swelling midsection, and a widely flaring mouth; the vertical divisions are made by four sets of powerful flanges that extend beyond the rim to end in massive architectonic projections. The midsection and foot are decorated with animal masks in high relief, those on the midsection have large ears and horns projecting far beyond the vessel surface to give a strongly sculptural effect. The inscription of six characters on the bottom of the interior translates as "Precious vessel made for Ancestor Yi."

Click here for a larger picture
(image size between 100k - 300K)
and use the [BACK] Function key back to this page

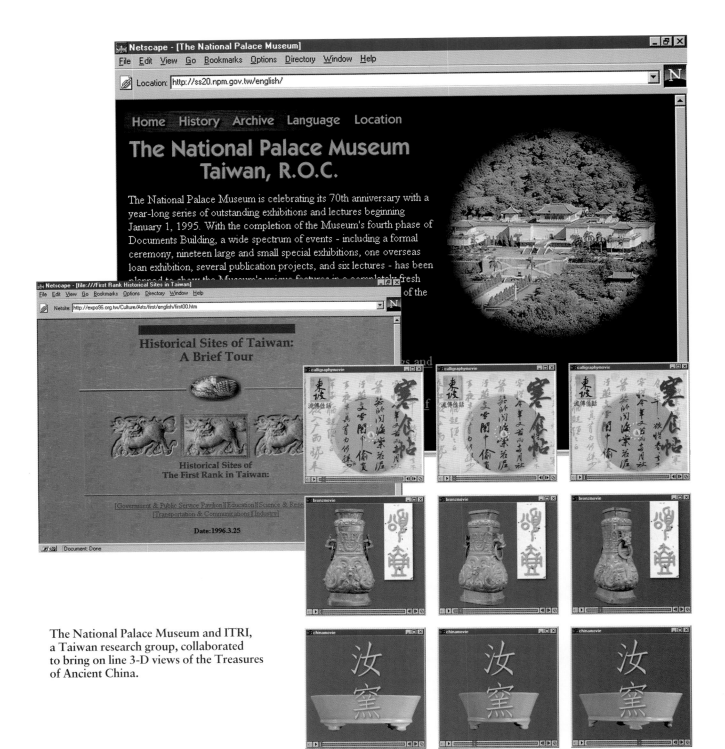

The National Palace Museum and ITRI, a Taiwan research group, collaborated to bring on line 3-D views of the Treasures of Ancient China.

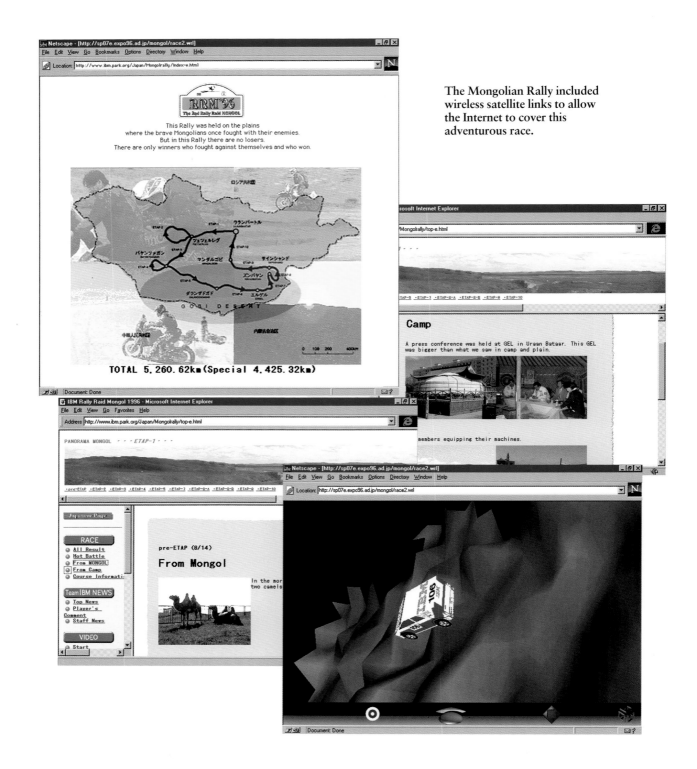

The Mongolian Rally included wireless satellite links to allow the Internet to cover this adventurous race.

The 2nd Rally Raid MONGOL.

The breeze and sweet memories are all that remain now on the Mongolian plains.

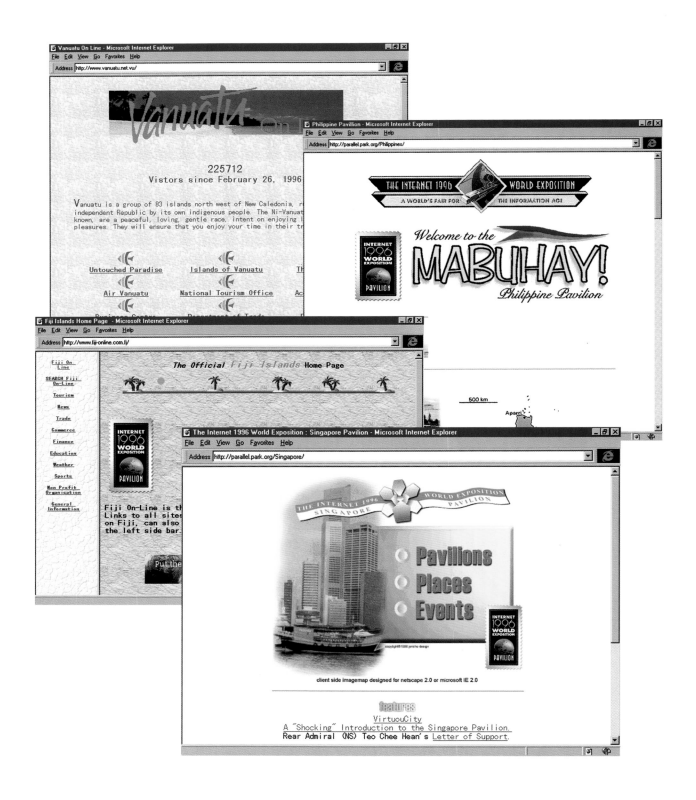

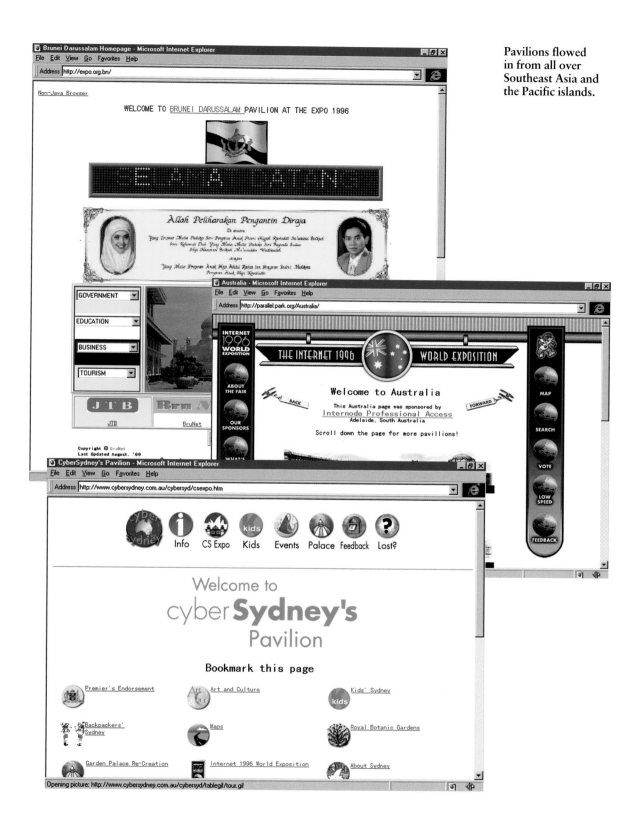

Pavilions flowed in from all over Southeast Asia and the Pacific islands.

Korea

전시관
주제전시관
공공전시관
기업전시관
개인전시관
어린이동산

공공이용시설

특별행사

I thank all those who worked hard to hold the Internet 1996 World Exposition and wish this event to be a great success.

—President
Kim Young Sam
Republic of Korea

Korea started in much the same way as Taiwan. Kil Nam Chon, a Korean computer science professor and long-time leader of networking Asia, handed the fair over to the country's National Computerization Agency. The agency, in turn, drafted participants ranging from government-spawned corporations such as Korea Telecom and the fiercely independent chaebols such as Samsung.

Korea Telecom worked a deal with KDD to get a 45-million-bit-per-second extension of the railroad installed. The National Computerization Agency teamed up with the telephone company to put in a big Central Park server. Professional web designers were hired to do the Korean National Home Page, and each of the groups put together its own projects.

Korea Telecom, for example, had a pavilion called "Look and Feel," put together by a team of 10 project managers and 32 additional staff. Snazzy graphics, all the latest plug-in modules, and lots of interactive scripts were put together in a slick corporate pavilion that offered a look at the year 2006. The corporate glimpse into the future was reminiscent of the corporate pavilions at the 1939 New York World's Fair, where GM sponsored a ride through the Futurama city of tomorrow, or the 1964 New York World's Fair, where AT&T showed off the future with the videophone.

What was unique about the Korean presence in the world's fair was the inward focus. In Taiwan, the fair served two purposes. First, it was a tool to spur development of local Internet activities. Just as important, however, was the outward focus, giving the rest of the world a view of Taiwan. In Korea, there seemed very little interest in projecting outward. Many of the sites were only in Korean, and the Korean secretariat didn't communicate with any of its colleagues around the world

The fair was big in Korea, but it was big in a way that was not very visible to the rest of us. A one-way fair, where the global efforts simply became the backdrop for a glorified trade show inside a country, was not our intention. There are dozens of world trade fairs, but we wanted the Internet 1996 World Exposition to go beyond that, to capture the spirit of global community that the great expositions of the last century demonstrated.

The global synergy that each region of the world received from participating in the fair was the result of a mutual self-help society. Each group made a lot of noise about its activities, shipped around computers whenever possible, and sent people back and forth. By creating enough noise, we were each able to get our local corporations and governments to take the project seriously because it truly did appear to be a world's fair. The world's fair only worked because we all helped each other. The Korean secretariat obviously did a tremendous amount of work, but it was an invisible fair to the rest of the world.

*It's just amazing and
challenging. I'm standing
right in front of the entrance
to Internet World.*

—Tatsuo Tokumitsu
Yokohama, Japan
tokmitsu@imasy.or.jp

Yoichi Shinoda

**Katsura Hattori of
Doors Magazine,
one of the leading
Japanese organizers.**

Japan

In Japan, the world's fair was truly everywhere. Expo 96 banners hung on the streets. Every magazine I picked up had articles about the expo and advertisements from corporate sponsors featured the logo prominently. I looked up one day to see my face on a banner in the subway, advertising a world's fair speech I was giving at an industry trade show. It was not a picture I would have expected to see in a Tokyo subway.

The activity was moving faster than a bullet train by the end of the fair. Internet traffic had surpassed voice and fax traffic on the United States–Japan international lines, and the national backbone was upgraded to the same speed as the backbones in the United States. Over $5 million was raised for the secretariat, and the donations of computers and volunteer time by people were truly staggering.

The fair activity in the Japan was the product of many people, but it was spurred by two in particular, Joichi Ito and Jun Murai. Together, they provided the spark and the enthusiasm that drove others to participate. The real work, the day-to-day engineering, was led by a whole cadre of capable workers, under the direction of Dr. Osamu Nakamura, a former student of Jun Murai and now an up-and-coming professor at Keio University. Another professor, Yoichi Shinoda, ran the Central Park team, and Tomoaki Sakurai of the WIDE project worked as event director. Digital Garage, Joichi Ito's firm, coordinated the technical working groups. I remember well one of the earliest planning meetings in Japan, where over 100 people showed up.

Trying to describe this level of activity in a few words is a daunting task. From Hiroshima, you could fly through the atom bomb dome. Nagasaki provided the very last event of the fair, broadcasting New Year's Eve live from the Huis Ten Bosch model city, complete with fireworks on the Internet. From the Neuro-Net site, you could go into a guy's living room where he ran a radio station as his pavilion in the fair. From Kyoto, you could learn about Japanese cuisine. And, in every corporate pavilion you could see original content, developed specifically for the fair.

Many of the fair's biggest events were in Japan. The Brain Opera had its last 1996 performance at a huge production in Tokyo. Ryuichi Sakamoto did several concerts with the fair, including live broadcasts of MIDI data from his concerts, a first on the net. Local magazines devoted monthly features to the fair, and the stack of press clippings got to be so large that the secretariat stopped circulating copies because the duplication cost was out of control.

Every once in a while, when I have a few minutes, I go and visit the fair, which I keep on a spare disk drive in my house. Each time I go, I see yet another Japanese pavilion that I hadn't noticed on previous visits.

The grand kickoff for the world's fair in Japan at the beginning of 1996.

I Guess You Just Had to Be There

Ultimately, it is almost impossible to tell the story of the world's fair in a few words. The Internet will never replace the book, but reading about a fair is not the same as traveling to visit it. One of the things that I find most appealing about the Internet 1996 World Exposition is that it is the first world's fair that will stay open as a ghost town on the Internet, a pristine structure that will remain forever present. The entire edifice is stored in Central Park, and people can walk through the silent halls of our world exposition and look at the marvelous exhibits that people constructed, truly an assemblage of any things and of all things.

Yet, like a real world's fair, the five million people who attended in 1996 will have memories that could only come from participating in the event. I guess, as the saying goes, you just had to be there.

For those people who were there, and especially for those who built pavilions, places, and events, it was an extrodinary experience, one they will not likely see repeated. Like those engineers who exhibited their wares at the Crystal Palace for the first time, there was a feeling that we were all participating

International World Expo, it's just my favorite event!

—Hiromichi Mori
Tokyo, Japan
hi-mori@kdd.co.jp

A weary and slightly giddy Network Operating Team after broadcasting a Sakamoto concert.

Geisha! Fuji-yama! Sukiyaki! and so on ...

—**Hiroshi Yoshida**
Suita, Osaka, Japan
yokun@sco.bekkoame.or.jp

in something new and very different. It is probable, indeed we hope, that others will build better fairs, more focused or more organized. Yet, we got to build our world's fair on unplowed ground, making mistakes but also trying to make a difference. We hope that others will follow.

This world's fair was very much in the spirit of the Internet itself. Our public park for the global village is just a reflection of the efforts of the broader Internet community. All over the world, people have been building public parks. In the gold rush of the Internet industry, it is gratifying to see that thousands of people are still dedicated to a broader sense of community, to building a vibrant, culturally rich, diverse world. It is to these engineers, artists, teachers, scientists, and all the others that we dedicate our world's fair for the information age and our public park for the global village.

LET US GO THEN, YOU AND I
WHEN THE EVENING IS SPREAD OUT AGAINST THE SKY...
OH, DO NOT ASK, "WHAT IS IT?"
LET US GO AND MAKE OUR VISIT.

T.S. ELIOT
THE LOVE SONG OF J. ALFRED PRUFROCK

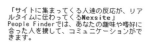

Click Me!

IWE公式イベント **BrainOpera in Tokyo.**

11月22（金）～11月24（日）

於：恵比寿ガーデンホール

あなたは、インターネットの本当の魅力を
知っていますか？

世界中のホームページを巡って情報を得るだけがインターネットではありません。あなた自身が情報の発信源となって世界中の人々と交流し、気のあった仲間と共に新しい世界を創造する、これこそ21世紀のインターネットの姿であり、魅力です。その世界へひと足早く私たちを誘ってくれるのが「Nexsite」。簡単な設問に答えるだけで自分の情報ページが開設でき、世界に向けて瞬時にメッセージを発信できる。メッセージに呼応した仲間とグループカプセルで共同作業を楽しんだり、ワールドフィクションであなたのオリジナルストーリーを"動く"マンガにして掲載することも可能です。今までのインターネットにはなかった私たちの創造力を刺激する未知なる空間、それが「Nexsite」。NTTデータ通信が提案する新しいコミュニティワールドへ、あなたもご一緒に…。

「むずかしいことを知らなくても、すぐに自分のページが作れる**Nexsite**」
Community Areaでは、あなた個人の情報発信ページ（カプセル）が簡単に作れます。

「サイトに集まってくる人達の反応が、リアルタイムに伝わってくる**Nexsite**」
People Finderでは、あなたの趣味や嗜好に合った人を捜して、コミュニケーションができます。

「アクセスすると、いつでも私の名前で迎えてくれる**Nexsite**」
ネット上でも、アクセスする一人一人に対して優しい心遣いがほっとさせます。

「いつの間にか話が膨らんで、予期せぬ展開**Nexsite**」
World Fictionでは、あなたの作った「ひとこまマンガ」に、みんながストーリーをつないでいきます。

n OperaはMIT（マサチューセッツ工科大学）メディアラボのトッドマコー教授によって開発されたインタラクティブ・ミュージック・パフォーマンス、このパフォーマンスは全く新しい発想の"楽器"を使って音づくりを楽しperience Space（次世代音楽創造体験ゾーン）と、それらの音をマルチィアネットワークにより合成し、奏でるPerformance Space（マルチメデコンサート体験ゾーン）の2つのスペースで構成されます。NTT DATAは、のネットワークメディアのクリエイティブな利用法を探査するNexsiteプロクトの一貫として今年11月22・23・24日の3日間、Brain Operaの公演を実施しました。

NTT DATA Presents
Brain Opera in Tokyo
インフォメーション

Photo/Madoka Sakaguchi

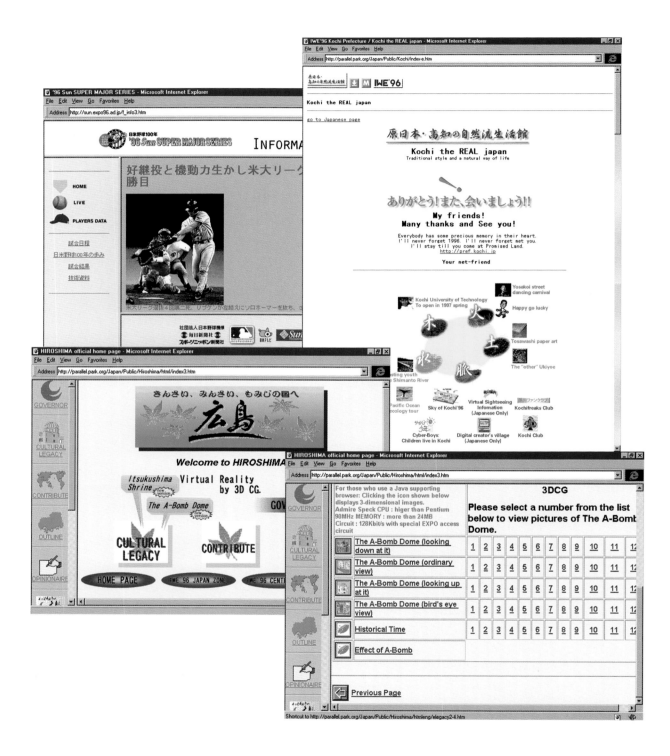

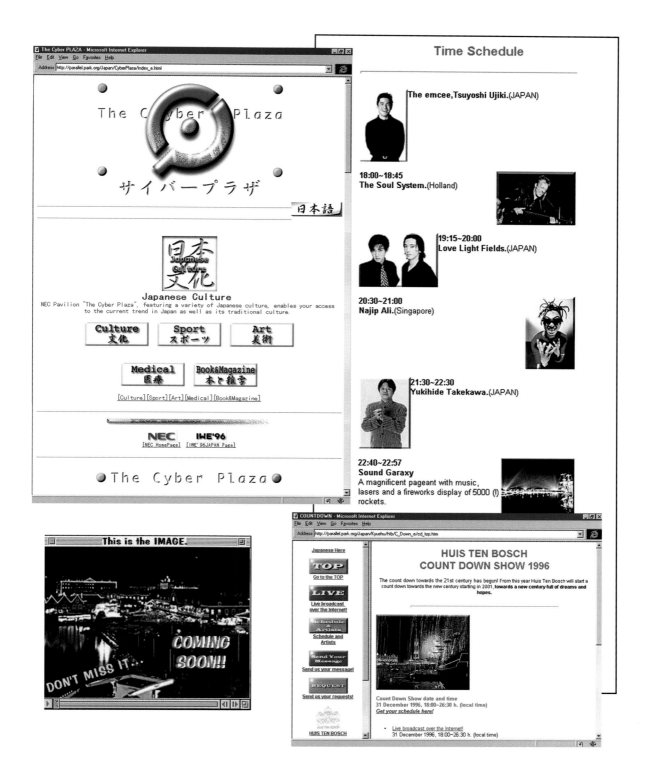

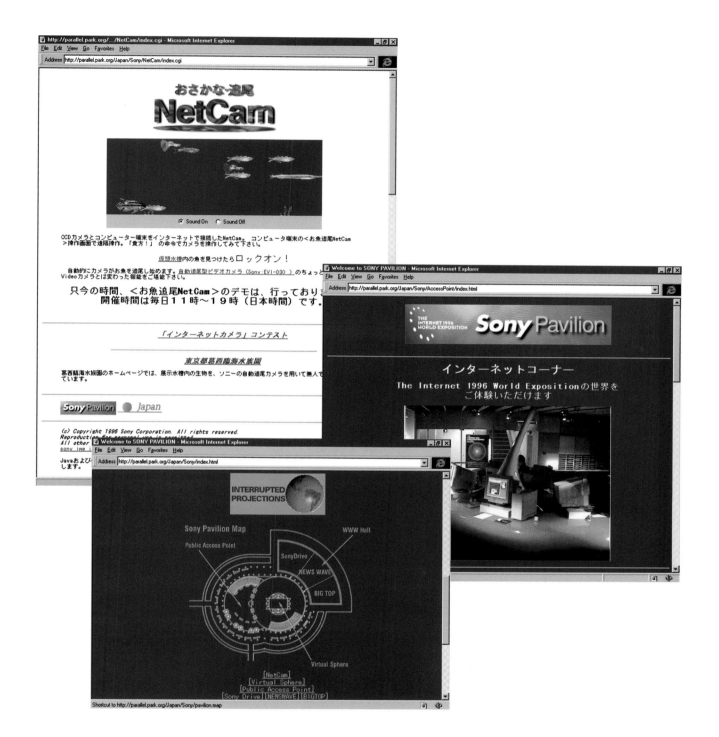

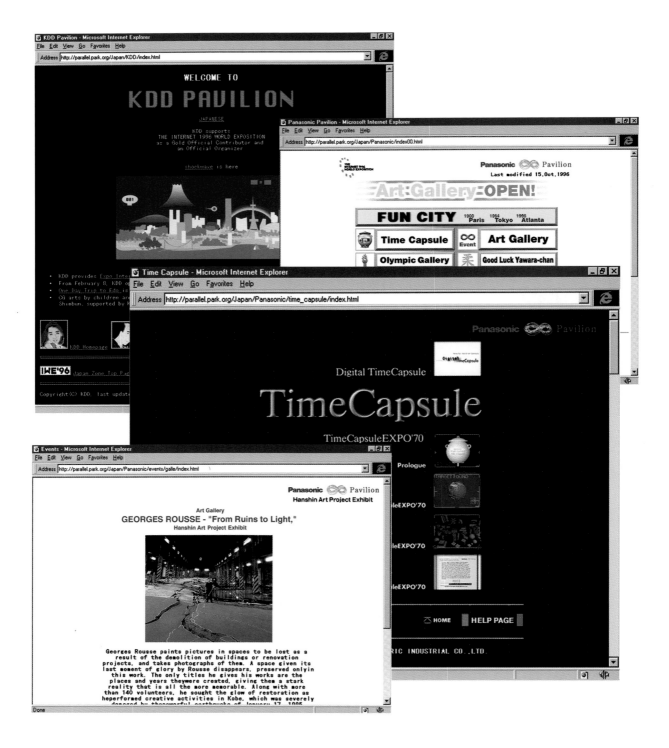

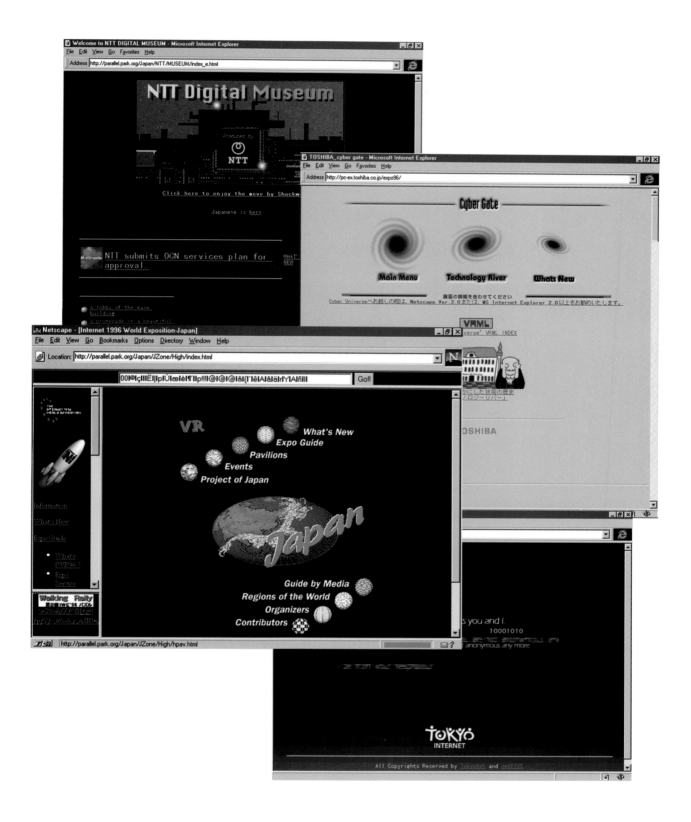

Illustration/Alan Brown/Photonics Graphics

Afterword

Laurie Anderson

A World's Fair in the Air

The free-form spirit of the Internet World's Fair seemed to be everywhere. Unlimited real estate meant that anything could be built there—parks, office buildings, little hovels, mindspaces, breeding grounds for cattle. It was a real free-for-all. I suppose that whenever a new technology is created, there is always a certain amount of time that goes by while people figure out what it actually is and what it's good for. The metaphors of highway and home were just beginnings. Is the net a mall? A stage? A library? Lots of roads leading out to suburbia? Maybe all of these things at once and many more. So why not see if the net would be a good place to produce a world's fair?

Of course, it would be easy to say that the net is already a permanent year-round world's fair. People from virtually every country in the world are represented there. But what was fun about the Internet 1996 World Exposition was watching people be playful with the definition of exhibitions and pavilions. This was not a fair that featured competition between nations for the coolest structure. "Randyland" was a great example of someone who decided to build his own personal pavilion starring himself. And why not? Maybe the days of identifying ourselves by nationalities are really beginning to break down.

In the past one of the purposes of the great world's fairs has been to introduce people to new ideas and technologies—from steam engines to hamburgers and Ferris wheels. Is this still a primary goal of a late-twentieth-century fair?

Getting information and finding out what is new doesn't seem to be a problem to most Americans who are plugged in, not just to the consumer culture but to mass culture. Increased speed in every medium has meant that we are constantly being updated on technological and cultural developments through the net, TV, radio, and print. It is not hard to find out what's going on in music, film, politics, spelunking, space exploration, or basketball.

For the specialists, there are huge and frequent conferences on everything from acoustical engineering to theme park construction. Communication networks abound so technical and scientific researchers rarely find themselves working in a vacuum. Technical expositions such as SIGGRAPH and MILIA are held with increasing frequency. The big art fairs such as Dokumenta in Kassel and the Venice Biennale present mammoth overviews every two years. Endless trade fairs of all kinds present the tools and engines of the future. Information processing is becoming more and more global every day.

In many ways, though, we are so inundated with information that many people simply want to be able to pare it down in some way, to make it at least a little bit more manageable. So a world's fair in the air, a fair that's democratic, open-ended and experimental, seems like a great way to focus some of this energy. Maybe it's the beginning of the construction of another floating world where borders are more porous and identities can shift more easily.

Another purpose of world's fairs in the past has been to present a hopeful vision of the future. Fairs are a celebration of progress. The image of fairgoers gazing up at the Eiffel Tower or the Crystal Palace is a picture of people looking into the future.

But, at the end of our own century, a lot of people are getting pretty bored of endlessly speculating about the future. Promises that technology will improve our future lives have been surrounded by the powerful drives of consumerism. There is an enormous pressure for people to get with the program, get up to speed, compete. Buy! Buy! Buy more bandwidth, more storage, more memory, more speed and if you don't you'll be left behind in the dust with the rest of the digital homeless. So what began as a promise becomes in fact a kind of threat. As technologies escalate and things get faster, a lot of people get caught up in what amounts to a sort of personal arms race, building up arsenals of equipment, and for what? So we have to keep getting more and more stuff endlessly: And we will never ever have enough. It's like we're in a race against speed itself.

The dark side of technology was a wonderful part of Malamud's story. He points out how cars destroyed the centers of many of our great cities and how technology backfired when a Santa project was threatened by intense high-speed spamming.

On the other hand, the speed that enabled the world's fair to happen in the first place left its mark. World's fairs have always featured speed. They have also left very visible and usable networks in the form of highways and trains. The networks left by the Internet 1996 World Exposition are harder to see but the high-speed data lines crisscrossing the Pacific created for the fair will certainly make future communication faster.

If the purpose of world's fairs has always been spectacle, there's no doubt that an Internet world's fair has a hard time competing with the real world. No matter how great the graphics and interface, images and sounds on a computer can't compete with the dazzle of a moon shot or the excitement of the Super Bowl, which have the additional advantage of happening in real time, live. Half-time at the Super Bowl has become an amazing demonstration of equipment, logistics, and camera choreography. The commercials that continually interrupt are demonstrations of the most advanced and sophisticated graphic techniques.

Two Super Bowls ago, I was talking to some artists who live in Bratislava. They had seen the game and while they had no interest whatsoever in football, they had been so astounded by the elaborate half-time show that they decided to emigrate to the United States, believing that any country that would put so much flamboyant energy into a ballgame must either be a nation of lunatics or else weirdly warped avant gardists. Either way, they decided to become Americans.

When they finally arrived, by the way, they weren't disappointed. One of the first things they noticed was the purple lights that various drivers attach to the bottoms of their cars, for no reason at all except maybe to create the illusion that their cars were floating around on little purple clouds.

The Internet 1996 World Exposition had much of that same playfulness. And when it tapped into real time events, like Kasparov vs Deep Blue, the crowds came out. In the end, this Internet world's fair almost seemed like it was the beginning of a construction of another strange and floating world, where borders are more porous, where identities can shift, and where time can slip from past to future. As the very first fair in the air, it was nowhere and everywhere. I had the feeling that many of the guests logging on were thrilled to have found their way there. It was an achievement just to have arrived out in the second dimension. And as we continue to shape this new world, the eclectic and democratic spirit of the fair will be important things to remember and to build on.

LAURIE ANDERSON
NEW YORK, NEW YORK

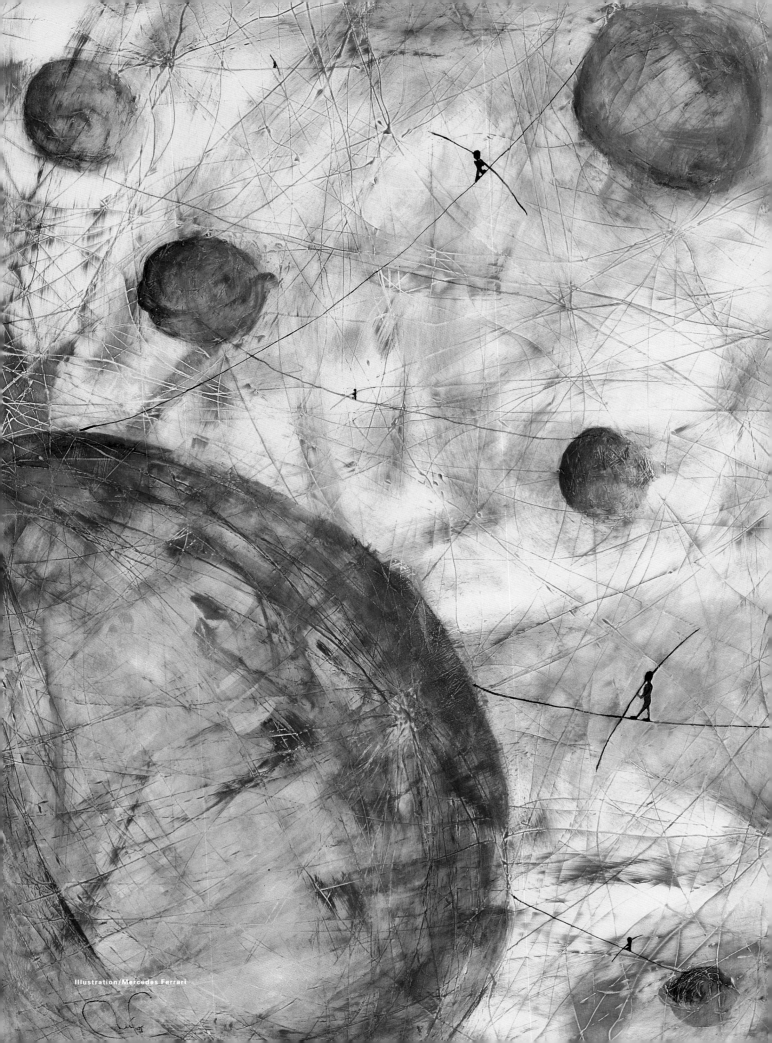

Illustration/Mercedes Ferrari

Appendix

About the Discs

Concert in the Park: An Audio CD

The first of the two discs included with this book is an audio CD. You can play it in your computer, but it is designed to work on any traditional CD player. Concert in the Park features original music composed for the fair and selections from around the world that were recorded for the Internet 1996 World Exposition. Many of the pieces on this disc were played at fair events or were broadcast live on the Internet.

Distances (5:36). The fair's theme song was written and produced by Becknell and Lucas Media. The music is performed by Ctrl-Z, the fair's house band, with special guest vocalist Tad Robinson, a Delmark recording artist. The lyrics to *Distances* are on the web at http://www.bigeastern.com/ and on the CD-ROM.

A Public Park/A Global Village (6:24). Prologue and fanfare for the Internet 1996 World Exposition composed and produced by Becknell and Lucas and featuring a scarlet tanager on lead vocals.

1919 (6:02). An ambient toccata by Japanese composer and electronic music luminary Ryuichi Sakamoto from his 1996 Trio tour, which was broadcast via the Internet. Sakamoto became internationally known for his electronic music explorations with the Yellow Magic Orchestra. He is best known for his stunning sound tracks, including *Merry Christmas, Mr. Lawrence* and his Academy award winning score for *The Last Emperor.* Ryuichi Sakamoto Trio live version of *1919* is included courtesy of For Life/güt Records (Japan) and Milan Records (outside of Japan). Ryuichi Sakamoto appearrs on For Life/güt Records (Japan) and Milan Records (outside of Japan). © Kab Inc./Japan, Kab America Inc./World Wide ex. Japan, used by permission. Recorded live in Tokyo.

Teida' (1:49). A classical Burmese song of praise played on the piano by Kit Young after an interpretation by Gita Luling Maung KoKo. Ms. Young, an accomplished student of Burmese music and language, played this piece in her Bangkok home.

Via Bo Shana (the Black Hat Dance) (5:16). A Tibetan tale of sorcerers who, through their knowledge and practice of cantrip, destroy the powers of evil. This series is symbolic and is associated with the assassination of the evil King Lampama by Halipeligoli in the seventh century A.D. Performed by the Tibetan Institute for the Performing Arts. Recorded live in Dharmsala, India.

Raga Sri (a Twilight Raga) (12:51). Master sarodist Uma Guha's rendition of this staple of the classical Indian repertoire was digitally recorded in her home in East Bengal in 1995 by Deb Roy. The sarod is constructed from a single piece of wood. The bridge rests on a goat skin covering. The sarod has 25 strings. The performer plucks the four main strings, which span three octaves. Fifteen additional strings enrich the sound through sympathetic vibration. Two strings maintain the tonic, the others drone. The sarod produces a softer, mellower tone than the more familiar sitar, and, mixed with the ambient sounds of traffic, trains, and insects, this recording captures the warmth, emotional yearning, and serenity that has kept Indian classical music vibrant for centuries.

Mr. Smith (10,000 Sworn Heroes) (5:16). On March 10, 1812, Mr. Smith, a Huddersfield manufacturer receives a letter of obscure origin.[1] This song is from the *Ballad of Ned Ludd,* a listener-directed techno-folk opera that was written and produced by Becknell and Lucas Media for the Internet Multicasting Service. The lyrics to *Mr. Smith* and the rest of the *Ballad of Ned Ludd* are available at http://www.bigeastern.com on the Internet. *Mr. Smith* is performed by Ctrl-Z.

A Unique Assemblage/Internet Railroad (11:09). The lyrics of Charlotte Brontë, sung by Corinne Becknell, the voice of the Internet 1996 World Exposition. This song features soundbytes of Gary Kasparov and the Dalai Lama and ends with a dub of the soundtrack of the Internet Railroad. The working title for this piece was "Fun With Subwoofers." Go figure.

Ctrl-Z is:
  Corinne Becknell: vocals, keyboards and Session8.
  Marty Lucas: synthesizers, vocals and sequencing.
  Trudie Cavey: guitar.
  Dirk Shorter: bass.
  John Zane: drums and percussion.
Concert in the Park was edited and mastered in North Judson, Indiana by Becknell and Lucas Media. Original music © and ℗ 1995–1996 Becknell and Lucas Media. Produced by Becknell and Lucas Media with Carl Malamud.

---

1. E.P. White, *The Rise of the English Working Class,* Vintage Books (New York, 1966), p. 558.

Disc 2: The World's Fair

The second disc included with this book is a computer CD-ROM, containing material gathered for the fair, much of it never published before. In addition to highlights from http://park.org, the disc includes video clips, long audio files, and other material that would have been especially painful on a web site.

You do not need an Internet connection to use this disc. It is compatible with most computer systems, including Macintosh®, Windows® 95, Windows NT, and many UNIX™ systems. If you have standard Internet software, this disc will work for you without any further ado. We assume an environment compatible with either Netscape Navigator 3.0 or Microsoft Internet Explorer 3.0 or higher. We assume at least a 2x CD-ROM drive and 8 megabytes of memory for adequate performance.

If you would like, the disc will install standard software and will update versions of plugins and other support routines for the Windows 95, Windows NT, Macintosh PPC, and Macintosh 68k environments.

On the Macintosh, you need to be running Mac® OS 7.1 or greater with 8 megabytes of memory to use the software we provide.

On a PC, you need to be running Windows 95 or Windows NT. Eight megabytes of memory is highly recommended to use the software we provide.

On a UNIX system, you need to have support for Rockridge Extensions, which allows for long file names. Since the browser we have rights to redistribute does not run on UNIX systems, you'll have to use a Java™-compatible browser of your own choosing.

The disc contains a tremendous amount of data, but here are just a few of the highlights:

- A special animated movie of the fair train and Quicktime video interviews with fair creators.
- The entire fair guestbook, with thousands of visitor comments.
- A techno-mola screensaver for your Macintosh or Windows 95 system.
- The Kasparov versus Deep Blue chess match.
- The Durga Puja festival from India, the Sensorium from Japan, and the World of Kimchi from Korea.

- Over 1,000 mail messages from the author's personal archive.
- Pictures of food from the Aw Taw Kaw market that will make you slobber like a water buffalo in a mango orchard.
- Randyland: First person on the planet to open a personal pavilion.
- The Big Eastern: Tales from the sand country of Northern Indiana.

The Java™ search engine used on the guestbook is by John Leach © 1996. Installer VISE for the Macintosh donated by MindVision Software.

A Unique Assemblage was a Thin Battle Lines production.

BANDWIDTH

◄HIGH

LOW►

Illustration/Rob Pierce

Index

Colophon

Production of this book, like management of the world's fair, was an exercise in distributed chaos. Before we descend into the sea of three-letter acronyms (TLAs), let's get the traditional colophon material out of the way. This book was set in Sabon, with Simoncini Garamond®, Univers, and ITC Anna® fonts used for section openers, picture labels, and titles. Screendumps were from Corel Capture 6 into Tiff bitmaps, photos were scanned onto Photo CDs, and the layout for the book was done in Quark XPress. Movie Cleaner Pro and Adobe Premiere were used for video post-processing. Awk, Grep, and PERL were used to post-process html.

Work on the book took part in three main locations in the United States, Enviromedia in Cincinnati, Ohio, the Big Eastern Studios in North Judson, Indiana, and a variety of facilities spread around Cambridge, Massachusetts. As Martin Lucas would often comment, our battle lines were awfully thin.

Cincinnati, Ohio

At EnviroMedia, page layout was executed on an 8100/100AV Power PC with 58 megs of RAM and a 20" Sony Trinitron monitor using QuarkXpress 3.32. Graphics were created, edited and processed on 2 Power Macintosh workstations: an 8100/80AV Power PC with 40 megs of RAM and a 7100/66AV with 58 megs of RAM, both equipped with professionally calibrated 17" Sony Trinitron monitors.

Color postcards, slides and transparencies were scanned on a Scitex drum scanner, while other artwork was scanned in-house using a UMAX 840 scanner and a Polaroid Sprintscan 35. Images were edited in Adobe Photoshop 4.0, while original artwork was created using a combination of Photoshop, Adobe Illustrator 6.0 and Lead Pencil 2.0. Creative work was fueled by a healthy dose of Diet Mountain Dew and vintage Frank Sinatra (the Capitol/Riddle era, 'natch).

Color proofing was done with IRIS digital proofs and an Epson Stylus ProXL, while anticipatory voicemail messages from Cambridge were regularly transmitted via Cincinnati Bell's ChoiceMail system. Across town, Rob Pierce worked on the fair train and other signature graphics using Electric Image and Adobe Photoshop 4.0. Nick Gressle brought Pipo, the fair mascot, to life with Macromedia Director 5.0 and Adobe Photoshop 4.0.

North Judson, Indiana

Big Eastern Studios, home of Becknell and Lucas Media, uses a vintage Korg Monopoly MP4 analog synthesizer with a Korg SQ-10 analog sequencer, a 1988 Korg M1 as a master keyboard, and an UltraProteus as the main rack unit. All digital patches were created using Unisys. The sequencer setup uses Cakewalk ProAudio for Windows 95 and a MIDI Express PC card linked to a Digidesign Session8, which was used for audio editing and multitrack mixing. Audio resampling and mastering was done in CoolEdit 96. Four Pentium PCs and an 80486 were used to edit, resample and upload audio and image data. Images and animations were made using Corel Graphics 6.0 and Macromedia's Director 5.0, Extreme 3D, and xRes packages.

John Zane played his Roland electronic kit through the UltraProteus along with a Yamaha RX11 drum machine. Dirk Shorter played a vintage Thunderbird bass, and Trudie Cavey played a Stratocaster. Both were patched through twin Korg A1 signal processors. Vocals used the same path with an Audio-Technica AT 4033 mic.

Network connections were through a dialup modem to a local service provider, with web hosting in Kansas. Lunch was created with 1 lb. of rooster comb mushrooms from the base of an undisclosed vintage black oak tree processed with IronSkillet 8SK, followed by sampling and resampling with Old Style 1.0.

Cambridge, Massachusetts

Global headquarters for the production of this book was a spare bedroom in the author's house. A T1 line donated by BBN Planet was used for Internet connectivity. Many days, over 1 gigabyte of files were transferred from Cincinnati to Cambridge and back. The file server was a dual-processor Sparcstation with 50 gigabytes of disk balanced on top of a file cabinet, big enough to stash a copy of the fair. Document production was on an IBM 350 donated by Intel, supplemented by a Thinkpad 760ED with 80 megabytes of RAM donated by IBM. Quark XPress 3.32 for Windows, Microsoft Word, Corel Graphics 6.0, Elm, and Vi were the primary document production tools. Awk, Gawk, Grep, Lib WWW, WebXref, and MHonArc were invaluable splicers and dicers. Fuel was provided by the Hi-Rise Bread Company and Formaggio Kitchen.

At the MIT Media Lab, I was fortunate to be located in the Interactive Cinema group, which has a Kodak Photo CD imaging workstation, an AVID video editing system, and more Macintoshes than you can shake a stick at. An IBM PC in my office was outfitted with 12 gigabytes of disk and a Sony Spressa CD-R drive. CDR Publisher HyCD was used for production of the CD-ROMs. A Digital Colorwriter LSR 2000 was used for color proofing.

The MIT Media Lab was extremely generous in the use of their facilities, but it was the unstinting advice and counsel from numerous people that was the most useful. Director Nicholas Negroponte and Associate Director Andrew Lippman provided me with a great place to work for a year to write this book and finish up the fair.

Special thanks are due to Glorianna Davenport of the Interactive Cinema group, administrative assistant Michelle Kemper, and students Freedom Baird, Brian Bradley, Kevin Brooks, Tara Rosenberger, A. Arjan Schütte, Flavia Sparacino, and Phillip R. Tiongson. Thanks are also due to Henry N. Holtzman, Joe Paradiso, Susan Murphy-Bottari, Greg Tucker, Jane Hsiung Wojcik, and Michail Bletsas for a profusion of small and large favors. Deb K. Roy and Natasha Tsarkova, in addition to their brilliant work as scholars, gave unstintingly to this book.

The Brain Opera team provided a great home away from home, and the team was always gracious and helpful. Special help was provided by Tod Machover, production director Maggie Orth, Tanya Bezreh, Peter Colao, Ben Denckla, Andrew Garcia, Ed Hammond, Teresa Marrin, Eric Metois, William Oliver, Josh Smith, and Josh Strickon. I'd also like to thank the following Media Lab faculty and students for their assistance and interest in this project: Nuria Oliver, Neil Gershenfeld, Michael Hawley, Hiroshi Ishii, Roger "Woja" Kermode, Sandy Pentland, and Mitchel Resnick.

In addition to the main facilities in Indiana, Ohio, and Massachusetts, additional processing on the data was performed in numerous locations throughout the world. Philippe Tabaux in Amsterdam analyzed the 16-Gbyte log files and maintained the fair master site and my mirror in Cambridge. Hiromi Kawakami in Tokyo directed the Japanese translation team. Brad Burdick in Virginia handled the installation routines for the discs and fixed the numerous misconfigurations caused by the author. Stephanie Faul in Washington, DC, provided developmental editing. All these people communicated with Cambridge almost exclusively through the Internet.

The MIT Press

After the data were bounced around the Internet, they were turned into three Jazz drives and two gold masters for production by the MIT Press. Theresa M. Lamoureux ably guided a fast-track production schedule, and Michael Sims handled the copy editing and proof reading of a messy manuscript in a capable, diligent fashion. Robert Prior was the acquisitions editor and patiently put up with the Sturm und Drang of a nervous author who expects same day service from a nanosecond world.

I WON'T SLAVE FOR BEGGAR'S PAY
LIKEWISE GOLD AND JEWELS
BUT I WOULD SLAVE TO LEARN THE WAY
TO SINK YOUR SHIP OF FOOLS.

Ship of Fools
Robert Hunter